SOCIAL SECURITY LEG
SUPPLEMENT 202

General Editor
Nick Wikeley, M.A. (Can

Commentary by
Ian Hooker, LL.B.
Formerly Lecturer in Law, University of Nottingham
Formerly Chairman, Social Security Appeal Tribunals

John Mesher, B.A., B.C.L. (Oxon), LL.M. (Yale)
Retired Judge of the Upper Tribunal

Edward Mitchell, LL.B.
Judge of the Upper Tribunal

Mark Rowland, LL.B.
Retired Judge of the Upper Tribunal

Tom Royston, M.A. (Cantab)
Barrister

Christopher Ward, M.A. (Cantab)
Judge of the Upper Tribunal

Nick Wikeley, M.A. (Cantab)
Judge of the Upper Tribunal,
Emeritus Professor of Law, University of Southampton

Consultant Editor
Child Poverty Action Group

SWEET & MAXWELL  **THOMSON REUTERS**

Published in 2022 by Thomson Reuters,
trading as Sweet & Maxwell.
Registered in England & Wales. Company No. 1679046.
Registered office 5 Canada Square, Canary Wharf, London E14 5AQ.

Typeset by Wright and Round Ltd., Gloucester
Printed and bound by CPI Group (UK) Ltd, Croydon, CR0 4YY

For further information on our products and services,
visit www.sweetandmaxwell.co.uk

No natural forests were destroyed to make this product.
Only farmed timber was used and re-planted.

A CIP catalogue record for this book is
available from the British Library

Print ISBN: 978–0–414–10222–4
Ebook ISBN 978–0–414–10224–8
Print and Ebook ISBN: 978–0–414–10223–1

PREFACE

This is the Supplement to the 2021/22 edition of the five-volume work, *Social Security Legislation*, which was published in September 2021. Part I of this Supplement contains new legislation, presented in the same format as in the main volumes. Parts II, III, IV, V and VI contain the standard updating material—a separate Part for each volume of the main work—which amends the legislative text and key aspects of the commentary, drawing attention to important recent case law, so as to be up to date as at December 6, 2021 (although we have squeezed in some more recent case law developments thanks to the generous understanding of our publishers Sweet & Maxwell). Finally, Part VII gives some notice of changes forthcoming between December 2021 and the date to which the main work (2022/23 edition) will be up to date (mid-April 2022) along with the April 2022 benefit rates.

The updating changes in this Supplement include a multitude of amendments to both the primary and secondary legislation governing social security provision. There is detailed analysis of further amendments to the rules for universal credit in the light of the Coronavirus pandemic as well as discussion of the Court of Appeal's decision in *Pantellerisco v Secretary of State for Work and Pensions* [2021] EWCA Civ 1454. As ever, the text also covers important developments in the Upper Tribunal jurisprudence relating to the descriptors for personal independence payment (PIP) (appeals for these benefits together form the great bulk of social security cases heard by the First-tier Tribunal (Social Entitlement Chamber)). There have in addition been significant changes to devolved social security provision in Scotland, including Disability Assistance for Children and Young People.

Finally, we have great pleasure in welcoming barrister Tom Royston to our expert team of authors and look forward to working with him on many future editions of these Volumes.

As always, we welcome comments from those who use this Supplement. Please address these to the General Editor, Nick Wikeley, c/o School of Law, The University of Southampton, Highfield, Southampton SO17 1BJ (njw@soton.ac.uk).

Ian Hooker
John Mesher
Edward Mitchell
Tom Royston

Mark Rowland
Christopher Ward
Nick Wikeley

February 4, 2022

CONTENTS

USING THE UPDATING MATERIAL IN THIS SUPPLEMENT

The amendments and updating material contained in Parts II-VI of this Supplement are keyed to the page numbers of the relevant main volume of *Social Security Legislation 2021/22*. Where there have been a significant number of changes to a provision, the whole section, subsection, paragraph or regulation, as amended will tend to be reproduced. Other changes may be noted by an instruction to insert or substitute new material or to delete part of the existing text. The date the change takes effect is also noted. Where explanation is needed of the change, or there is updating relating to existing annotations but no change to the legislation, you will also find commentary in this Supplement. The updating material explains new statutory material, takes on board Upper Tribunal or court decisions, or gives prominence to points which now seem to warrant more detailed attention.

For the most part any relevant new legislation since the main volumes were published is contained in Part I, while amendments to existing legislative provisions are contained in Parts II-VI respectively, together with commentary on new case law. This Supplement amends the text of the main volumes of *Social Security Legislation 2021/22* to be up-to-date as at December 6, 2021.

Nick Wikeley
General Editor

PAGES OF MAIN VOLUMES AFFECTED
BY MATERIAL IN THIS SUPPLEMENT

Main volume page affected	Relevant paragraph in supplement
VOLUME I	
p.53	2.001
p.63	2.002
p.110	2.003
pp.201–206	2.004
p.237	2.005
p.243	2.006
p.248	2.007
p.319	2.008
pp.339–341	2.009
pp.373–374	2.010
pp.761–763	2.011
p.771	2.012
p.789	2.013
p.850	2.014
p.860	2.015
p.869	2.016
p.869	2.017
p.873	2.018
p.897	2.019
p.914	2.020
p.943	2.021
pp.943–944	2.022
p.1043	2.023
p.1104	2.024
pp.1126–1128	2.025
pp.1151–1153	2.026
p.1156	2.027
p.1159	2.028
p.1161	2.029
p.1173	2.030
p.1241	2.031
p.1296	2.032
p.1328	2.033
p.1336	2.034
pp.1406–1417	2.035
p.1408	2.036
p.1412	2.037
p.1473	2.038
p.1502	2.039
pp.1599–1600	2.040
pp.1599–1600	2.041

VOLUME IV

Pages of Main Volumes Affected by Material in this Supplement

VOLUME V

TABLE OF ABBREVIATIONS USED IN THIS SERIES

1975 Act	Social Security Act 1975
1977 Act	Marriage (Scotland) Act 1977
1979 Act	Pneumoconiosis (Workers' Compensation) Act 1979
1986 Act	Social Security Act 1986
1996 Act	Employment Rights Act 1996
1998 Act	Social Security Act 1998
2002 Act	Tax Credits Act 2002
2004 Act	Gender Recognition Act 2004
2006 Act	Armed Forces Act 2006
2008 Act	Child Maintenance and Other Payments Act 2008
2013 Act	Marriage (Same Sex Couples) Act 2013
2014 Act	Marriage and Civil Partnership (Scotland) Act 2014
2018 Act	Social Security (Scotland) Act 2018
A1P1	Art.1 of Protocol 1 to the European Convention on Human Rights
AA	Attendance Allowance
AA 1992	Attendance Allowance Act 1992
AAC	Administrative Appeals Chamber
AACR	Administrative Appeals Chamber Reports
A.C.	Law Reports, Appeal Cases
A.C.D.	Administrative Court Digest
Admin	Administrative Court
Admin L.R.	Administrative Law Reports
Administration Act	Social Security Administration Act 1992
Administration Regulations	Statutory Paternity Pay and Statutory Adoption Pay (Administration) Regulations 2002
AIP	assessed income period
All E.R.	All England Reports
All E.R. (E.C.)	All England Reports (European Cases)
AMA	Adjudicating Medical Authorities
AO	Adjudication Officer
AOG	*Adjudication Officers Guide*
art.	article
Art.	Article
ASD	Autistic Spectrum Disorder

ASPP	Additional Statutory Paternity Pay
A.T.C.	Annotated Tax Cases
Attendance Allowance Regulations	Social Security (Attendance Allowance) Regulations 1991
AWT	All Work Test
BA	Benefits Agency
Benefits Act	Social Security Contributions and Benefits Act 1992
B.H.R.C.	Butterworths Human Rights Cases
B.L.G.R.	Butterworths Local Government Reports
Blue Books	*The Law Relating to Social Security*, Vols 1–11
B.P.I.R.	Bankruptcy and Personal Insolvency Reports
B.T.C.	British Tax Cases
BTEC	Business and Technology Education Council
B.V.C.	British Value Added Tax Reporter
B.W.C.C.	Butterworths Workmen's Compensation Cases
c.	chapter
C	Commissioner's decision
C&BA 1992	Social Security Contributions and Benefits Act 1992
CAA 2001	Capital Allowances Act 2001
CAB	Citizens Advice Bureau
CAO	Chief Adjudication Officer
CB	Child Benefit
CBA 1975	Child Benefit Act 1975
CBJSA	Contribution-Based Jobseeker's Allowance
C.C.L. Rep.	Community Care Law Reports
CCM	HMRC *New Tax Credits Claimant Compliance Manual*
C.E.C.	European Community Cases
CERA	cortical evoked response audiogram
CESA	Contribution-based Employment and Support Allowance
CFS	chronic fatigue syndrome
Ch.	Chancery Division Law Reports; Chapter
Charter	Charter of Fundamental Rights of the European Union
Citizenship Directive	Directive 2004/38/EC of the European Parliament and of the Council of April 29, 2004
CJEC	Court of Justice of the European Communities

Table of Abbreviations used in this Series

CJEU	Court of Justice of the European Union
Claims and Payments Regulations	Social Security (Claims and Payments) Regulations 1987
Claims and Payments Regulations 1979	Social Security (Claims and Payments) Regulations 1979
Claims and Payments Regulations 2013	Universal Credit, Personal Independence Payment, Jobseeker's Allowance and Employment and Support Allowance (Claims and Payments) Regulations 2013
CM	Case Manager
CMA	Chief Medical Adviser
CMEC	Child Maintenance and Enforcement Commission
C.M.L.R.	Common Market Law Reports
C.O.D.	Crown Office Digest
COLL	*Collective Investment Schemes Sourcebook*
Community, The	European Community
Computation of Earnings Regulations	Social Security Benefit (Computation of Earnings) Regulations 1978
Computation of Earnings Regulations 1996	Social Security Benefit (Computation of Earnings) Regulations 1996
Consequential Provisions Act	Social Security (Consequential Provisions) Act 1992
Contributions and Benefits Act	Social Security Contributions and Benefits Act 1992
Contributions Regulations	Social Security (Contributions) Regulations 2001
COPD	chronic obstructive pulmonary disease
CP	Carer Premium; Chamber President
CPAG	Child Poverty Action Group
CPR	Civil Procedure Rules
Cr. App. R.	Criminal Appeal Reports
CRCA 2005	Commissioners for Revenue and Customs Act 2005
Credits Regulations 1974	Social Security (Credits) Regulations 1974
Credits Regulations 1975	Social Security (Credits) Regulations 1975
Crim. L.R.	Criminal Law Review
CRU	Compensation Recovery Unit
CSA 1995	Children (Scotland) Act 1995
CSIH	Inner House of the Court of Session (Scotland)
CSM	Child Support Maintenance
CS(NI)O 1995	Child Support (Northern Ireland) Order 1995

CSOH	Outer House of the Court of Session (Scotland)
CSPSSA 2000	Child Support, Pensions and Social Security Act 2000
CTA	Common Travel Area
CTA 2009	Corporation Tax Act 2009
CTA 2010	Corporation Tax Act 2010
CTB	Council Tax Benefit
CTC	Child Tax Credit
CTC Regulations	Child Tax Credit Regulations 2002
CTF	child trust fund
CTS	Carpal Tunnel Syndrome
DAC	Directive 2011/16/ EU (Directive on administrative co-operation in the field of taxation)
DAT	Disability Appeal Tribunal
dB	decibels
DCA	Department for Constitutional Affairs
DCP	Disabled Child Premium
Decisions and Appeals Regulations 1999	Social Security Contributions (Decisions and Appeals) Regulations 1999
Dependency Regulations	Social Security Benefit (Dependency) Regulations 1977
DfEE	Department for Education and Employment
DHSS	Department of Health and Social Security
Disability Living Allowance Regulations	Social Security (Disability Living Allowance) Regulations
DIY	do it yourself
DLA	Disability Living Allowance
DLA Regs 1991	Social Security (Disability Living Allowance) Regulations 1991
DLAAB	Disability Living Allowance Advisory Board
DLADWAA 1991	Disability Living Allowance and Disability Working Allowance Act 1991
DM	Decision Maker
DMA	Decision-making and Appeals
DMG	*Decision Makers' Guide*
DMP	Delegated Medical Practitioner
DP	Disability Premium
DPT	diffuse pleural thickening
DPTC	Disabled Person's Tax Credit
DRO	Debt Relief Order
DSD	Department for Social Development (Northern Ireland)

DSM IV; DSM-5	Diagnostic and Statistical Manual of Mental Disorders of the American Psychiatric Association
DSS	Department of Social Security
DTI	Department of Trade and Industry
DWA	Disability Working Allowance
DWP	Department for Work and Pensions
DWPMS	Department for Work and Pensions Medical Service
EAA	Extrinsic Allergic Alveolitis
EAT	Employment Appeal Tribunal
EC	European Community
ECHR	European Convention on Human Rights
ECJ	European Court of Justice
E.C.R.	European Court Reports
ECSC	European Coal and Steel Community
ECSMA	European Convention on Social and Medical Assistance
EEA	European Economic Area
EEA EFTA Separation Agreement	Agreement on arrangements between Iceland, the Principality of Liechtenstein, the Kingdom of Norway and the United Kingdom of Great Britain and Northern Ireland following the withdrawal of the United Kingdom from the European Union, the EEA Agreement and other agreements applicable between the United Kingdom and the EEA EFTA States by virtue of the United Kingdom's membership of the European Union
EEA Regulations 2016	Immigration (European Economic Area) Regulations 2016
EEC	European Economic Community
EESSI	Electronic Exchange of Social Security Information
E.G.	Estates Gazette
E.G.L.R.	Estates Gazette Law Reports
EHC plan	education, health and care plan
EHIC	European Health Insurance Card
EHRC	European Human Rights Commission
E.H.R.R.	European Human Rights Reports
EL	employers' liability
E.L.R	Education Law Reports
EMA	Education Maintenance Allowance
EMP	Examining Medical Practitioner
Employment and Support Allowance Regulations	Employment and Support Allowance Regulations 2008

EPS	extended period of sickness
Eq. L.R.	Equality Law Reports
ERA	evoked response audiometry
ERA scheme	Employment, Retention and Advancement scheme
ES	Employment Service
ESA	Employment and Support Allowance
ESA Regs 2013	Employment and Support Allowance Regulations 2013
ESA Regulations	Employment and Support Allowance Regulations 2008
ESA WCAt	Employment and Support Allowance Work Capability Assessment
ESC	employer supported childcare
ESE Scheme	Employment, Skills and Enterprise Scheme
ESE Regulations	Jobseeker's Allowance (Employment, Skills and Enterprise Scheme) Regulations 2011
ESES Regulations	Jobseeker's Allowance (Employment, Skills and Enterprise Scheme) Regulations 2011
ETA 1973	Employment and Training Act 1973
ETA(NI) 1950	Employment and Training Act (Northern Ireland) 1950
ETS	European Treaty Series
EU	European Union
Eu.L.R.	European Law Reports
EWCA Civ	Civil Division of the Court of Appeal (England and Wales)
EWHC Admin	Administrative Court, part of the High Court (England and Wales)
FA 1993	Finance Act 1993
FA 1996	Finance Act 1996
FA 2004	Finance Act 2004
Fam. Law	Family Law
FAS	Financial Assistance Scheme
F.C.R.	Family Court Reporter
FEV	forced expiratory volume
FIS	Family Income Supplement
FISMA 2000	Financial Services and Markets Act 2000
F.L.R.	Family Law Reports
FME	further medical evidence
F(No.2)A 2005	Finance (No.2) Act 2005
FOTRA	Free of Tax to Residents Abroad

FRAA	flat rate accrual amount
FRS Act 2004	Fire and Rescue Services Act 2004
FSCS	Financial Services Compensation Scheme
FTT	First-tier Tribunal
General Benefit Regulations 1982	Social Security (General Benefit) Regulations 1982
General Regulations	Statutory Shared Parental Pay (General) Regulations 2014
GMCA	Greater Manchester Combined Authority
GMFRA	Greater Manchester Fire and Rescue Authority
GMP	Guaranteed Minimum Pension
GMWDA	Greater Manchester Waste Disposal Authority
GNVQ	General National Vocational Qualification
GP	General Practitioner
GRA	Gender Recognition Act 2004
GRB	Graduated Retirement Benefit
GRP	Graduated Retirement Pension
HB	Housing Benefit
HB (WSP) R (NI) 2017	Housing Benefit (Welfare Social Payment) Regulations (Northern Ireland) 2017
HBRB	Housing Benefit Review Board
HCA	Homes and Communities Agency
HCD	House of Commons Debates
HCP	healthcare professional
HCV	Hepatitis C virus
Health Service Act	National Health Service Act 2006
Health Service (Wales) Act	National Health Service (Wales) Act 2006
HIV	Human Immunodeficiency Virus
HL	House of Lords
H.L.R.	Housing Law Reports
HMIT	Her Majesty's Inspector of Taxes
HMRC	Her Majesty's Revenue and Customs
HMSO	Her Majesty's Stationery Office
Hospital In-Patients Regulations 1975	Social Security (Hospital In-Patients) Regulations 1975
HP	Health Professional
HPP	Higher Pensioner Premium
HRA 1998	Human Rights Act 1998
H.R.L.R.	Human Rights Law Reports
HRP	Home Responsibilities Protection
HSE	Health and Safety Executive

IAC	Immigration and Asylum Chamber
IAP	Intensive Activity Period
IB	Incapacity Benefit
IB PCA	Incapacity Benefit Personal Capability Assessment
IB Regs	Social Security (Incapacity Benefit) Regulations 1994
IB Regulations	Social Security (Incapacity Benefit) Regulations 1994
IB/IS/SDA	Incapacity Benefits Regime
IBJSA	Income-Based Jobseeker's Allowance
IBS	Irritable Bowel Syndrome
ICA	Invalid Care Allowance
I.C.R.	Industrial Cases Reports
ICTA 1988	Income and Corporation Taxes Act 1988
IFW Regulations	Incapacity for Work (General) Regulations 1995
IH	Inner House of the Court of Session
I.I.	Industrial Injuries
IIAC	Industrial Injuries Advisory Council
IIDB	Industrial Injuries Disablement Benefit
ILO	International Labour Organization
Imm. A.R.	Immigration Appeal Reports
Incapacity for Work Regulations	Social Security (Incapacity for Work) (General) Regulations 1995
Income Support General Regulations	Income Support (General) Regulations 1987
IND	Immigration and Nationality Directorate of the Home Office
I.N.L.R.	Immigration and Nationality Law Reports
I.O.	Insurance Officer
IPPR	Institute of Public Policy Research
IRESA	Income-Related Employment and Support Allowance
I.R.L.R.	Industrial Relations Law Reports
IS	Income Support
IS Regs	Income Support Regulations
IS Regulations	Income Support (General) Regulations 1987
ISA	Individual Savings Account
ISBN	International Standard Book Number
ITA 2007	Income Tax Act 2007
ITEPA 2003	Income Tax, Earnings and Pensions Act 2003
I.T.L. Rep.	International Tax Law Reports

I.T.R.	Industrial Tribunals Reports
ITS	Independent Tribunal Service
ITTOIA 2005	Income Tax (Trading and Other Income) Act 2005
IVB	Invalidity Benefit
IW (General) Regs	Social Security (Incapacity for Work) (General) Regulations 1995
IW (Transitional) Regs	Incapacity for Work (Transitional) Regulations
Jobseeker's Allowance Regulations	Jobseeker's Allowance Regulations 1996
Jobseeker's Regulations 1996	Jobseeker's Allowance Regulations 1996
JSA	Jobseeker's Allowance
JSA 1995	Jobseekers Act 1995
JSA (NI) Regulations	Jobseeker's Allowance (Northern Ireland) Regulations 1996
JSA (Transitional) Regulations	Jobseeker's Allowance (Transitional) Regulations 1996
JSA Regs 1996	Jobseeker's Allowance Regulations 1996
JSA Regs 2013	Jobseeker's Allowance Regulations 2013
JS(NI)O 1995	Jobseekers (Northern Ireland) Order 1995
J.S.S.L.	Journal of Social Security Law
J.S.W.L.	Journal of Social Welfare Law
K.B.	Law Reports, King's Bench
L.& T.R.	Landlord and Tenant Reports
LCW	limited capability for work
LCWA	Limited Capability for Work Assessment
LCWRA	limited capability for work-related activity
LDEDC Act 2009	Local Democracy, Economic Development and Construction Act 2009
LEA	local education authority
LEL	Lower Earnings Limit
LET	low earnings threshold
LGA 2003	Local Government Act 2003
L.G. Rev.	Local Government Review
L.G.L.R.	Local Government Reports
L.J.R.	Law Journal Reports
LRP	liable relative payment
L.S.G.	Law Society Gazette
Luxembourg Court	Court of Justice of the European Union (also referred to as CJEC and ECJ)
MA	Maternity Allowance
MAF	Medical Assessment Framework
Maternity Allowance Regulations	Social Security (Maternity Allowance) Regulations 1987

MDC	Mayoral development corporation
ME	myalgic encephalomyelitis
Medical Evidence Regulations	Social Security (Medical Evidence) Regulations 1976
MEN	Mandatory Employment Notification
Mesher and Wood	*Income Support, the Social Fund and Family Credit: the Legislation* (1996)
M.H.L.R.	Mental Health Law Reports
MHP	mental health problems
MIF	minimum income floor
MIG	minimum income guarantee
Migration Regulations	Employment and Support Allowance (Transitional Provisions, Housing Benefit and Council Tax Benefit (Existing Awards) (No.2) Regulations 2010
MP	Member of Parliament
MRSA	methicillin-resistant Staphylococcus aureus
MS	Medical Services
MWA Regulations	Jobseeker's Allowance (Mandatory Work Activity Scheme) Regulations 2011
MWAS Regulations	Jobseeker's Allowance (Mandatory Work Activity Scheme) Regulations 2011
NCB	National Coal Board
NDPD	Notes on the Diagnosis of Prescribed Diseases
NHS	National Health Service
NI	National Insurance
N.I..	Northern Ireland Law Reports
NICA	Northern Ireland Court of Appeal
NICom	Northern Ireland Commissioner
NICs	National Insurance Contributions
NINO	National Insurance Number
NIRS 2	National Insurance Recording System
N.L.J.	New Law Journal
NMC	Nursing and Midwifery Council
Northern Ireland Contributions and Benefits Act	Social Security Contributions and Benefits (Northern Ireland) Act 1992
N.P.C.	New Property Cases
NRCGT	non-resident capital gains tax
NTC Manual	Clerical procedures manual on tax credits
NUM	National Union of Mineworkers
NUS	National Union of Students
OCD	obsessive compulsive disorder

Table of Abbreviations used in this Series

Ogus, Barendt and Wikeley	A. Ogus, E. Barendt and N. Wikeley, *The Law of Social Security* (1995)
Old Cases Act	Industrial Injuries and Diseases (Old Cases) Act 1975
OPB	One Parent Benefit
O.P.L.R.	Occupational Pensions Law Reports
OPSSAT	Office of the President of Social Security Appeal Tribunals
Overlapping Benefits Regulations	Social Security (Overlapping Benefits) Regulations 1975
P	retirement pension case
P. & C.R.	Property and Compensation Reports
para.	paragraph
Pay Regulations	Statutory Paternity Pay and Statutory Adoption Pay (General) Regulations 2002; Statutory Shared Parental Pay (General) Regulations 2014
PAYE	Pay As You Earn
PC	Privy Council
PCA	Personal Capability Assessment
PCC	Police and Crime Commissioner
PD	Practice Direction; prescribed disease
Pens. L.R.	Pensions Law Reports
Pensions Act	Pension Schemes Act 1993
PEP	Personal Equity Plan
Persons Abroad Regulations	Social Security Benefit (Persons Abroad) Regulations 1975
Persons Residing Together Regulations	Social Security Benefit (Persons Residing Together) Regulations 1977
PIE	Period of Interruption of Employment
PILON	pay in lieu of notice
Pilot Scheme Regulations	Universal Credit (Work-Related Requirements) In Work Pilot Scheme and Amendment Regulations 2015
PIP	Personal Independence Payment
P.I.Q.R.	Personal Injuries and Quantum Reports
Polygamous Marriages Regulations	Social Security and Family Allowances (Polygamous Marriages) Regulations 1975
PPF	Pension Protection Fund
Prescribed Diseases Regulations	Social Security (Industrial Injuries) (Prescribed Diseases) Regulations 1985
PSCS	Pension Service Computer System
Pt	Part
PTA	pure tone audiometry
P.T.S.R.	Public and Third Sector Law Reports

PTWR 2000	Part-time Workers (Prevention of Less Favourable Treatment) Regulations 2000
PVS	private and voluntary sectors
Q.B.	Queen's Bench Law Reports
QBD	Queen's Bench Division
QCS Board	Quality Contract Scheme Board
QEF	qualifying earnings factor
QYP	qualifying young person
r.	rule
R	Reported Decision
R.C.	Rules of the Court of Session
REA	Reduced Earnings Allowance
Reciprocal Agreement with Ireland	Convention on Social Security between the Government of the United Kingdom and Northern Ireland and the Government of Ireland
reg.	regulation
RIPA	Regulation of Investigatory Powers Act 2000
RMO	Responsible Medical Officer
rr.	rules
RR	reference rate
RSI	repetitive strain injury
RTI	Real Time Information
R.V.R.	Rating & Valuation Reporter
s.	section
S	Scottish Decision
SAP	Statutory Adoption Pay
SAPOE Regulations	Jobseeker's Allowance (Schemes for Assisting Persons to Obtain Employment) Regulations 2013
SAWS	Seasonal Agricultural Work Scheme
SAYE	Save As You Earn
SB	Supplementary Benefit
SBAT	Supplementary Benefit Appeal Tribunal
SBC	Supplementary Benefits Commission
S.C.	Session Cases
S.C. (H.L.)	Session Cases (House of Lords)
S.C. (P.C.)	Session Cases (Privy Council)
S.C.C.R.	Scottish Criminal Case Reports
S.C.L.R.	Scottish Civil Law Reports
Sch.	Schedule
SDA	Severe Disablement Allowance
SDP	Severe Disability Premium

SEC	Social Entitlement Chamber
SEN	special educational needs
SERPS	State Earnings Related Pension Scheme
ShPP	statutory shared parental pay
ShPP Regulations	Statutory Shared Parental Pay (General) Regulations 2014
SI	Statutory Instrument
SIP	Share Incentive Plan
S.J.	Solicitors Journal
S.J.L.B.	Solicitors Journal Law Brief
SLAN	statement like an award notice
S.L.T.	Scots Law Times
SMP	Statutory Maternity Pay
SMP (General) Regulations 1986	Statutory Maternity Pay (General) Regulations 1986
Social Security Directive	Council Directive 79/7/EEC of 19 December 1978 on the progressive implementation of the principle of equal treatment for men and women in matters of social security
SPC	State Pension Credit
SPC Regulations	State Pension Credit Regulations 2002
SPCA 2002	State Pension Credit Act 2002
SPL Regulations	Shared Parental Leave Regulations 2014
SPP	Statutory Paternity Pay
ss.	sections
SS (No.2) A 1980	Social Security (No.2) Act 1980
SSA 1975	Social Security Act 1975
SSA 1977	Social Security Act 1977
SSA 1978	Social Security Act 1978
SSA 1979	Social Security Act 1979
SSA 1981	Social Security Act 1981
SSA 1986	Social Security Act 1986
SSA 1988	Social Security Act 1988
SSA 1989	Social Security Act 1989
SSA 1990	Social Security Act 1990
SSA 1998	Social Security Act 1998
SSAA 1992	Social Security Administration Act 1992
SSAC	Social Security Advisory Committee
SSAT	Social Security Appeal Tribunal
SSCBA 1992	Social Security Contributions and Benefits Act 1992
SSCB(NI)A 1992	Social Security Contributions and Benefits (Northern Ireland) Act 1992

SSCPA 1992	Social Security (Consequential Provisions) Act 1992
SSD	Secretary of State for Defence
SSHBA 1982	Social Security and Housing Benefits Act 1982
SSHD	Secretary of State for the Home Department
SSI	Scottish Statutory Instrument
SS(MP)A 1977	Social Security (Miscellaneous Provisions) Act 1977
SSP	Statutory Sick Pay
SSP (General) Regulations	Statutory Sick Pay (General) Regulations 1982
SSPA 1975	Social Security Pensions Act 1975
SSPP	statutory shared parental pay
SS(S)A 2018	Social Security (Scotland) Act 2018
SSWP	Secretary of State for Work and Pensions
State Pension Credit Regulations	State Pension Credit Regulations 2002
S.T.C.	Simon's Tax Cases
S.T.C. (S.C.D.)	Simon's Tax Cases: Special Commissioners' Decisions
S.T.I.	Simon's Tax Intelligence
STIB	Short-Term Incapacity Benefit
subpara.	subparagraph
subs.	subsection
Swiss Citizens' Rights Agreement	Agreement between the United Kingdom of Great Britain and Northern Ireland and the Swiss Confederation on citizens' rights following the withdrawal of the United Kingdom from the European Union and the Free Movement of Persons Agreement
T	Tribunal of Commissioners' Decision
T.C.	Tax Cases
TCA 1999	Tax Credits Act 1999
TCA 2002	Tax Credits Act 2002
TCC	Technology and Construction Court
TCEA 2007	Tribunals, Courts and Enforcement Act 2007
TCGA 1992	Taxation of Chargeable Gains Act 2002
TCTM	*Tax Credits Technical Manual*
TEC	Treaty Establishing the European Community
TENS	transcutaneous electrical nerve stimulation
TEU	Treaty on European Union
TFC	tax-free childcare

TFEU	Treaty on the Functioning of the European Union
TIOPA 2010	Taxation (International and Other Provisions) Act 2010
TMA 1970	Taxes Management Act 1970
T.R.	Taxation Reports
Transfer of Functions Act	Social Security Contributions (Transfer of Functions etc.) Act 1999
Tribunal Procedure Rules	Tribunal Procedure (First-tier Tribunal)(Social Entitlement Chamber) Rules 2008
UB	Unemployment Benefit
UC	Universal Credit
UC Regs 2013	Universal Credit Regulations 2013
UCITS	Undertakings for Collective Investments in Transferable Securities
UKAIT	UK Asylum and Immigration Tribunal
UKBA	UK Border Agency of the Home Office
UKCC	United Kingdom Central Council for Nursing, Midwifery and Health Visiting
UKFTT	United Kingdom First-tier Tribunal Tax Chamber
UKHL	United Kingdom House of Lords
U.K.H.R.R.	United Kingdom Human Rights Reports
UKSC	United Kingdom Supreme Court
UKUT	United Kingdom Upper Tribunal
UN	United Nations
Universal Credit Regulations	Universal Credit Regulations 2013
URL	uniform resource locator
USI Regs	Social Security (Unemployment, Sickness and Invalidity Benefit) Regulations 1983
USI Regulations	Social Security (Unemployment, Sickness and Invalidity Benefit) Regulations 1983
UT	Upper Tribunal
VAT	Value Added Tax
VCM	vinyl chloride monomer
Vol.	Volume
VWF	Vibration White Finger
W	Welsh Decision
WCA	Work Capability Assessment
WCAt	limited capability for work assessment
WFHRAt	Work-Focused Health-Related Assessment
WFI	work-focused interview
WFTC	Working Families Tax Credit

Wikeley, Annotations	N. Wikeley, "Annotations to Jobseekers Act 1995 (c.18)" in *Current Law Statutes Annotated* (1995)
Wikeley, Ogus and Barendt	Wikeley, Ogus and Barendt, *The Law of Social Security* (2002)
Withdrawal Agreement	Agreement on the Withdrawal of the United Kingdom of Great Britain and Northern Ireland from the European Union and the European Atomic Energy Community 2019
W.L.R.	Weekly Law Reports
WLUK	Westlaw UK
Workmen's Compensation Acts	Workmen's Compensation Acts 1925 to 1945
WP	Widow's Pension
WPS	War Pensions Scheme
WRA 2007	Welfare Reform Act 2007
WRA 2009	Welfare Reform Act 2009
WRA 2012	Welfare Reform Act 2012
W-RA Regulations	Employment and Support Allowance (Work-Related Activity) Regulations 2011
WRAAt	Work-Related Activity Assessment
WRPA 1999	Welfare Reform and Pensions Act 1999
WRP(NI)O 1999	Welfare Reform and Pensions (Northern Ireland) Order 1999
WRWA 2016	Welfare Reform and Work Act 2016
WSP (LCP) R (NI) 2016	Welfare Supplementary Payment (Loss of Carer Payments) Regulations (Northern Ireland) 2016
WSP (LDRP) R (NI) 2016	Welfare Supplementary Payment (Loss of Disability-Related Premiums) Regulations (Northern Ireland) 2016
WSPR (NI) 2016	Welfare Supplementary Payment Regulations (Northern Ireland) 2016
WTC	Working Tax Credit
WTC Regulations	Working Tax Credit (Entitlement and Maximum Rate) Regulations 2002

TABLE OF CASES

Table of Cases

TABLE OF SOCIAL SECURITY COMMISSIONERS' DECISIONS

TABLE OF EUROPEAN LEGISLATION

TABLE OF STATUTES

TABLE OF STATUTORY INSTRUMENTS

PART I

NEW LEGISLATION

NEW REGULATIONS

The Universal Credit (Coronavirus) (Restoration of the Minimum Income Floor) Regulations 2021

SI 2021/807

Made by the Secretary of State in exercise of powers conferred by sections 22(2) and 42(1) to (3) of, and paragraph 4(1), (3)(a) and (4) of Schedule 1 to, the Welfare Reform Act 2012, the Social Security Advisory Committee having agreed that the proposals in respect of these Regulations should not be referred to it.

Citation, commencement and interpretation

1.—(1) These Regulations may be cited as the Universal Credit (Coronavirus) (Restoration of the Minimum Income Floor) Regulations 2021 and come into force on 31st July 2021.   1.001

(2) In these Regulations—

(a) "the Universal Credit Regulations" means the Universal Credit Regulations 2013;

(b) "the Coronavirus Further Measures Regulations" means the Social Security (Coronavirus) (Further Measures) Regulations 2020,

and other words and expressions in these Regulations have the same meaning as in regulation 2 of the Coronavirus Further Measures Regulations.

Restoration of the minimum income floor

2.—(1) Regulation 2 (universal credit—minimum income floor) of the Coronavirus Further Measures Regulations is, apart from sub-paragraphs (1)(c) and (d), to continue to have effect up to and including 31st July 2022, subject to the following provisions.   1.002

(2) Where the MIF easement is being applied to a claimant on the coming into force of these Regulations, the Secretary of State must, subject to paragraph (3), cease to apply that easement from the assessment period immediately after the assessment period in which the following conditions are met—

(a) the Secretary of State has determined that the claimant continues to be in gainful self-employment; and

(b) if the claimant was in a start-up period on 13th March 2020, the same number of complete months of that period that remained on that date have elapsed since the determination in sub-paragraph (a).

3

(3) The Secretary of State may continue to apply the MIF easement after the assessment period in which the conditions mentioned in paragraph (2) are met, but only if it appears that the trade, profession or vocation carried on by the claimant remains adversely affected by the outbreak of coronavirus disease, and not for more than two consecutive assessment periods on a single occasion and not for more than six assessment periods in total.

(4) The Secretary of State may, if satisfied that economic conditions have sufficiently improved, determine that the MIF easement is no longer to apply to any claimant.

(5) The application of the MIF easement for a specific period in relation to a particular claimant by virtue of paragraph (2)(b) or (3) is not to be affected by the expiry of this regulation or by a determination of the Secretary of State under paragraph (4).

(6) References in this regulation to the MIF easement are to the individual threshold or the couple threshold in regulation 62 (minimum income floor) of the Universal Credit Regulations 2013 being treated by the Secretary of State as if it were a lesser amount (including zero) in accordance with regulation 2(1)(a) of the Coronavirus Further Measures Regulations.

GENERAL NOTE

1.003   See the entry in this Supplement for pp.372-73 of Vol.II for discussion of the effect of reg.2.

NEW SCOTTISH STATUTORY INSTRUMENTS

The Disability Assistance for Children and Young People (Consequential Amendment and Transitional Provision) (Scotland) Regulations 2021

(SSI 2021/73)

Made	*10th February 2021*
Laid before the Scottish Parliament	*12th February 2021*
Coming into force	*26th July 2021*

The Scottish Ministers make the following Regulations in exercise of the powers conferred by section 95 of the Social Security (Scotland) Act 2018 and all other powers enabling them to do so.

1. to 17. *Omitted.*   1.004

18. *Omitted–this regulation amends the Winter Heating Assistance for Children and Young People (Scotland) Regulations 2020 and the amendments are set out in Part V of this Supplement.*

Transitional provision–extinguishment of right to apply for Disability Living

19.—(1) No person may claim disability living allowance who is under   1.005
the age of 16 years and—
  (a) during the initial period for applications for child disability pay-
      ment, is resident in the local authority area of Perthshire and
      Kinross, City of Dundee or the Western Isles, or
  (b) after the expiry of that period—
      (i) is resident in Scotland, or
      (ii) is a person to whom regulation 5(4) or (6) (residence and
           presence conditions–individuals resident in Ireland, mem-
           bers of Her Majesty's forces and civil servants) or regulation
           9 (persons residing outside the United Kingdom to whom a
           relevant EU regulation applies) of the Child Disability Pay-
           ment Regulations applies.
  (2) Paragraph (1) does not apply to a person who has an award of
disability living allowance which is of—
  (a) both the mobility component and the care component and the
      award in respect of either or both is for a fixed term period, or

5

(b) one of those components only and the award is for a fixed term period,

if the person has been notified by the Secretary of State for Work and Pensions that, because the fixed term period is due to come to an end, the person needs to claim disability living allowance again, or to apply for a supersession of the award, if the person wishes to continue to be entitled to disability living allowance in respect of the component or components subject to the fixed term period.

(3) In this regulation—

"child disability payment" means disability assistance for children and young people given in accordance with the Child Disability Payment Regulations,

"Child Disability Payment Regulations" means the Disability Assistance for Children and Young People (Scotland) Regulations 2021,

"disability living allowance" means a disability living allowance under section 71 of the Social Security Contributions and Benefits Act 1992,

"initial period for applications" means the period referred to in regulation 44 (transitory provision—initial period for applications) of the Child Disability Payment Regulations, beginning with 26 July 2021 and ending with 21 November 2021.

GENERAL NOTE

1.006   This regulation was made in anticipation of the making of the Disability Assistance for Children and Young People (Scotland) Regulations 2021. Its effect is that those entitled to make a claim for child disability payment under Scottish legislation are not entitled to claim disability living allowance under Great Britain legislation, unless a fixed term award of disability living allowance is coming to an end and they would prefer to make a continuation claim for that allowance rather than claim child disability payment.

The current intention is that, for almost all those under the age of 16 and ordinarily resident in Scotland, entitlement to disability living allowance will be converted into entitlement to child disability payment by the end of 2022 (see Pt 3 of the Schedule of the Disability Assistance for Children and Young People (Scotland) Regulations 2021, below).

The Disability Assistance for Children and Young People (Scotland) Regulations 2021

(SSI 2021/174)

Made   *24th March 2021*
Coming into force   *26th July 2021*

The Scottish Ministers make the following Regulations in exercise of the powers conferred by sections 31(2), 36(2), 41(4)(a), 43(5), 51(1), 52 and 95 of the Social Security (Scotland) Act 2018 and all other powers enabling them to do so.

In accordance with section 96(2) of that Act, a draft of these Regulations has been laid before and approved by resolution of the Scottish Parliament.

In accordance with section 97(2) of that Act, the Scottish Ministers have informed the Scottish Commission on Social Security of their proposals, notified the Scottish Parliament that they have done so and made their proposals publicly available by such means as they consider appropriate.

Citation and commencement

1. These Regulations may be cited as the Disability Assistance for Children and Young People (Scotland) Regulations 2021 and come into force on 26 July 2021.

       1.007

Interpretation—general

2. In these Regulations—   **1.008**
"the 2018 Act" means the Social Security (Scotland) Act 2018,
"armed forces independence payment" means the disability benefit paid in accordance with article 24A of the Armed Forces and Reserve Forces (Compensation Scheme) Order 2011,
"authorised provider of vehicles" means a supplier of vehicles for persons with disabilities approved under an accreditation scheme run by the Scottish Ministers,
"award" means that a determination has been made that an individual is entitled to be given assistance under section 24 of the 2018 Act in accordance with these Regulations, and cognate expressions are to be construed accordingly,
"bodily functions" means the normal actions of any organ of the body, including the brain, or of a number of organs acting together,
"care component" means the care component of Child Disability Payment within the meaning of regulation 11,
"care home" means an establishment which provides a care home service as defined in paragraph 2 of schedule 12 of the Public Services Reform (Scotland) Act 2010 and includes a residential educational establishment,
"Child Disability Payment" means disability assistance for children and young people given in accordance with section 31 of the 2018 Act,
"determination" or "determination of entitlement" has the meaning in section 25 of the 2018 Act,

"Disability Living Allowance" means a disability living allowance under—

    (a) section 71 of the Social Security Contributions and Benefits Act 1992, or

    (b) section 71 of the Social Security Contributions and Benefits (Northern Ireland) Act 1992,

"EEA State" means—

    (a) any member state of the European Union, or

    (b) any other state that is party to the agreement on the European Economic Area signed at Oporto on 2 May 1992, together with the Protocol adjusting that Agreement signed at Brussels on 17 March 1993, as modified or supplemented from time to time,

"hospice" means a hospital or other institution whose primary function is to provide palliative care for persons resident there who are suffering from a progressive disease in its final stages other than—

    (a) a health service hospital (within the meaning of section 108(1) of the National Health Service (Scotland) Act 1978) in Scotland,

    (b) a health service hospital (within the meaning of section 275(1) of the National Health Service Act 2006) in England,

    (c) a hospital in Wales vested in—

        (i) an NHS trust,

        (ii) a Local Health Board, or

        (iii) the Welsh Ministers,

    for the purpose of functions under the National Health Service (Wales) Act 2006,

    (d) a hospital maintained or administered by the Defence Council, or

    (e) an institution similar to a hospital mentioned in any of the preceding paragraphs,

[1 "legal detention" means detention in legal custody within the meaning of section 295 of the Criminal Procedure (Scotland) Act 1995,]

"mobility component" means the mobility component of Child Disability Payment within the meaning of regulations 12 and 13,

"personal independence payment" means personal independence payment under—

    (a) Part 4 of the Welfare Reform Act 2012, or

    (b) article 82 of the Welfare Reform (Northern Ireland) Order 2015,

"qualifying services" means accommodation, board and personal care,

"relevant EU Regulation" means—

    (a) one of the following Regulations—

        (i) Council Regulation (EC) No 1408/71 of 14 June 1971 on the application of social security schemes to employed persons, to self-employed persons and to members of their families moving within the Community,

    (ii) Regulation (EC) No 883/2004 of the European Parliament and of the Council of 29 April 2004 on the coordination of social security systems, or

(b) in relation to an individual to whom the agreement constituted by the exchange of letters set out in the schedule of the Family Allowances, National Insurance and Industrial Injuries (Gibraltar) Order 1974 applies, a Regulation mentioned in paragraph (a) of this definition as it forms part of domestic law by virtue of section 3 of the European Union (Withdrawal) Act 2018,

"residential educational establishment" means a care home which provides education or training except for one where the costs of any qualifying services are borne wholly or partly out of public or local funds by virtue of—

(a) [¹ section 485 of the Education Act 1996 or section 14 of the Education Act 2002 (which relate to grants and financial assistance for education),]

(b) sections 49 or 73 of the Education (Scotland) Act 1980 (which relate respectively to the power of education authorities to assist persons to take advantage of educational facilities and the powers of the Secretary of State to make grants to education authorities and others),

(c) section 65 of the Further and Higher Education Act 1992, sections 39 or 40 of the Higher Education and Research Act 2017 or sections 4 or 11 of the Further and Higher Education (Scotland) Act 2005 (which relate respectively to the funding of further education and the administration of funds), or

(d) section 22 of the Teaching and Higher Education Act 1998,

"transferring individual" has the meaning set out in paragraph 7 of the schedule, and

"week" means a period of 7 days.

AMENDMENTS

1. Disability Assistance for Children and Young People (Scotland) Amendment Regulations 2021 (SSI 2021/416) regs 2 and 3 (November 22, 2021).

Overview

3.—(1) An individual is entitled to Child Disability Payment in accordance with these Regulations if they meet the eligibility rules in—   1.009

(a) regulation 4 (age criteria),

(b) regulations 5 to 9 (residence and presence conditions, etc.),

(c) regulation 10 (entitlement to other benefits),

(d) one or more of the following—

    (i) regulation 11 (care component criterion: lowest, middle and highest rate of care component),

(ii) regulation 12 (mobility requirements: lower rate mobility component),

(iii) regulation 13 (mobility requirements: higher rate mobility component),

(iv) regulation 15 (entitlement under special rules for terminal illness),

(v) regulation 16 (entitlement to care component when undergoing dialysis).

(2) Child Disability Payment is to consist of a care component and a mobility component.

(3) There are 3 weekly rates of the care component and 2 weekly rates of the mobility component and those rates are specified in regulation 23 (amount and form of Child Disability Payment).

Age criteria

1.010   **4.**—(1) Subject to [¹ paragraph (1A), (1B) and (2)], Child Disability Payment may be paid in respect of an individual who is aged at least 3 months and is under the age of 18 years.

[¹ (1A) Where regulation 15 (entitlement under special rules for terminal illness) applies, the requirement in paragraph (1) to be aged at least 3 months does not apply.

(1B) Child Disability Payment may continue to be paid in respect of an individual who is over the age of 17 years—

(a) where they are an individual to whom regulation 15 (entitlement under special rules for terminal illness) applies,

(b) until the age of 19 years where—

(i) the individual is awaiting a determination of their entitlement to disability assistance for working age people under regulations made under section 31 of the 2018 Act,

(ii) they are an individual mentioned in regulation 35 (individuals in respect of whom Disability Living Allowance is paid in another part of the United Kingdom immediately before moving to Scotland), or

(iii) they are a transferring individual in terms of Part 3 of the schedule.]

(2) [¹ Where an individual's entitlement to Child Disability Payment is first determined on the basis of an application made in accordance with section 38 of the 2018 Act,] Child Disability Payment may only be paid in respect of an individual who is under the age of 16 years on the day on which entitlement begins in accordance with regulation 24 (when an application is to be treated as made and beginning of entitlement to assistance).

(3) Where an individual was born on 29 February, the individual's birthday is to be taken to fall on 28 February in a year which is not a leap year.

Amendments

1. Disability Assistance for Children and Young People (Scotland) Amendment Regulations 2021 (SSI 2021/416) regs 2 and 4 (November 22, 2021).

10

Residence and presence conditions

5.—(1) An individual satisfies the residence and presence conditions   1.011
where on any day that individual—
- (a) is ordinarily resident in Scotland,
- (b) is habitually resident in the common travel area,
- (c) is not a person to whom section 115(3) of the Immigration and Asylum Act 1999 applies, within the meaning of section 115(9) of that Act [² . . .],
- (d) is present in the common travel area, and
- (e) has been present in the common travel area for a period of, or for periods amounting in the aggregate to, not less than 26 weeks in the 52 weeks immediately preceding that day.

(2) In the case of a child under the age of 6 months, paragraph (1) is to apply as if in sub-paragraph (e) for the reference to 26 weeks there was substituted a reference to 13 weeks.

(3) Where in any particular case a child has by virtue of paragraph (2) entitlement to the care component immediately before the day the child attains the age of 6 months, then until the child attains the age of 12 months, paragraph (1)(e) shall continue to apply in that child's case as if for the reference to 26 weeks there was substituted a reference to 13 weeks.

(4) The residence condition set out in paragraph (1)(a) does not apply in relation to the care component where on any day the individual—
- (a) is habitually resident in Ireland,
- (b) has a genuine and sufficient link to Scotland, and
- (c) is an individual—
  - (i) to whom the Convention on Social Security between the Government of the United Kingdom of Great Britain and Northern Ireland and the Government of Ireland signed at Dublin on 1 February 2019, as modified from time to time in accordance with any provision of it, applies, and
  - (ii) in respect of whom the United Kingdom is, as a result, competent for payment of long term care benefits.

(5) The reference in paragraph (4)(b) to an individual's link to Scotland being sufficient is to it being sufficiently close that if the individual were not entitled to Child Disability Payment, paragraph (4) would be incompatible with Convention on Social Security between the Government of the United Kingdom of Great Britain and Northern Ireland and the Government of Ireland signed at Dublin on 1 February 2019.

(6) A relevant individual is treated as satisfying the residence and presence conditions set out in paragraph (1)(a), [² (b) and (d)] where on any day that individual is outside the common travel area—
- (a) by reason of their capacity mentioned in paragraph (7)(b) provided that individual satisfied the residence and presence conditions set out in paragraph (1)(a), [² (b) and (d)] immediately prior to the start of their employment mentioned in paragraph (7)(b), or
- (b) by reason of being a person mentioned in paragraph (7)(a) living with an individual to whom sub-paragraph (a) applies.

(7) A "relevant individual" in paragraph (6) means an individual who is—

    (a) living with a person mentioned in sub-paragraph (b) and—
        (i) is the child, step-child or a child in care of that person, or
        (ii) is married to or in a civil partnership with that person, or is living together with that person as if they were married or in a civil partnership, or
    (b) outside the common travel area in their capacity as a—
        (i) serving member of Her Majesty's forces, or
        (ii) civil servant.

(8) An individual is to be treated as meeting the presence conditions set out in paragraphs (1)(d) and (e) for any period where that individual is—

    (a) outside the common travel area in their capacity as an aircraft worker or mariner, or
    (b) in employment prescribed for the purposes of section 120 (employment at sea (continental shelf operations)) of the Social Security Contributions and Benefits Act 1992 in connection with continental shelf operations.

(9) Where an individual—

    (a) does not meet the [² either or both of the presence conditions] set out in paragraph [² (1)(d) and (e)] on the date the application is received by the Scottish Ministers, and
    (b) appears to the Scottish Ministers likely to meet [² both of those conditions], unless there is a change of circumstances, on a date not later than 3 months after the application was received,

the Scottish Ministers may choose the date within that 3 month period on which the application is to be treated as being made.

(10) The past presence condition in paragraph (1)(e) does not apply where an individual—

    (a) has a terminal illness within the meaning of regulation 15, [² . . .]
    (b) has—
        (i) been granted refugee status or humanitarian protection under the immigration rules, or
        (ii) leave to enter or remain in the United Kingdom as the dependant of a person granted refugee status or humanitarian protection under the immigration rules, [² or
    (c) is a person described in paragraph 7].

[¹ (10A) The habitual residence condition in paragraph (1)(b) and the past presence condition in paragraph (1)(e) do not apply where an individual—

    (a) has leave to enter or remain in the United Kingdom granted under the immigration rules by virtue of—
        (i) the Afghan Relocations and Assistance Policy, or
        (ii) the previous scheme for locally-employed staff in Afghanistan (sometimes referred to as the ex-gratia scheme),
    (b) has been granted discretionary leave outside the immigration rules as a dependant of a person referred to in sub-paragraph (a); or
    (c) has leave granted under the Afghan Citizens Resettlement Scheme.]

(11) [¹ For the purposes of paragraphs (10) and (10A)—
(a) "immigration rules" means the rules laid before Parliament under
    section 3(2) of the Immigration Act 1971,
(b) "the Afghan Citizens Resettlement Scheme" means the scheme
    announced by the United Kingdom Government on 18 August
    2021.]

AMENDMENTS

1. Social Security (Residence Requirements) (Afghanistan) (Scotland) Regulations 2021 (SSI 2021/320) reg.6 (September 15, 2021).
2. Disability Assistance for Children and Young People (Scotland) Amendment Regulations 2021 (SSI 2021/416) regs 2 and 5 (November 22,
   2021).

Interpretation—residence and presence conditions

6. In regulation 5—   1.012
"aircraft worker" means a person who is, or has been, employed under
    a contract of service either as a pilot, commander, navigator or
    other member of the crew of any aircraft, or in any other capacity
    on board any aircraft where—
    (a) the employment in that other capacity is for the purposes of
        the aircraft or its crew or of any passengers or cargo or
        mails carried on that aircraft, and
    (b) the contract is entered into in the United Kingdom with a
        view to its performance (in whole or in part) while the
        aircraft is in flight,
    but does not include a person in so far as that employment is as
    a serving member of Her Majesty's forces,
"child in care" means—
    (a) under the law of Scotland, a child in respect of whom a
        relevant individual listed in regulation 5(7)(a)—
        (i) Is a foster carer within the meaning of regulation 2 of
            the Looked After Children (Scotland) Regulations
            2009,
        (ii) is a kinship carer within the meaning of regulation 2 of
            the Looked After Children (Scotland) Regulations
            2009,
        (iii) has a kinship care order within the meaning of section
            72 of the Children and Young People (Scotland) Act
            2014, or
    (b) under the law of England and Wales and Northern Ireland,
        a child in respect of whom a person listed in regulation
        5(7)(a) has a relationship equivalent to those listed in para-
        graph (a) under the law of Scotland,
"civil partnership" is to be read as including a reference to marriage of
    a same sex couple and a reference to civil partners or to a person
    who is in a civil partnership is to be construed accordingly,

"civil servant" has the meaning given by section 1(4) of the Constitutional Reform and Governance Act 2010,

"common travel area" has the meaning given in section 1(3) of the Immigration Act 1971,

"mariner" means a person who is, or has been, in employment under a contract of service either as a master or member of the crew of any ship or vessel, or in any other capacity on board any ship or vessel where—

(a) the employment in that other capacity is for the purposes of that ship or vessel or its crew or any passengers or cargo or mails carried by the ship or vessel, and

(b) the contract is entered into in the United Kingdom with a view to its performance (in whole or in part) while the ship or vessel is on its voyage,

but does not include a person in so far as that employment is as a serving member of Her Majesty's forces,

"person who is living with another person as if they were in a civil partnership" is to be read as including a reference to a person who is living with another person of the same sex as if they were married, and

"serving member of Her Majesty's forces" means a member of a regular force or reserve force ("M") as defined, in each case, by section 374 (definitions applying for purposes of the whole Act) of the Armed Forces Act 2006, unless—

(a) M is under the age of 16,

(b) M is committing an offence under section 8 of the Armed Forces Act 2006 (desertion),

(c) the force concerned is one of Her Majesty's naval forces which M locally entered at an overseas base without [¹ . . .]—

  (i) [¹ previously being] an insured person under the National Insurance Act 1965, or

  [(ii) paying or having previously paid one or more of the following classes of contributions under the Social Security Act 1975 or the Social Security Contributions and Benefits Act 1992—

  (aa) primary Class 1,

  (bb) Class 2, or

  (cc) Class 3, or]

(d) the force concerned is one of Her Majesty's military forces or Her Majesty's air forces which M entered, or was recruited for, outside the United Kingdom and—

  (i) where that force is one of Her Majesty's military forces, the depot for M's unit is outside the United Kingdom, or

  (ii) where that force is one of Her Majesty's air forces, M is liable under the terms of M's engagement to serve only in a specified area outside the United Kingdom.

1. Disability Assistance for Children and Young People (Scotland) Amendment Regulations 2021 (SSI 2021/416) regs 2 and 6 (November 22, 2021).

Temporary absence from the common travel area

7.—(1) Where an individual is temporarily absent from the common travel area, the individual is to be treated as present in the common travel area for—   **1.013**
    (a) the first 13 weeks of that absence for any reason, or
    (b) the first 26 weeks of that absence where—
        (i) after the first 13 weeks, the absence is in connection with arrangements made for the medical treatment of the individual for a disease or bodily or mental disablement which commenced before leaving the common travel area, and
        (ii) the arrangements relate to medical treatment—
           (aa) outside the common travel area,
           (bb) during the period when the individual is temporarily absent from the common travel area, and
           (cc) by, or under the supervision of, a person appropriately qualified to carry out that treatment.
(2) For the purposes of paragraph (1)—
    (a) an individual is "temporarily absent" if, at the beginning of the period of absence, that absence is unlikely to exceed 52 weeks, and
    (b) "medical treatment" means medical, surgical, psychological or rehabilitative treatment (including any course, diet or regimen).

Persons residing in the United Kingdom to whom a relevant EU regulation applies

8. The past presence condition set out in regulation 5(1)(e) does not apply where on any day the individual is—   **1.014**
    (a) ordinarily resident in Scotland,
    (b) habitually resident in the United Kingdom,
    (c) an individual—
        (i) to whom the rules set out in a relevant EU regulation applies by virtue of—
           (aa) Title III of Part 2 of the EU withdrawal agreement,
           (bb) Part 3 or Article 23(4) of the Swiss citizens' rights agreement (as defined in section 39(1) of the European Union (Withdrawal Agreement) Act 2020) ("the 2020 Act")),
           (cc) Title III of the EEA EFTA separation agreement (as defined in section 39(1) of the 2020 Act), or
           (dd) the agreement constituted by the exchange of letters set out in the schedule of the Family Allowances, National Insurance and Industrial Injuries (Gibraltar) Order 1974,

(ii) in respect of whom the United Kingdom is, as a result, competent for payment of sickness benefits in cash.

Persons residing outside the United Kingdom to whom a relevant EU regulation applies

1.015   **9.**—(1) The residence and presence conditions set out in regulation 5(1) do not apply in relation to the care component where on any day the individual satisfies the conditions in paragraph (2).

(2) The conditions referred to in paragraph (1) are that the individual must—

(a) be an individual—

    (i) to whom the rules set out in a relevant EU regulation apply by virtue of—

      (aa) Title III of Part 2 of the EU withdrawal agreement,

      (bb) Part 3 or Article 23(4) of the Swiss citizens' rights agreement (as defined in section 39(1) of the European Union (Withdrawal Agreement) Act 2020 ("the 2020 Act")),

      (cc) Title III of the EEA EFTA separation agreement (as defined in section 39(1) of the 2020 Act), or

      (dd) the agreement constituted by the exchange of letters set out in the schedule of the Family Allowances, National Insurance and Industrial Injuries (Gibraltar) Order 1974, and

    (ii) in respect of whom the United Kingdom is, as a result, competent for payment of sickness benefits in cash,

(b) be habitually resident in—

    (i) Switzerland,

    (ii) an EEA state, or

    (iii) Gibraltar, and

(c) have a genuine and sufficient link to Scotland.

(3) The reference in paragraph (2)(c) to an individual's link to Scotland being sufficient is to it being sufficiently close that if the individual were not entitled to Child Disability Payment, paragraph (2) would be incompatible with the applicable agreement mentioned in sub-paragraph (a)(i) of that paragraph.

Entitlement to other benefits

1.016   **10.** An individual is not entitled to Child Disability Payment while they are entitled to—

(a) Disability Living Allowance,

(b) Personal Independence Payment, or

(c) armed forces independence payment.

Care component criterion: lowest, middle or highest rate care component

1.017   **11.**—(1) An individual satisfies the care component criterion in respect of any period throughout which at least one of the following conditions is satisfied—

16

(a) the individual is so severely disabled physically or mentally that they require in connection with their bodily functions attention from another person for a significant portion of the day (whether during a single period or a number of periods),

(b) the individual is 16 years old or older and is so severely disabled physically or mentally that they cannot prepare a cooked main meal for themselves if they have the ingredients,

(c) the individual is so severely disabled physically or mentally that they require from another person—

    (i) frequent attention throughout the day in connection with their bodily functions, or

    (ii) continual supervision throughout the day in order to avoid substantial danger to the individual or others, or

(d) the individual is so severely disabled physically or mentally that they require—

    (i) prolonged or repeated attention from another person [¹ at] night in connection with their bodily functions, or

    (ii) another person to be awake for a prolonged period or at frequent intervals for the purpose of watching over the individual [¹ at] night in order to avoid substantial danger to the individual or others.

(2) No condition mentioned in paragraph (1) is to be taken to be satisfied unless—

(a) the individual has requirements of a description mentioned in the condition substantially in excess of the normal requirements of a person of the same age, or

(b) the individual has substantial requirements of such a description which younger persons in normal physical and mental health may also have but which persons of the individual's age and in normal physical and mental health would not have.

(3) An individual is not entitled to the care component unless—

(a) throughout the period of 13 weeks immediately preceding the date on which the award of that component would begin, the individual has satisfied or is likely to satisfy at least one of the conditions mentioned in paragraph (1) as read with paragraph (2), and

(b) the individual is likely to continue to satisfy at least one of those conditions throughout the period of 26 weeks beginning with that date.

(4) In the case of an individual who is under the age of 16 on the date on which the award of the care component would begin, paragraph (2) only applies in relation to so much of any period mentioned in that paragraph as falls before the day on which the individual reaches the age of 16.

(5) The amount of the care component that an individual is entitled to be given for each week in the period for which they are awarded that component is—

(a) the highest rate (see regulation 23(1)(a)), if the individual falls within paragraph (3) by virtue of having satisfied or being likely to satisfy both the conditions mentioned in paragraph (1)(c) and (d)

above throughout both the period mentioned in paragraph (3)(a)
and that mentioned in paragraph (3)(b),

(b) the middle rate (see regulation 23(1)(b)), if the individual falls
within paragraph (3) by virtue of having satisfied or being likely to
satisfy one of those conditions mentioned in paragraph (1)(c) or
(d) throughout both those periods, and

(c) the lowest rate (see regulation 23(1)(c)) in any other case.

(6) In paragraph (1)—

(a) references to "day" and "night" are to be construed in relation to
the ordinary domestic routine of the household in which the
individual lives, and

(b) "attention" means the provision of personal care, prompting or
motivation in relation to bodily functions or assistance with communication needs.

(7) In paragraph (1) and regulation 12, "supervision" means the
precautionary or anticipatory presence of another person to monitor an
individual's physical, mental or emotional health including monitoring
for obstacles or dangerous places or situations.

(8) In this regulation and regulations 12 and 13, "require" means
reasonably require and cognate expressions are to be construed
accordingly.

AMENDMENTS

1. Disability Assistance for Children and Young People (Scotland) Amendment Regulations 2021 (SSI 2021/416) regs 2 and 7 (November 22,
2021).

GENERAL NOTE

1.018   This regulation substantially re-enacts s.72(1) to (4) of the Social Security
Contributions and Benefits Act 1992, which provides for the care component of
disability living allowance throughout Great Britain, but there are some differences apart from the use of gender-neutral language.

In particular, paras (6) to (8) make explicit in the legislation points that are
only implicit in the 1992 Act and are made explicit for the purposes of that Act
only in case law. In addition, the term "bodily functions" is defined in reg.2.
Case law under the 1992 Act (see the annotations in Vol I of the main work) will
nonetheless continue to be relevant.

The amendments to para.(1)(d) correct a drafting error that would have made
the sub-paragraph disadvantageous to some claimants by comparison with
s.72(1)(c) of the 1992 Act.

Mobility requirements: lower rate mobility component

1.019   **12.**—(1) An individual aged 5 years or more is entitled to be given the
mobility component at the lower rate (see regulation 23(2)(b)) if the
individual satisfies the condition set out in paragraph (2).

(2) The condition referred to in paragraph (1) is that the individual,
though able to walk, cannot move around outdoors without requiring
guidance or supervision from another person most of the time as a result
of a physical or mental impairment.

(3) The guidance or supervision required must be—

(a) substantially in excess of the normal requirements of a person of the same age, or

(b) of such a description which younger persons in normal physical and mental health may also require but which persons of the individual's age and in normal physical and mental health would not require.

(4) In the case of an individual who is under the age of 16 on the date on which the award of the mobility component would begin, paragraph (3) only applies in relation to so much of any period mentioned in that paragraph as falls before the day on which the individual reaches the age of 16.

(5) Whether the individual satisfies the condition in paragraph (2), no account is to be taken of any ability which the individual has to use routes with which they are familiar, without guidance or supervision from another person.

(6) An individual is not entitled to the lower rate of the mobility component unless—

(a) throughout the period of 13 weeks immediately preceding the date on which the award of that component would begin, the individual has satisfied or is likely to satisfy the condition mentioned in paragraph (2), and

(b) the individual is likely to continue to satisfy the condition mentioned in paragraph (2) throughout the period of 26 weeks beginning with that date.

(7) In this regulation, "guidance" means direction or leading by physical means or verbal suggestion or persuasion.

GENERAL NOTE

This regulation substantially re-enacts s.73(1)(d), (1A)(b), (4A) and (9) of the   1.020
Social Security Contributions and Benefits Act 1992, which provides for the
mobility component of disability living allowance throughout Great Britain.
Paragraph (7) makes explicit in the legislation the meaning of "guidance"
suggested only in case law in relation to s.73. Note also that reg.11(7) and (8)
define "supervision" and "require" for the purposes of reg.12 as well as reg.11.
Case law under the 1992 Act will nonetheless continue to be relevant (see the
annotations in Vol I of the main work).

Mobility requirements: higher rate mobility component

13.—(1) An individual aged 3 years or more is entitled to be given the   1.021
mobility component at the higher rate (see regulation 23(2)(a)) if the
individual satisfies at least one of the conditions mentioned in paragraph (2).

(2) The conditions referred to in paragraph (1) are—

(a) taking account of the individual's physical condition as a whole, the individual's condition is such that, without having regard to the nature of the location where the individual resides—

(i) the individual is unable to walk,

(ii) the individual's ability to walk out of doors is so limited, as regards the distance over which or the speed at which or the length of time for which or the manner in which the individual can make progress on foot without severe discomfort, that the individual is virtually unable to walk, or

   (iii) the exertion required to walk would constitute a danger to the individual's life, or would be likely to lead to a serious deterioration in the individual's health, from which there would no recovery, or from which recovery would take a significant period of time,

(b) the individual has no legs or no feet (regardless of the use of artificial limbs),

(c) the individual has a severe visual impairment,

(d) the individual is blind and deaf,

(e) the individual has a severe mental impairment and severe behavioural difficulties and satisfies both of the conditions mentioned in regulation 11(1)(c) and (d).

(3) Where paragraph (2)(a) applies in relation to an individual, the test of being unable or virtually unable to walk is not met where the individual—

(a) is not unable or virtually unable to walk with the use of an artificial limb or artificial aid which the individual normally wears or uses, or

(b) would not be unable or virtually unable to walk if the individual wore or used an artificial limb or artificial aid which is suitable to the individual's circumstances.

(4) Paragraph (3) is not relevant for the purpose of determining whether an individual is to be taken to satisfy the conditions set out in paragraphs (2)(b) to (e).

(5) An individual is to be taken to have a severe visual impairment, for the purpose of paragraph (2)(c), if the individual has a severe visual impairment fulfilling the definition given by the Visual Impairment Network for Children and Young People.

(6) An individual is taken to be blind and deaf, for the purpose of paragraph (2)(d), if the individual is—

(a) blind where the loss of vision amounts to an absolute loss of vision,

(b) deaf where loss of hearing when using any artificial aid which they habitually use or which is suitable in their case amounts to not less than 80% on a scale where 100% represents absolute deafness, and

(c) unable, without the assistance of another person, to walk to any intended or required destination while out of doors.

(7) An individual is to be taken to have a severe mental impairment, for the purpose of paragraph (2)(e), if the individual has a severe impairment of intelligence and social functioning resulting from—

(a) a state of arrested development as a result of a failure of the individual's brain to grow or develop in the way normally expected, or

(b) a deficiency in the functionality of the brain as a result of its incomplete physical development.

(8) An individual is to be taken to have severe behavioural difficulties, for the purpose of paragraph (2)(e), if the individual exhibits disruptive behaviour which—

(a) is extreme,

(b) regularly requires another person to intervene in order to prevent or reduce the likelihood of physical injury to the individual or another person, and

(c) is so unpredictable that another person requires to be awake and watching over the individual while the individual is awake.

(9) In paragraph (8)(b), reference to another person intervening relates to the provision of care and support of, or treatment provided to, the individual.

(10) An individual is not entitled to the [¹ higher rate of the] mobility component unless—

(a) throughout the period of 13 weeks immediately preceding the date on which the award of that component would begin, the individual has satisfied or is likely to satisfy one of the conditions mentioned in paragraph (2), and

(b) the individual is likely to continue to satisfy one of those conditions throughout the period of 26 weeks beginning with that date.

AMENDMENT

1. Disability Assistance for Children and Young People (Scotland) Amendment Regulations 2021 (SSI 2021/416) regs 2 and 8 (November 22, 2021).

GENERAL NOTE

This regulation substantially re-enacts the provisions of s.73 of the Social **1.022** Security Contributions and Benefits Act 1992 relating to the higher rate of the mobility component of disability living allowance but, in place of the regulation-making powers in that section, it effectively re-enacts reg.12 of the Social Security (Disability Regulations 1991 which was made in the exercise of those powers. Although there are some differences of language, case law interpreting s.73 of the 1992 Act and reg.12 of the 1991 Regulations and their forerunners is likely to remain relevant (see the annotations to those provisions in Vol I of the main work).

A footnote to reg.13(5) states that the Visual Impairment Network for Children and Young People is a "National Managed Clinical Network forming part of NHS Scotland" and provides a link to their definition of "visual impairment", which is to be found at https://www.vincyp.scot.nhs.uk/vincyp-definition/ and is—

Best corrected visual acuity (both eyes open) equal to or worse than 6/18/0.5 logmar

Requires N18 print or larger to read comfortably

Visual field loss with both eyes open which significantly affects function

Any eye movement disorder which significantly affects visual function

Any form of cognitive visual dysfunction due to disorders of the brain which can be demonstrated to significantly affect function

Note that reg.11(8) defines "require" for the purposes of regs.12 and 13 as well as reg.11.

Exclusion of entitlement to mobility component

1.023   **14.** An individual is not entitled to the mobility component of Child Disability Payment for a period unless, during most of that period, the individual's physical or mental condition is such that they are able, from time to time, to benefit from assistance for movement.

GENERAL NOTE

This regulation substantially re-enacts s.73(8) of the Social Security Contributions and Benefits Act 1992. See the annotations to that provision in Vol.I of the main work.

Entitlement under special rules for terminal illness

1.024   **15.**—(1) An individual who has a terminal illness is—
   (a) to be treated as satisfying the conditions for the highest rate of the care component of Child Disability Payment in regulation 11(5)(a), and
   (b) from the date on which the individual reaches the age of 3, to be treated as satisfying the conditions for the higher rate of the mobility component in regulation 13.

(2) Paragraph (1) applies regardless of—
   (a) the period of time for which the individual has had the terminal illness, and
   (b) any period of time spent by the individual in a hospital or hospice while in receipt of the assistance.

(3) Subject to paragraphs (4) and (5), the individual's entitlement to the rates referred to in paragraph (1) begins on the date on which—
   (a) the individual's application for Child Disability Payment was made, where the application included information about the individual's terminal illness,
   (b) the Scottish Ministers became aware of the individual's terminal illness (whether as a result of the individual notifying a change in circumstances or otherwise), where the individual was previously awarded, and has an ongoing entitlement to, Child Disability Payment, on the basis of a determination that the individual was entitled to the care component or the mobility component or both in relation to a condition other than terminal illness, or
   (c) the clinical judgement was made in accordance with paragraphs (6) and (7) ("the judgement"),
whichever is the earlier.

(4) Where the judgement mentioned in paragraph (3)(c) is dated not more than 26 weeks earlier than whichever date in paragraph (3)(a) or (b) applies ("the relevant date"), the Scottish Ministers have the power, when making their determination, to specify that an individual's entitlement begins—
   (a) up to a maximum of 26 weeks prior to the relevant date, and
   (b) on or after the day these Regulations come into force.

(5) Where the judgement mentioned in paragraph (3)(c)—

    (a) is dated more than 26 weeks earlier than whichever date in paragraph (3)(a) or (b) applies ("the relevant date"), and

    (b) an appropriate healthcare professional confirms that the judgement is still accurate by making a judgement in accordance with paragraphs (6) and (7),

an individual's entitlement can only begin—

    (c) up to a maximum of 26 weeks prior to the relevant date, and

    (d) on or after the day these Regulations come into force.

(6) For the purpose of this regulation, an individual is to be regarded as having a terminal illness for the purpose of determining entitlement to Child Disability Payment if it is the judgement of an appropriate healthcare professional that the individual has a progressive disease that can reasonably be expected to cause the individual's death.

(7) Subject to paragraph (8), an appropriate healthcare professional exercising the judgement described in paragraph (6) must have regard to the guidance prepared and made publicly available by the Chief Medical Officer of the Scottish Administration in accordance with paragraph 1(3) of schedule 5 of the 2018 Act.

(8) Where regulation 9 (persons residing outside the United Kingdom to whom a relevant EU regulation applies) applies to the individual, an appropriate healthcare professional mentioned in paragraph (9)(b) need not have regard to the guidance mentioned in paragraph (7) where it would not be reasonable in the circumstances to insist on the judgement being formed with regard to that guidance.

(9) In this regulation, "an appropriate healthcare professional" means—

    (a) a registered medical practitioner or a registered nurse who is—

        (i) involved in the diagnosis or care of the individual, and

        (ii) acting in their professional capacity, or

    (b) where regulation 9 applies to the individual, a person who—

        (i) has equivalent qualifications to a registered medical practitioner or a registered nurse in an EEA state, Gibraltar or Switzerland,

        (ii) is a member of the professional body equivalent to the General Medical Council or Nursing and Midwifery Council in that EEA state, Gibraltar or Switzerland, and

        (iii) meets the requirements of sub-paragraph (a)(i) and (ii).

[¹ (10) Where an individual has previously received Child Disability Payment for a period and a determination is subsequently made that the same individual is entitled to Child Disability Payment at a higher rate for that period by virtue of this regulation, that individual will be entitled to the difference between the value of entitlement to Child Disability Payment under the subsequent determination and the value of Child Disability Payment to which that individual was previously entitled for that period.]

AMENDMENT

1. Disability Assistance for Children and Young People (Scotland) Amendment Regulations 2021 (SSI 2021/416) regs 2 and 9 (November 22, 2021).

Entitlement to care component when undergoing dialysis

1.025   **16.**—(1) Subject to paragraph (5), an individual who is at least 3 months old is to be treated as satisfying the conditions for the care component in regulation 11 (care component criterion: lowest, middle or highest rate of care component) where the individual undergoes renal dialysis—

(a) where at least one of the conditions in paragraph (2) is met, and

(b) at least twice a week,

as a consequence of a disability or physical impairment.

(2) The conditions are that—

(a) the renal dialysis is of a type which normally requires the attendance or supervision of another person, or

(b) due to particular circumstances, the individual requires another person to attend—

   (i) in connection with the individual's bodily functions, or

   (ii) to supervise the individual in order to avoid substantial danger to the individual,

during the period of the dialysis.

(3) Where the renal dialysis mentioned in paragraph (2) takes place by day or at night, the individual is entitled to the middle rate care component.

(4) Where the renal dialysis mentioned in paragraph (2) takes place both by day and at night, the individual is entitled to the highest rate care component.

(5) An individual is not entitled to the care component unless—

(a) throughout the period of 13 weeks immediately preceding the date on which the award of that component would begin, the individual has satisfied or is likely to satisfy the requirements in paragraph (1) as read with paragraph (2), and

(b) the individual is likely to continue to satisfy those requirements throughout the period of 26 weeks beginning with that date.

Effect of admission to a care home on ongoing entitlement to care component

1.026   **17.**—(1) This regulation applies where an individual who has an ongoing entitlement to the care component of Child Disability Payment, becomes a resident of a care home.

(2) Subject to paragraphs (4) and (5), [¹ on the day after] the day on which the individual has been resident in a care home for 28 days, and for so long as the individual continues to reside in such a home, the value of the care component of Child Disability Payment that is to be given to the individual is £0 instead of the values set out in regulation 23 (amount and form of Child Disability Payment).

(3) The 28 days referred to in paragraph (2) may comprise two or more separate periods, provided that there is no more than 28 days between each period.

(4) Paragraph (2) does not apply to a resident in a care home, where the full costs of any qualifying services are met—

(a) entirely out of the resources of the individual for whom the qualifying services are provided,

(b) partly out of the resources of the individual for whom the qualifying services are provided and partly out of the resources of another person (other than a local authority) or assistance from a charity, or

(c) entirely out of the resources of another person (other than a local authority) or assistance from a charity.

(5) For the purposes of this regulation, an individual is not resident in a care home during any period when the individual is being looked after by a local authority and—

(a) has been placed temporarily in a private dwelling with a family, relative or some other suitable person while—

(i) under the age of 16, or

(ii) aged between 16 and 18 and receiving services under Part II of the Children (Scotland) Act 1995 by virtue of being a child in need within the meaning of section 93(4)(a)(ii) (impairment of health), or 93(4)(a)(iii) (disability) of that Act, or

(b) is accommodated in a care home outside the United Kingdom, where the costs of any qualifying services are met by a local authority exercising its powers under section 25 of the Education (Additional Support for Learning) (Scotland) Act 2004.

(6) For the purposes of this regulation and regulation 20 (entitlement [¹ to care component] beginning while in alternative accommodation), reference to an individual being "looked after by a local authority" is to be construed, as the case may be, in accordance with—

(a) section 17(6) of the Children (Scotland) Act 1995,

(b) section 105(4) of the Children Act 1989, or

(c) article 25 of the Children (Northern Ireland) Order 1995.

AMENDMENT

1. Disability Assistance for Children and Young People (Scotland) Amendment Regulations 2021 (SSI 2021/416) regs 2 and 10 (November 22, 2021).

Effect of legal detention on ongoing entitlement to care component

18.—(1) This regulation applies where an individual who has an ongoing entitlement to the care component of Child Disability Payment is in legal detention.   1.027

[¹ (1A) For the purposes of this regulation, an individual is to be treated as though they are not in legal detention on any day on which they are an in-patient in a hospital or hospice.]

(2) [¹ On the day after] the day on which an individual has been in legal detention for 28 days, and for so long as the individual continues to be in legal detention, the value of the care component of Child Disability Payment that is to be given to the individual is to be £0, instead of the values set out in regulation 23 (amount and form of Child Disability Payment).

AMENDMENTS

1. Disability Assistance for Children and Young People (Scotland) Amendment Regulations 2021 (SSI 2021/416) regs 2 and 11 (November 22, 2021).

Calculation of periods of time spent in a care home or in legal detention

1.028   **19.**—(1) Subject to paragraphs (2) and (3), a period during which an individual is resident in a care home for the purpose of regulation 17 or in legal detention for the purpose of regulation 18 is to be taken to—

(a) begin on the day after the day on which the individual enters the care home or legal detention, and

(b) end on the day before the day on which the individual leaves the care home or legal detention.

(2) Where an individual who is resident in a care home takes a period of leave from the home, the days on which the individual begins and returns from leave are not to be counted as days of residence in the home.

(3) Days constituting a period of leave are not to be counted as days of residence in a care home.

(4) Where an individual enters or returns to a care home as a result of a transfer from a hospital or a hospice, or from another care home, the day of transfer is to be counted as a day of residence in a care home.

(5) Where an individual enters legal detention as a result of a transfer from a hospital or a hospice, or from a care home, the day of transfer is to be counted as a day in legal detention.

[¹ Entitlement to care component beginning while in alternative accommodation]

1.029   **20.**—(1) This regulation applies where an individual is resident in a care home or in legal detention on the day on which entitlement to [¹ the care component of] Child Disability Payment begins.

(2) On and after that day, and for so long as the individual continues to reside in a care [¹home], or be in legal detention, the value of the care component of Child Disability Payment that is to be given to the individual is £0 instead of the values set out in regulation 23 (amount and form of Child Disability Payment).

(3) Paragraphs (1) and (2) do not apply where the costs of any qualifying services whilst resident in a care home are met—

(a) entirely out of the resources of the individual for whom the qualifying services are provided,

(b) partly out of the resources of the individual for whom the qualifying services are provided and partly out of the resources of another person (other than a local authority) or assistance from a charity, or

(c) entirely out of the resources of another person (other than a local authority) or assistance from a charity.

(4) For the purposes of this regulation an individual is not resident in a care home during any period when the individual is being looked after by a local authority and—

(a) has been placed temporarily in a private dwelling with a family, relative or some other suitable person while—
    (i) under the age of 16,
    (ii) aged between 16 and 18 and receiving services under Part II of the Children (Scotland) Act 1995 by virtue of being a child in need within the meaning of section 93(4)(a)(ii) (impairment of health), or 93(4)(a)(iii) (disability) of that Act, or
(b) is accommodated in a care home outside the United Kingdom, where the costs of any qualifying services are met by a local authority exercising its powers under section 25 of the Education (Additional Support for Learning) (Scotland) Act 2004.

AMENDMENTS

1. Disability Assistance for Children and Young People (Scotland) Amendment Regulations 2021 (SSI 2021/416) regs 2 and 12 (November 22, 2021).

Entitlement to care component of Child Disability Payment while an in-patient

21. For the avoidance of doubt, any period when an individual is an in-patient in a hospice or hospital, has no effect on the individual's entitlement to the care component of Child Disability Payment.   1.030

Making payments

22.—(1) Where Child Disability Payment is payable in respect of an individual, the Scottish Ministers may, where they consider it appropriate, make the payment to another person to be used for the benefit of the individual.   1.031

(2) Where the Scottish Ministers consider, for any reason, that it is no longer appropriate for a particular person who falls within paragraph (1) to continue to receive the payment, they may cease making payment to that person.

Amount and form of Child Disability Payment

23.—(1) The weekly rate of payment of the care component is where the individual is entitled to—   1.032

(a) the highest rate, £89.60,
(b) the middle rate, £60.00, or
(c) the lowest rate, £23.70.

(2) The weekly rate of payment of the mobility component is where the individual is entitled to—

(a) the higher rate, £62.55, or
(b) the lower rate, £23.70.

(3) Where an individual is entitled to payment of the care component or the mobility component for a period shorter than one week, payment

of that component is to be made at one-seventh of the relevant weekly rate, for each day of entitlement.

(4) For any week where an individual is entitled to—

(a) the care component of Child Disability Payment, and

(b) payment of an amount in respect of constant attendance under section 61 of the Social Security Act 1975,

the amount of the care component of Child Disability Payment that is to be given to the individual is to be reduced by the amount paid under that section.

(5) For the purpose of calculating the amount of the care component that is to be given to the individual, in accordance with paragraph (4), where the amount in respect of constant attendance is equal to or greater than the amount of the care component of Child Disability Payment the value of Child Disability Payment that is to be given to the individual is to be £0.

(6) For any week where an individual is entitled to—

(a) the mobility component of Child Disability Payment, and

(b) payment of War Pensioners' Mobility Supplement within the meaning of—

(i) the Naval, Military and Air Forces etc. (Disablement and Death) Service Pensions Order 1983 ("1983 Order"),

(ii) the Personal Injuries (Civilians) Scheme 1983,

(iii) the 1983 Order by virtue of the War Pensions (Naval Auxiliary Personnel) Scheme 1964,

(iv) the Pensions (Polish Forces) Scheme 1964,

(v) the War Pensions (Mercantile Marine) Scheme 1964, or

(vi) an Order of Her Majesty in relation to the Home Guard dated 21 December 1964 or 22 December 1964, or in relation to the Ulster Defence Regiment dated 4 January 1971,

the amount of the mobility component of Child Disability Payment that is to be given to the individual is to be £0.

(7) For each week in the period of 8 weeks ending with the death of the individual—

(a) the amount of Child Disability Payment that is to be given to that individual is the relevant weekly rate of each component to which the individual is entitled in that week, multiplied by two, and

tli1(b)

any provision in these Regulations reducing the amount to £0 has no effect.

(8) Child Disability Payment may only be given as money, except as provided for by regulation 27(1) (form of payment—giving Child Disability Payment by way of deduction).

When an application is to be treated as made and beginning of entitlement to assistance

1.033   **24.**—(1) An application for Child Disability Payment is to be treated as made—

(a) on the day it is received by the Scottish Ministers, or

(b) if applicable, on the day identified by the Scottish Ministers in accordance with paragraph (2).

(2) If, before making a determination on the basis of an application, the Scottish Ministers consider that the individual in respect of whom the application is made—

(a) would not satisfy the requirement in—

    (i) regulation 4 (age criteria),

    (ii) regulations 5 to 9 (residence and presence conditions etc.),

    (iii) regulation 10 (entitlement to other benefits),

    (iv) regulation 11 (care component criterion: lowest, middle or highest rate of care component),

    (v) regulation 12 (mobility requirements: lower rate mobility component),

    (vi) regulation 13 (mobility requirements: higher rate mobility component), or

    (vii) regulation 16 (entitlement to care component when undergoing dialysis),

if the application were treated as made on the day it was received, and

(b) would likely be entitled to receive Child Disability Payment if those requirements were satisfied within a 13-week period beginning on the day it was received,

the Scottish Ministers may choose the date within that 13 week period on which the application is to be treated as having been made.

(3) Where, on the basis of an application, a determination is made that an individual is entitled to Child Disability Payment, the date on which entitlement begins is to be identified in accordance with paragraphs (4) to (6).

(4) Where an application is made within 6 weeks of the day on which the full name and date of birth of an individual ("the required data") is submitted by, or on behalf of, the individual to the Scottish Ministers for the purpose of an application for Child Disability Payment, entitlement begins on whichever is the later of the day—

(a) on which the required data was submitted, or

(b) identified in accordance with paragraph (2).

(5) Subject to paragraph (6), where an application is made after the 6 week period described in paragraph (4), entitlement begins on the day on which the application is treated as having been made in accordance with paragraph (1).

(6) Where the Scottish Ministers are satisfied that there is good reason why an application was made after the 6 week period described in paragraph (4), they may treat the application as having been made within that period.

(7) For the purposes of section 38(3) (application for assistance) of the 2018 Act, the period covered by an application for Child Disability Payment—

(a) under paragraph (1)(a)—

    (i) begins on the day on which the application is treated as having been made, and

    (ii) ends on the day on which the determination of entitlement is made, and

(b) under paragraph (1)(b)—

    (i) is deemed to begin on the day before the determination is made provided that the requirements are satisfied, and

    (ii) ends on the day on which the determination is made.

Time of payment

1.034   **25.** Where an award of Child Disability Payment is made, the Scottish Ministers are to make—

(a) the first payment of assistance on a date specified in the notice of determination, and

(b) any subsequent payment—

    (i) 4 weekly in arrears, or

    (ii) where regulation 15 (entitlement under special rules for terminal illness) applies, weekly in advance.

Continuing eligibility

1.035   **26.**—(1) Subject to paragraphs (3) and (4), a determination that an individual is entitled to Child Disability Payment in respect of a period is to be made on the basis that the individual has an ongoing entitlement to Child Disability Payment after the end of that period, except where paragraph (2) applies.

(2) This paragraph applies where, after the end of the period mentioned in paragraph (1), the individual no longer satisfies the eligibility rules.

(3) A determination of ongoing entitlement is made on the basis that—

(a) the individual will continue to be entitled to Child Disability Payment for a fixed or indefinite period as specified in the notice of determination, and

(b) the decision that the individual is entitled to Child Disability Payment for each subsequent 4-week period is to be taken in accordance with these Regulations, on the strength of the assumptions set out in paragraph (4).

(4) The assumptions are that—

(a) the individual continues to satisfy the eligibility criteria which were satisfied to be entitled to Child Disability Payment under the determination mentioned in paragraph (1),

(b) the information on which the determination mentioned in paragraph (1) was made still applies and is relevant in the individual's case, and

(c) there is no change in circumstances of the individual which would require to be notified under section 56 (duty to notify change of circumstances) of the 2018 Act.

Form of payment—giving Child Disability Payment by way of deduction

27.—(1) Where an individual has a liability to the Scottish Ministers   **1.036** under section 63 of the 2018 Act (liability for assistance given in error), the individual's payment of Child Disability Payment may be given (in whole or in part) by way of deduction, at a reasonable level, from that liability either—

  (a) with the agreement of the individual, or

  (b) without the individual's agreement, where the individual has unreasonably refused to agree to the assistance being given in that form.

(2) For the purpose of paragraph (1), "reasonable level" means a level that is reasonable having regard to the financial circumstances of the individual.

When an increase in level of entitlement takes effect

28.—(1) Where, as a result of a determination without an application,   **1.037** the amount of Child Disability Payment payable in respect of an individual is increased or their entitlement to a component is awarded, the [¹ change takes effect]—

  (a) in the case of an increase pursuant to a determination made under regulation [¹ 31(c) or (d)] (determination following change of circumstances etc.) on the day after the day on which Disability Living Allowance ceased to be paid in respect of the individual,

  (b) in the case of an award of entitlement to a component or an increase pursuant to a determination made in accordance with regulation 31(a) [¹ . . .] that affects their eligibility under regulation 11 (care component criterion: lowest, middle or highest rate of care component), 12 (mobility requirements: lower rate mobility component) or 13 (mobility requirements: higher rate mobility component), on the date when—

    [¹(i) if as a result of the individual reporting the change—

      (aa) if the individual reports the change within one month of the change occurring, the individual first satisfies the requirements for a higher rate of the care or mobility component,

      (bb) if the individual reports the change more than one month but not more than 13 months of the change occurring, the individual first satisfies the requirements for a higher rate of the care or mobility component, but only if the Scottish Ministers consider that the individual had good reason for not notifying the change within one month,

      (cc) in any other case, the individual reports the change,

    (ii) if as a result of the Scottish Ministers becoming aware that an earlier determination of an individual's entitlement was made in ignorance of a material fact, on the date when the Scottish Ministers make the determination.]

(c) in the case of an earlier determination which was based on official error within the meaning of regulation 32 (determination following official error—underpayments) or on error within the meaning of regulation 33 (determination following error—overpayments), begins on the date when the earlier determination took effect, or

(d) in any other case, on the date when Scottish Ministers make the determination.

(2) Where the Scottish Ministers consider that in all the circumstances it would be unjust not to do so, they may, when making their determination, set an earlier date for the purposes of paragraph 1(b), (c) or (d).

[¹ (2A) Where an individual has previously received Child Disability Payment for a period and a determination without application has been subsequently made that the same individual is entitled to Child Disability Payment at a higher rate for that period, that individual will be entitled to the difference between the value of entitlement to Child Disability Payment under the subsequent determination and the value of Child Disability Payment to which that individual was previously entitled for that period.]

(3) This regulation does not apply to an individual to whom regulation 15 (entitlement under special rules for terminal illness) applies.

AMENDMENTS

1. Disability Assistance for Children and Young People (Scotland) Amendment Regulations 2021 (SSI 2021/416) regs 2 and 13 (November 22, 2021).

When a decrease in level or cessation of entitlement takes effect

1.038   **29.**—(1) Where, as a result of a determination without an application, the amount of Child Disability Payment payable in respect of an individual is decreased or their entitlement to a component is ceased, the [¹ change takes effect]—

(a) in the case of a decrease pursuant to a determination made under regulation [¹ 31(c) or (d)] (determination following change of circumstances etc.) on the day after the day on which Disability Living Allowance ceased to be paid in respect of the individual,

(b) in the case of a determination without application under [¹ regulation 30 or] 31(a), on the date [¹ on which]—

[¹(i) where the individual was required to notify a change under section 56 of the 2018 Act, if the individual—

(aa) knowingly fails to notify a change, or

(bb) fails to notify the change as soon as reasonably practicable after it occurred,

the individual should have notified the Scottish Ministers of the change,]

(ii) in any other case, the Scottish Ministers make the determination,

(c) in the case of an earlier determination which was based on official error within the meaning of regulation 32 (determination following official error—underpayments) or on error within the meaning of regulation 33 (determination following error—overpayments), begins on the date when the earlier determination took effect,

(d) in any other case, on the date when Scottish Ministers make the determination.

(2) Where the Scottish Ministers consider that in all the circumstances it would be unjust not to do so, they may, when making their determination, set a later date for the purposes of paragraph 1(b), (c) or (d).

AMENDMENTS

1. Disability Assistance for Children and Young People (Scotland) Amendment Regulations 2021 (SSI 2021/416) regs 2 and 14 (November 22, 2021).

Consideration of entitlement after specified period

30. The Scottish Ministers must make a determination of an individual's entitlement to Child Disability Payment, without receiving an application, after the end of the period specified (if any) in—

1.039

(a) the individual's notice of determination under section 40 or notice of re-determination under section 44 (as the case may be), or

(b) a determination made by the First-tier Tribunal for Scotland under section 49, of the 2018 Act.

Determination following change of circumstances etc.

31. The Scottish Ministers must make a determination of an individual's entitlement to Child Disability Payment, without receiving an application, where the individual has an ongoing entitlement to Child Disability Payment and they become aware—

1.040

(a) of a change of circumstances, whether or not notified by the individual in accordance with section 56 of the 2018 Act, [¹ or where the Scottish Ministers become aware that a determination of an individual's entitlement was made in ignorance of a material fact,] which would possibly result in an alteration to the component or rate of Child Disability Payment payable to the individual or which is likely to mean that the individual is no longer entitled to Child Disability Payment,

(b) that the individual has died,

(c) of an alteration of the component or rate of award of Disability Living Allowance which the individual was entitled to immediately before the date of transfer to Child Disability Payment in accordance with Part 3 of the schedule (transitional provisions), as a result of a decision made pursuant to—

(i) a revision under regulation 3 of the Social Security and Child Support (Decisions and Appeals) Regulations 1999 ("the 1999 Regulations"),

(ii) a supersession under regulation 6of the 1999 Regulations,

(iii) an appeal under section 12 of the Social Security Act 1998 ("the 1998 Act"),

(iv) a re-consideration under section 13 of the 1998 Act, [¹ . . .]

    (v) an appeal to the Upper Tribunal under section 14 of the 1998 Act,

    [1(vi) a revision under article 10 of the Social Security (Northern Ireland) Order 1998 ("the 1998 Order"),

    (vii) a supersession under article 11 of the 1998 Order,

    (viii) an appeal under article 13 of the 1998 Order, or

    (ix) an appeal to the Commissioner under article 15 of the 1998 Order,]

(d) of an alteration of the rate of award of Disability Living Allowance which the individual was entitled to immediately before moving to Scotland in circumstances in which regulation 35 (individuals in respect of whom Disability Living Allowance is paid in another part of the United Kingdom immediately before moving to Scotland) applies, as a result of a decision made pursuant to—

    (i) a revision under regulation 3 of the Social Security and Child Support (Decisions and Appeals) Regulations 1999,

    (ii) a supersession under regulation 6 of those Regulations,

    (iii) an appeal under section 12 of the Social Security Act 1998 ("the 1998 Act"),

    (iv) a re-consideration under section 13 of the 1998 Act,

    (v) an appeal to the Upper Tribunal under section 14 of the 1998 Act,

    (vi) a revision under article 10 of the Social Security (Northern Ireland) Order 1998 ("the 1998 Order"),

    (vii) a supersession under article 11 of the 1998 Order,

    (viii) an appeal under article 13 of the 1998 Order, or

    (ix) an appeal to the Commissioner under article 15 of the 1998 Order.

AMENDMENTS

1. Disability Assistance for Children and Young People (Scotland) Amendment Regulations 2021 (SSI 2021/416) regs 2 and 15 (November 22, 2021).

Determination following official error—underpayments

1.041   **32.**—(1) The Scottish Ministers are to make a determination of an individual's entitlement to Child Disability Payment, without receiving an application, where—

(a) they have previously made a determination of the individual's entitlement to Child Disability Payment ("the original determination"),

(b) they establish that, due to an official error, the original determination was incorrect resulting in the individual—

    (i) not being given an award of Child Disability Payment, or

    (ii) being given a lower award than that,

to which the individual was entitled,

(c) the Scottish Ministers are not considering a request for a re-determination of the individual's entitlement to the Payment, and

(d) the individual has not appealed to the First-tier Tribunal for Scotland against the Scottish Ministers' determination of the individual's entitlement to Child Disability Payment.

(2) In making a determination required by paragraph (1) the Scottish Ministers are to use—

(a) the information—

    (i) provided in the application that led to the original determination,

    (ii) any other information they have obtained in connection with that application, or

(b) any other information they have obtained in connection with the individual's entitlement to Child Disability Payment.

(3) In this regulation "official error" means an error made by someone acting on behalf of the Scottish Ministers or on behalf of a Minister of the Crown that was not materially contributed to by anyone else.

Determination following error—overpayments

33.—(1) The Scottish Ministers are to make a determination of an individual's entitlement to Child Disability Payment, without receiving an application, where—   **1.042**

(a) they have previously made a determination of the individual's entitlement to Child Disability Payment ("the original determination"),

(b) they establish that, due to an error, the original determination was incorrect resulting in the individual being given—

    (i) an award of Child Disability Payment to which the individual was not entitled, or

    (ii) a higher award than that to which the individual was entitled.

(c) the Scottish Ministers are not considering a request for a re-determination of the individual's entitlement to the Payment, and

(d) the individual has not made an appeal to the First-tier Tribunal for Scotland or Upper Tribunal against the Scottish Ministers' determination of the individual's entitlement to Child Disability Payment, that has not yet been determined.

(2) In making a determination required by paragraph (1) the Scottish Ministers are to use—

(a) the information—

    (i) provided in the application that led to the original determination, and

    (ii) any other information they have obtained in connection with that application,

(b) any other information they have obtained in connection with the individual's entitlement to Child Disability Payment, and

(c) any other information available to them that is relevant to their consideration of whether the individual is entitled to Child Disability Payment.

(3) In this regulation references to an "error" are to—

    (a) an error in the performance of a function conferred by these Regulations or the 2018 Act, including a determination being made—

        (i) wrongly, or

        (ii) correctly but on the basis of—

            (aa) incorrect information, or

            (bb) an assumption which proves to be wrong, or

    (b) a new determination not being made after an assumption on the basis of which an earlier determination was made has proved to be wrong.

Determination to effect a deduction decision

1.043   **34.**—(1) The Scottish Ministers are to make a determination of an individual's entitlement to Child Disability Payment, without receiving an application, where the circumstances in paragraphs (2) and (3) apply.

(2) This paragraph applies where—

    (a) regulation 27 (form of payment—giving Child Disability Payment by way of deduction) allows Child Disability Payment to be given to the individual by way of deduction, or

    (b) Child Disability Payment is being given to the individual by way of deduction, and the Scottish Ministers consider that may no longer be appropriate.

(3) This paragraph applies where the Scottish Ministers have decided to—

    (a) vary the amount of Child Disability Payment to be given by way of deduction (including introducing a deduction, where the full amount of Child Disability Payment was previously given as money),

    (b) vary any period for which the individual's Child Disability is to be given by way of deduction, that may have been specified in a previous determination of the individual's entitlement, or

    (c) cease making deductions, and instead give the individual's Child Disability Payment in the form of money.

(4) The Scottish Ministers are to make a determination, without receiving an application, where an individual who is receiving Child Disability Payment by way of deduction under a previous determination of entitlement notifies the Scottish Ministers that the individual—

    (a) withdraws their agreement to their Child Disability Payment being given by way of deduction,

    (b) wishes the Scottish Ministers to increase the amount of their Child Disability Payment that is given by way of deduction,

    (c) wishes the Scottish Ministers to decrease the amount of their Child Disability Payment that is given by way of deduction (including ceasing the deduction), or

    (d) wishes the Scottish Ministers to amend the length of any period referred to in paragraph (3)(b).

Individuals in respect of whom Disability Living Allowance is paid in another part of the United Kingdom immediately before moving to Scotland

35.—(1) Where an individual—   1.044

(a) is under 18 years of age,

(b) becomes resident in Scotland,

(c) was resident in another part of the United Kingdom, and

(d) was entitled to Disability Living Allowance immediately before the date of the move,

the Scottish Ministers are to make a determination without application of the individual's entitlement to Child Disability Payment.

(2) Entitlement to Child Disability Payment under paragraph (1) begins on the day after the day on which [¹ the individual's entitlement to Disability Living Allowance ends].

(3) In this regulation, "the date of the move" is the date when the individual becomes resident in Scotland as notified by the individual [¹ or otherwise communicated] to the Scottish Ministers (whether the notification takes place before or after the date of the move).

AMENDMENTS

1. Disability Assistance for Children and Young People (Scotland) Amendment Regulations 2021 (SSI 2021/416) regs 2 and 16 (November 22, 2021).

Individuals in respect of whom Child Disability Payment is paid at the time of moving to another part of the United Kingdom

36.—(1) Where the Scottish Ministers [¹ become aware] that an   1.045
individual who is entitled to Child Disability Payment has moved or is to move to become [¹ . . .] resident in another part of the United Kingdom, the individual is to be treated as though the individual meets the condition [¹ under regulation 5(1)(a)] of being ordinarily resident in Scotland for a period of 13 weeks beginning [¹ in accordance with paragraph (4)].

(2) Subject to Part 5 (effect of time spent in care homes and in legal detention), where the Scottish Ministers [¹ become aware that an individual has moved or is to move to another part of the United Kingdom as] mentioned in paragraph (1), they are to make a determination without application at the end of the 13-week period mentioned in paragraph (1) that the individual's entitlement to Child Disability Payment is to terminate.

(3) Where before the end of the 13-week period, the Scottish Ministers [¹ become aware] that the individual is no longer to move to become [¹ . . .] resident in another part of the United Kingdom, [¹ . . .] the duty in paragraph (2) does not apply.

[¹ (4) The 13-week period mentioned in paragraph (1) begins—

(a) if the Scottish Ministers become aware that the individual is to become resident in another part of the United Kingdom, on the date the individual ceases to be ordinarily resident in Scotland,

(b) if the Scottish Ministers become aware after the date when the individual becomes resident in another part of the United Kingdom, but before they have been resident there for 13 weeks, on the date the individual notifies the Scottish Ministers of the move, or

(c) in any other case, on the date that the individual ceases to be ordinarily resident in Scotland.

(5) On the day after the 13-week period specified in paragraph (4) ends—

(a) entitlement to Child Disability Payment ends, and

(b) regulation 33 (determination following error—overpayments) applies to any Child Disability Payment paid to an individual in relation to a period after the end of that 13-week period.]

AMENDMENTS

1. Disability Assistance for Children and Young People (Scotland) Amendment Regulations 2021 (SSI 2021/416) regs 2 and 17 (November 22, 2021).

Periods in respect of a re-determination request

1.046 37.—(1) The period for requesting a re-determination of entitlement to Child Disability Payment under section 41 (right to request re-determination) of the 2018 Act is 42 days beginning with the day that the individual is informed, in accordance with section 40 of the 2018 Act (notice of determination), of the right to make the request.

(2) In relation to determining entitlement to Child Disability Payment, the period allowed for re-determination (within the meaning of section 43 of the 2018 Act (duty to re-determine)) is 56 days beginning with—

(a) the day that the request for a re-determination is received by the Scottish Ministers, [¹ . . .]

(b) in a case where the request for a re-determination is received by the Scottish Ministers outwith the period prescribed in paragraph (1), the day on which it is decided by the Scottish Ministers or (as the case may be) the First-tier Tribunal for Scotland that the individual in question has a good reason for not requesting a re-determination sooner [¹ , or

(c) in a case where the Scottish Ministers have informed the individual of their decision that the request for a re-determination was not made in such form as the Scottish Ministers require, the day on which it is subsequently decided by the First-Tier Tribunal for Scotland that the individual in question has made the request in such form as the Scottish Ministers require.]

AMENDMENTS

1. Disability Assistance for Children and Young People (Scotland) Amendment Regulations 2021 (SSI 2021/416) regs 2 and 18 (November 22, 2021).

Payment of mobility component to authorised providers of vehicles for individuals with disabilities

38.—(1) Where—   1.047
  (a) an individual is entitled to the higher rate of the mobility component of Child Disability Payment, and
  (b) the individual has entered into an agreement with an authorised provider of vehicles for persons with disabilities for the hire or hire-purchase of a vehicle,
the Scottish Ministers may, with the consent of the individual, pay that component (in whole or in part) to the provider to be used to meet, or contribute towards meeting, the individual's liability under the agreement.

(2) The Scottish Ministers must cease to make payments to the provider in accordance with paragraph (1) in the event that—
  (a) the agreement is brought to an end in accordance with the terms of the agreement, or
  (b) the individual withdraws their consent.

Vehicles for persons with disabilities—powers of appointees

39.—(1) Where a person (an "appointee") is appointed by the Scot-   1.048
tish Ministers under the 2018 Act to act on an individual's behalf in connection with the determination of the individual's entitlement to assistance under section 24 of the 2018 Act (duty to give assistance), in addition to the powers conferred on the appointee by that Act the appointee can, on behalf of the individual—
  (a) enter into an agreement with an authorised provider of vehicles for the hire or hire-purchase of a vehicle,
  (b) terminate any such agreement,
  (c) for the purpose of regulation 38(1), give consent to the Scottish Ministers to pay (in whole or in part) the mobility component to which the individual is entitled to the provider, and
  (d) withdraw any such consent.

(2) An appointee may exercise the powers conferred by paragraph (1)(b) and (d) whether the agreement was entered into, or the consent given, by the appointee or by any other person.

Initial period for applications

40. Part 2 of the schedule makes provision about the initial period for   1.049
applications.

Transfer to Child Disability Payment

41. Part 3 of the schedule makes provision about transferring from   1.050
Disability Living Allowance to Child Disability Payment.

Entitlement to short-term assistance

42. Part 1 of the schedule makes provision about short-term assis-   1.051
tance.

Consequential amendment

1.052   43. The amendment specified in Part 4 of the schedule has effect.

Transitory provision—initial period for applications

1.053   44.—(1) During the initial period for applications, in addition to meeting the residence and presence conditions in regulation 5, an individual must be resident in one of the local authority areas specified in paragraph 6 of Part 2 of the schedule on the date their application is received by the Scottish Ministers.

(2) In this regulation and in Part 2 of the schedule, "initial period for applications" means the period beginning with 26 July 2021 and ending with 21 November 2021.

Exclusion to transitory provision

1.054   45.—(1) An individual who has made a claim for Disability Living Allowance prior to 26 July 2021 which has not yet been decided is not entitled to be paid Child Disability Payment during the initial period for applications.

(2) In paragraph (1) a claim for Disability Living Allowance is decided if it has—

(a) been decided by the Secretary of State under section 8 (decisions by Secretary of State) of the Social Security Act 1998,

(b) been withdrawn in accordance with regulation 5(2) of the Social Security (Claims and Payments) Regulations 1987, or

(c) otherwise is no longer to be decided by the Secretary of State as mentioned in sub-paragraph (a).

SCHEDULE

Regulation 42

PART 1

SHORT-TERM ASSISTANCE

Entitlement to short-term assistance

1.055   1.—(1) Subject to sub-paragraph (2), an individual who is, or was, entitled to Child Disability Payment under a determination made on the basis that the individual has ongoing entitlement is entitled to short-term assistance where—

(a) a determination of the individual's entitlement to Child Disability Payment ("earlier determination") has been superseded by a subsequent determination ("subsequent determination") which has the effect that the individual is—

(i) no longer entitled to Child Disability Payment, or

(ii) entitled to a lower amount of Child Disability Payment,

[¹ (b) the individual's entitlement to Child Disability Payment is under review within the meaning of—

(i) paragraph 1(2) of schedule 10 of the 2018 Act, or

(ii) sub-paragraph (1A), and]

(c) the individual—

(i) continues to meet the conditions as to residence and presence set out in regulations 5 to 9, or

(ii) has transferred to become [¹ . . .] resident in another part of the United Kingdom, and the matter under review is the determination of entitlement for the 13-week period beginning [¹ . . .] in accordance with regulation 36[¹ (4)] (individuals in respect of whom Child Disability Payment is paid at the time of moving to another part of the United Kingdom).

[¹ (1A) An individual's entitlement to Child Disability Payment is under review in terms of sub-paragraph (1)(b)(ii) if—

(a) a decision of the First-Tier Tribunal for Scotland under section 49 of the 2018 Act, in relation to the subsequent determination of the individual's entitlement to Child Disability Payment mentioned in paragraph 1(1)(a), is set aside after a review under section 43(2) of the Tribunals (Scotland) Act 2014 (review of decisions), and

(b) the First-Tier Tribunal for Scotland decides not to uphold a determination of an individual's entitlement to Child Disability Payment in an appeal under section 46 of the 2018 Act and the First-Tier Tribunal for Scotland is to make a determination of the individual's entitlement to Child Disability Payment under section 49 of the 2018 Act.

(1B) Where an individual's entitlement to Child Disability Payment is set aside after a review in terms of sub-paragraph (1A)(a), the Scottish Ministers are to make a determination without application of the individual's entitlement to short-term assistance.]

(2) An individual is not entitled to short-term assistance where the individual is no longer entitled to Child Disability Payment as a result of a subsequent determination made under regulation 31(b) (determination following change of circumstances etc.).

(3) An individual to whom regulation 17(2) (effect of admission to a care home on ongoing entitlement to care component) [¹ , 18(2)] (effect of legal detention on ongoing entitlement to care component) [¹ , or 20(2) (entitlement to care component beginning while in alternative accommodation)] applies is not entitled to short-term assistance in respect of the care component of Child Disability Payment.

(4) Where the Scottish Ministers have made a determination under section 37 of the 2018 Act (duty to make determination) that an individual is entitled to short-term assistance, entitlement to short-term assistance begins—

(a) where a request is made under section 41 of the 2018 Act (right to request re-determination) for a re-determination [¹ . . .] of the individual's entitlement to Child Disability Payment mentioned in paragraph 1(1)(a), on the day that request is made,

(b) where a notice of appeal is submitted under section 47 of the 2018 Act (initiating an appeal) against the determination of the individual's entitlement to Child Disability Payment mentioned in paragraph 1(1)(a), on the day that request is made,

(c) where a decision of the Scottish Ministers is made not to accept a request for a re-determination of the individual's entitlement to Child Disability Payment mentioned in paragraph 1(1)(a), on the day that decision is set aside by the First-tier Tribunal for Scotland, [¹ . . .]

(d) [¹ where] a request is made under section 48(1)(b) of the 2018 Act (deadline for appealing) for permission to appeal the determination of the individual's entitlement to Child Disability Payment mentioned in paragraph 1(1)(a), on the day that request is made [¹ , or

(e) where a decision of the First-tier Tribunal for Scotland under section 49 of the 2018 Act, in relation to the subsequent determination of the individual's entitlement to Child Disability Payment mentioned in paragraph 1(1)(a), is set aside after review under section 43(2) of the Tribunals (Scotland) Act 2014 (review of decisions) and the First-tier Tribunal for Scotland is to make a determination of the individual's entitlement to Child Disability Payment under section 49 of the 2018 Act, on the day that the decision is set aside.

(5) Regulation 37 (periods in respect of a re-determination request) applies to short-term assistance in the same way as it applies to Child Disability Payment.

Value and form

2.—(1) The value of short-term assistance payable is to be the difference between the amount of Child Disability Payment to which the individual was entitled under the earlier determination mentioned in paragraph 1(1)(a), and the amount of Child Disability Payment the individual is entitled to under the subsequent determination mentioned in paragraph 1(1)(a).

(2) The form in which the short term assistance is to be given is to be the same as the form in which Child Disability Payment was given under the earlier determination.

(3) Where the mobility component was being paid by the Scottish Ministers to an authorised provider of vehicles for persons with disabilities in accordance with regulation 38(1) (payment of mobility component to authorised provider of vehicles for individuals with disabilities) on the day before an individual's entitlement to the mobility component ended as a result of a subsequent determination mentioned in paragraph 1(1)(a)—

    (a) the amount of short-term assistance that is payable in respect of the mobility component may be paid by the Scottish Ministers to the authorised provider, and

    (b) paragraphs (1) and (2) of regulation 38 apply to the payment of short-term assistance as they had applied to the payment of mobility component prior to the individual's entitlement ending.

(4) Regulations 27 (form of payment—giving Child Disability Payment by way of deduction), 32 (determination following official error—underpayments), 33 (determination following error—overpayments) and 34 (determination to effect a deduction decision) apply to short-term assistance in the same way as they apply to Child Disability Payment.

End of entitlement

3.—(1) Entitlement to short-term assistance ends on the day—

    (a) a determination of an individual's entitlement to short-term assistance is cancelled under section 26(2) of the 2018 Act (individual's right to stop receiving assistance),

    [¹ (b) a re-determination of an individual's entitlement to Child Disability Payment is made by the Scottish Ministers under section 43 of the 2018 Act (duty to re-determine),]

    (c) the First-tier Tribunal for Scotland makes a [¹ determination] under section 49 of the 2018 Act (First-tier Tribunal's power to determine entitlement) in relation to the subsequent determination of the individual's entitlement to Child Disability Payment mentioned in paragraph 1(1)(a), [¹ . . .]

    (d) that the First-tier Tribunal for Scotland makes a determination to refuse permission under section 48(1)(b) of the 2018 Act (deadline for appealing) to bring an appeal against the subsequent determination of the individual's entitlement to Child Disability Payment mentioned in paragraph 1(1)(a) [¹ , or

    (e) where the individual withdraws their application to bring an appeal against the subsequent determination of the individual's entitlement to Child Disability Payment mentioned in paragraph 1(1)(a), on that day.]

[¹ (2) Where an individual's entitlement to short-term assistance is to end under sub-paragraph (1), the Scottish Ministers are to make a determination without application.]

Reduction of payment of Child Disability Payment where short-term assistance is paid

4. Where an individual has received short-term assistance for a period and a determination is subsequently made that that individual is entitled to Child Disability Payment at the same rate or at a higher rate for that period, any payment of Child Disability Payment to be made for that period is to be reduced by any short-term assistance and any Child Disability Payment already paid to that individual for that period.

Regulation 40

Part 2

Initial Period For Applications

Initial period for applications

1.056   **5.**—(1) These Regulations apply to an individual who is resident in one of the local authority areas mentioned in paragraph 6 when they make an application for Child Disability Payment during the initial period for applications.

(2) An individual who is awarded Child Disability Payment pursuant to an application made during the initial period for applications will continue to be entitled if that person moves to another local authority area in Scotland.

Local authority areas for initial period for applications

6. The local authority areas are Perthshire and Kinross, City of Dundee and the Western Isles.

Part 3

Transfer To Child Disability Payment

Interpretation

7. In this Part of the schedule— 1.057

"date of transfer" means the date when a transferring individual's entitlement to Child Disability Payment begins by virtue of a determination made under paragraph 9(1),

"relevant individual" means an individual—

(a) who has an award of Disability Living Allowance who appears to the Scottish Ministers to be likely to be eligible for Child Disability Payment,

(b) who is—

(i) ordinarily resident in Scotland, or

(ii) someone to whom regulation 5(4) (residence and presence conditions) or 9(2) (persons residing outside the United Kingdom to whom a relevant EU regulation applies) applies,

"sufficient" means a link to Scotland that is sufficiently close that regulations 5(4) or 9(2) would be incompatible with the applicable agreement mentioned in that regulation, if the relevant individual were not entitled to Child Disability Payment,

"transfer notice" means the notice required by paragraph 8, and

"transferring individual" means a relevant individual on whom the Scottish Ministers have served a notice of intention to transfer in accordance with paragraph 8.

Notice of intention to transfer to Child Disability Payment

8.—(1) The Scottish Ministers are to notify each relevant individual of their intention to transfer that individual's entitlement to disability assistance from an entitlement to Disability Living Allowance to an entitlement to Child Disability Payment.

(2) Notice under sub-paragraph (1) must—

(a) be given in a way that leaves the relevant individual with a record of the information which they can show to, or otherwise share with, others,

(b) inform the relevant individual that—

(i) they have been identified as a relevant individual for the purposes of transfer to Child Disability Payment,

(ii) the Scottish Ministers will make a determination without application to transfer the individual's entitlement to Disability Living Allowance to an entitlement to Child Disability Payment within [¹ 17] weeks of the date of the notice (the individual will be notified when the determination is made and informed about their award and start date of Child Disability Payment), and

(iii) the individual's award of Disability Living Allowance will cease immediately before the award of Child Disability Payment begins.

(3) Where a notice under sub-paragraph (1) is given in error where the individual is neither—

(a) ordinarily resident in Scotland, nor

(b) an individual who is habitually resident in an EEA state, Gibraltar or Switzerland and has a genuine and sufficient link to Scotland,

the duty on the Scottish Ministers in paragraph 9(1) does not apply.

(4) Where sub-paragraph (3) applies in respect of an individual and a determination under paragraph 9(1) has not been made, the Scottish Ministers are to notify the individual that the duty on the Scottish Ministers in paragraph 9(1) does not apply.

Determination without application of entitlement to Child Disability Payment

9.—(1) The Scottish Ministers are to make a determination without application in respect of a transferring individual of that individual's entitlement to Child Disability Payment.

(2) Entitlement to Child Disability Payment under a determination under sub-paragraph (1) begins on the date specified in the notice of determination given to the transferring individual in accordance with section 40 of the 2018 Act.

(3) The determination under sub-paragraph (1) is to be made on the basis of—

(a) such information as the Scottish Ministers have received from the Secretary of State for Work and Pensions in respect of the transferring individual's entitlement to Disability Living Allowance, and

(b) any other information available to the Scottish Ministers that appears to them to be relevant.

(4) Subject to paragraph 11, a determination under sub-paragraph (1) must be made on the basis that the transferring individual is entitled to the components and rates of Child Disability Payment that are equivalent to those components and rates of Disability Living Allowance to which the individual was entitled immediately before the date of transfer.

(5) A determination under sub-paragraph (1)—

(a) may be made on the assumption that whatever can be discerned about the transferring individual's circumstances from the information mentioned in sub-paragraph (3) remains accurate on the date on which the determination is made,

(b) notwithstanding the generality of head (a), is to be made on the assumption that the conditions relating to residence and presence set out in regulations 5 to 9 (residence and presence conditions etc.) are satisfied in the individual's case, and

(c) must be made not later than 13 weeks after the date of the notice under paragraph 8(1) unless the Scottish Ministers have—

    (i) good reason to extend that period,

    (ii) agreed the period for extension with the Secretary of State for Work and Pensions, and

    (iii) notified the transferring individual of the extension and the reason for it.

Effect of determination on entitlement to Disability Living Allowance

[¹ **10.** Where a determination is made under paragraph 9 that the transferring individual is entitled to Child Disability Payment, the transferring individual's entitlement to Disability Living Allowance will end on—

(a) the date their entitlement to Child Disability Payment begins,

(b) where paragraph 11 applies, the date of the determination under paragraph 9(1), or

(c) where paragraph 12(1) applies, the date their entitlement to Child Disability Payment would have begun had paragraph 12(2) not applied to set an earlier date of entitlement.]

Exceptions to paragraph 9(4)

11.—(1) The following circumstances are exceptions to paragraph 9(4)—

[¹ (a) where the Scottish Ministers have—

    (i) received information from the Secretary of State for Work and Pensions that the transferring individual is terminally ill in terms of section 82 of the Welfare Reform Act 2012 immediately before the date of transfer, or

    (ii) not received information from the Secretary of State for Work and Pensions that the transferring individual is terminally ill in terms of section 82 of the Welfare Reform Act 2012, but become aware, before they have made a determination under paragraph 9(1), that the individual has a terminal illness in terms of regulation 15(6) (entitlement under special rules for terminal illness),

the determination made under paragraph 9(1) must be made on the basis that the transferring individual satisfies the conditions for the higher rate of the mobility component and highest rate of the care component of Child Disability Payment,]

(b) a transferring individual who is not awarded the care component of Disability Living Allowance and meets the condition in regulation 11(1)(b) (care component criterion: lowest, middle or highest rate of care component) is entitled to the lowest rate of the care component of Child Disability Payment,

(c) a transferring individual whose entitlement to [¹ one or both components] of Disability Living Allowance was affected because they were under 16 and did not meet the [¹ requirements in either or both sections 72(1A)(b) or 73(4A)] of the Social Security Contributions and Benefits Act 1992, who is aged 16 or over is entitled to an increased rate of either component or both components [¹ as the case may be] of Child Disability Payment, and

(d) a transferring individual, whose entitlement to the mobility component of Disability Living Allowance was affected by not meeting the requirement of regulation 12(1A) of the Social Security (Disability Living Allowance) Regulations 1991, who meets the condition in regulation 13(5) (mobility requirements: higher rate mobility component), is entitled [to the higher rate of the mobility component of Child

Disability Payment where the individual was either not entitled to the mobility component of Disability Living Allowance or entitled to the lower rate of that component.]

[¹ (2) Where sub-paragraph (1)(a) applies—

(a) paragraphs (7), (8) and (9) of regulation 15 (entitlement under special rules for terminal illness) are to be treated as satisfied for the individual, and

(b) the beginning of their entitlement is to be determined in terms of regulation 15(3), as modified by paragraph 13(zb).

(3) Where a transferring individual mentioned in sub-paragraph (1)(b), (c) or (d) whose entitlement to Child Disability Payment is determined under paragraph 9(1) to be at a higher value than their entitlement to Disability Living Allowance paid immediately before that determination, entitlement is to begin before the date of that determination but not before the later of—

(a) the date on which—

(i) sub-paragraph (1)(b) or (d) applies to a transferring individual by virtue of evidence supplied in relation to the transferring individual which is satisfactory to the Scottish Ministers, or

(ii) where sub-paragraph (1)(c) applies, when the transferring individual reaches the age of 16,

(b) 11 October 2021.

(4) Where an individual has previously received Disability Living Allowance for a period and a determination is subsequently made that the same individual is entitled to Child Disability Payment at a higher rate for that period by virtue of this paragraph, that individual will be entitled to the difference between the value of entitlement to Child Disability Payment under the subsequent determination and the value of Disability Living Allowance to which that individual was previously entitled for that period.]

Effect of legal custody on payment of the mobility component

12.—(1) Where a transferring individual is in legal detention immediately before the date of transfer and payment of the mobility component of Disability Living Allowance is suspended under regulation 3 of the Social Security (General Benefit) Regulations 1982, the mobility component of Child Disability Payment is to be paid at the rate equivalent to the rate of Disability Living Allowance paid to the transferring individual immediately prior to the suspension.

[¹ (2) Entitlement to the mobility component of Child Disability Payment of a transferring individual mentioned in sub-paragraph (1) is to begin before the date of the determination without application made under regulation 5(1) but not before the later of the date on which—

(a) the suspension of payment of the mobility component of Disability Living Allowance began,

(b) 11 October 2021.

(3) Where a transferring individual is in legal detention immediately before the date of transfer and entitlement to Child Disability Payment is determined under paragraph 9(1) to be at a higher rate than the Disability Living Allowance paid immediately before that determination, paragraph 11(4) does not apply for the purposes of determining the amount of the mobility component to be paid.]

Modification of these Regulations: transferring individuals

13. These Regulations apply to a transferring individual on and after the date of transfer with the following modifications—

[¹(za) where paragraph 11(3) or 12(2) applies, for the period between the date when entitlement to Child Disability Payment begins and the date of the determination under paragraph 9(1), regulation 10 (entitlement to other benefits) is treated as omitted,

(zb) regulation 15 (entitlement under special rules for terminal illness) is to be read as if—

(i) paragraph (3)(a) reads "the individual transferred by virtue of a determination under paragraph 9(1) ("the date of transfer")", where that determination is made in accordance with paragraph 11(1)(a) of the schedule",

(ii) paragraph (3)(b) is omitted,

(iii) in paragraphs (4) and (5) for "whichever date in paragraph (3)(a) or (b) applies" reads "the date in paragraph (3)(a),

(iv) paragraph (10) reads "Where an individual has previously received Child Disability Payment or Disability Living Allowance for a period and a determination is subsequently made that the same individual is entitled to Child Disability Payment at a higher rate for that period by virtue of this regulation, that individual will be entitled to the difference between the value of entitlement to Child Disability Payment under the subsequent determination and the value of Child Disability Payment or Disability Living Allowance to which that individual was previously entitled for that period.]

(a) regulation 17 (effect of admission to a care home on ongoing entitlement to care component) and regulation 18 (effect of legal detention on ongoing entitlement to care component) are to be read as if the period of 28 days begins on the date of transfer, and

[¹(aa) regulation 20 (entitlement to care component beginning while in alternative accommodation) is to be read as if—

(i) in paragraph (1) after "begins" there are the words "in terms of part 3 of the schedule",

(ii) in paragraph (2) "that day" reads "the day on which the individual has been entitled to Child Disability Payment for 28 days,]

(b) regulation 24 (when an application is to be treated as made and beginning of entitlement to assistance) is treated as omitted.

Appointees

14.—(1) A person appointed by the Secretary of State for Work and Pensions under regulation 33 or 43 of the Social Security (Claims and Payments) Regulations 1987(5) to receive Disability Living Allowance on behalf of a transferring individual is to be treated on and after the date of transfer as though appointed by the Scottish Ministers to act on behalf of that transferring individual under section 58 (or 85B(6)) or 85A of the 2018 Act.

(2) As soon as reasonably practicable after the date of transfer, the Scottish Ministers must—

(a) consider whether the conditions for making an appointment in respect of the transferring individual are met (having regard to whichever of section 58(4), 85A(3) or 85B(3) of the 2018 Act applies in the transferring individual's case),

(b) consider whether to terminate the appointment that is treated as having been made by virtue of sub-paragraph (1) and terminate it if they consider it appropriate, and

(c) if they have terminated an appointment in pursuance of head (b), appoint under section 58 (or 85B) or 85A of the 2018 Act another person to act on the transferring individual's behalf if they consider it appropriate to do so.

Regulation 43

PART 4

CONSEQUENTIAL AMENDMENT

15.—(1) The Social Security Contributions and Benefits Act 1992 is amended in accordance with paragraph (2).

(2) In section 70(2) (invalid care allowance), after "enhanced rate" insert "or disability assistance by virtue of entitlement to the care component at the middle or highest rate under regulations made under section 31 of the Social Security (Scotland) Act 2018".

AMENDMENTS

1. Disability Assistance for Children and Young People (Scotland) Amendment Regulations 2021 (SSI 2021/416) regs 2, 19 and 20 (November 22, 2021).

The Social Security Information-sharing (Scotland) Regulations 2021

(SSI 2021/178)

Made	*24th March 2021*
Coming into force	*26th July 2021*

The Scottish Ministers make the following Regulations in exercise of the powers conferred by sections 85(2)(g) and (5) and 95 of the Social Security (Scotland) Act 2018 and all other powers enabling them to do so.

In accordance with section 96(2) of that Act, a draft of this instrument has been laid before and approved by resolution of the Scottish Parliament.

Citation, commencement and interpretation

1.—(1) These Regulations may be cited as the Social Security Information-sharing (Scotland) Regulations 2021 and come into force on 26 July 2021.

(2) In these Regulations—

"the 1978 Act" means the National Health Service (Scotland) Act 1978,

"the 2018 Act" means the Social Security (Scotland) Act 2018,

"the Public Guardian" is to be construed in accordance with section 6 of the Adults with Incapacity (Scotland) Act 2000 (the Public Guardian and his functions).

Specification of persons who may be required to supply information

2.—(1) The persons described in paragraph (2) are specified for the purposes of section 85(2)(g) of the 2018 Act (persons who may be required to supply information).

(2) The persons are—

(a) any supplier of vehicles approved by the Scottish Ministers under an accreditation scheme run by Ministers to supply vehicles for the benefit of individuals who are entitled to the higher rate of the mobility component of Child Disability Payment in accordance with regulation 13 of the Disability Assistance for Children and Young People (Scotland) Regulations 2021 (mobility requirements: higher rate mobility component),

(b) the contractor under a general medical services contract within the meaning of section 17J of the 1978 Act (Health Boards' power to enter into general medical services contracts),

(c) the contractor under an arrangement under section 2C(2) of the 1978 Act (functions of Health Boards: primary medical services),

(d) the provider under an agreement under section 17C(1)(a) of the 1978 Act (agreement for provision of primary medical services), and

(e) the Public Guardian.

1.058

1.059

47

Supplying information to receive information in return

1.060   **3.**—(1) Paragraph (2) applies where the Scottish Ministers require information to be supplied under section 85(1) of the 2018 Act (requirement to supply information) by—

(a) a Health Board constituted under section 2(1)(a) of the 1978 Act (Health Boards) or a Special Health Board constituted under section 2(1)(b) of the 1978 Act,

(b) a contractor or provider of primary medical services described in regulation 2(2)(b), (c) or (d), or

(c) a local authority,

for the purpose of determining an individual's entitlement to social security assistance in accordance with section 37 of the 2018 Act (duty to make determination).

(2) The Scottish Ministers may supply to the person such information relating to the individual as is necessary for the purpose of enabling the person to comply with the requirement under section 85(1) of the 2018 Act.

(3) Information may be supplied by the Scottish Ministers under paragraph (2) only with the authorisation of the individual to whom the information relates.

Use of information supplied by the Scottish Ministers

1.061   **4.**—(1) Information held by the Scottish Ministers for the purpose of a social security function may be supplied by Ministers under section 85(5) of the 2018 Act (specification of functions) to—

(a) a supplier of vehicles described in regulation 2(2)(a) for use for the purposes of the function of that person specified in paragraph (2),

(b) a local authority for use for the purposes of the functions of the local authority specified in paragraph (3).

(2) The specified function referred to in paragraph (1)(a) is the provision of a vehicle.

(3) The specified functions referred to in paragraph (1)(b) are—

(a) the assessment of liability to pay local taxes used to fund local authority expenditure,

(b) the administration under section 134(1) of the Social Security Administration Act 1992 (arrangements for housing benefit) of housing benefit provided by virtue of a scheme under section 123(1)(d) of the Social Security Contributions and Benefits Act 1992 (income-related benefit),

(c) the administration of the national travel concession scheme provided for by the National Bus Travel Concession Scheme for Older and Disabled Persons (Scotland) Order 2006,

(d) the administration of a travel concession scheme established under section 93 of the Transport Act 1985 (travel concession schemes),

(e) determining whether a person falls within the description of person prescribed for the purposes of section 21(2) of the Chronically Sick and Disabled Persons Act 1970 (issue of badges for display on motor vehicles to disabled persons falling within prescribed descriptions) by regulation 4(2)(ad) of the Disabled Persons (Badges for Motor Vehicles) (Scotland) Regulations 2000 (descriptions of disabled persons),

(f) determining whether to provide occasional financial or other assistance for the purpose described in section 2(1)(a) or (b) of the Welfare Funds (Scotland) Act 2015 (use of welfare funds: assistance for short term need and community care),

(g) determining—
    (i) whether to make discretionary housing payments under regulation 2(1) of the Discretionary Financial Assistance Regulations 2001 (provision of additional financial assistance towards meeting housing costs),
    (ii) the amount of any such payments.

5. Where the Scottish Ministers supply information under these Regulations, which relates to an individual, the information supplied must be no more than is necessary for the purpose for which it is to be used by the recipient.

PART II

UPDATING MATERIAL
VOLUME I

NON MEANS TESTED BENEFITS

Commentary by

Ian Hooker

John Mesher

Edward Mitchell

Christopher Ward

Nick Wikeley

p.53, *annotation to the Social Security Contributions and Benefits Act 1992 s.39A (Widowed Parent's Allowance)*

Appeals coming before an FTT in respect of claims made by the survivor of a couple who were not married or living in a civil partnership should be left open until after the remedial order that will be made in consequence of the decision of the Supreme Court in *McLaughlin, Re Judicial Review (Northern Ireland)* [2018] UKSC 48 has become available; see *JG v SSWP (BB)* [2021] UKUT 194 (AAC). 2.001

p.63, *annotation to the Social Security Contributions and Benefits Act 1992 s.44 (Category A retirement pension)*

Note that the declaration in subs.(1) that a person retains entitlement to a Category A pension "throughout his life" does not necessarily mean that the person has the right to be paid the pension at the same rate throughout his life. This was illustrated by the Upper Tribunal's decision in *BB v Secretary of State for Work & Pensions (RP)* [2021] UKUT 141 (AAC). Upper Tribunal Judge Wikeley held that a pensioner's 7% enhancement to the rate of his Category A pension, referable to his receipt of New Zealand national superannuation, ceased to be payable once he began to reside outside the EU (he had moved from Malta to Turkey). While the pensioner's entitlement to a 7% enhancement persisted, the enhancement was only payable in accordance with the Social Security (New Zealand) Order 1983 (SI 1983/1894) (as modified by the Social Security (Application of Reciprocal Agreements with Australia, Canada and New Zealand) (EEA States and Switzerland) Regulations 2015 (SI 2015/349)). This reflects the distinction sometimes drawn by the 1992 Act between entitlement to benefit and its payability (*Campbell v Secretary of State for Work and Pensions* [2005] EWCA Civ 989). 2.002

p.110, *amendment to the Social Security Contributions and Benefits Act 1992 s.70(2) (Invalid care allowance)*

With effect from November 17, 2021, reg.2 of the Social Security (Scotland) Act 2018 (Disability Assistance for Children and Young People) (Consequential Modifications (No.2) Order 2021 (SI 2021/1301) amended subs.(2) by inserting after the words "Armed Forces and Reserve Forces (Compensation Scheme) Order 2011" the words "or a child disability payment by virtue of entitlement to the care component at the highest or middle rate by virtue of regulations made under section 31 of the Social Security (Scotland) Act 2018". This amendment applies only in respect of England and Wales. 2.003

A similar though not identically worded amendment is made in respect of Scotland with effect from July 26, 2021, by reg.43 and paragraph 15 of the Schedule to the Disability Assistance for Children and Young People (Scotland) Regulations 2021 (SSI 2021/174) by inserting after the words "enhanced rate" the words "or disability assistance by virtue of entitlement to the care component at the middle or highest rate under regulations made under section 31 of the Social Security (Scotland) Act 2018".

pp.201-206, *annotation to the Social Security Contributions and Benefits Act 1992 s.94 (Right to industrial injuries benefit)*

2.004   For further consideration of the test of "arising out of and in the course of his employment", where the location poses a particular risk, see *NE v SSWP (II)* [2021] UKUT 240 (AAC) (claimant having accident while showering before contracted working hours when living on-site).

p.237, *annotation to the Social Security Contributions and Benefits Act 1992, s.113 (General provisions as to disqualification and suspension)— Reciprocal agreements*

2.005   With effect from July 28, 2021, the Social Security (Application of Reciprocal Agreements with Australia, Canada and New Zealand) (EEA States and Switzerland) Regulations 2015 (SI 2015/349) are amended by reg.3 of the Social Security (Reciprocal Agreements) (Miscellaneous Amendments) (EU Exit) Regulations 2021 (SI 2021/811) (and then, with effect from December 31, 2021, by reg.4 of the 2021 Regulations, are to be repealed).

p.243, *amendment to the Social Security Contributions and Benefits Act 1992, s.122 (Interpretation of Parts I to VI and supplementary provisions)*

2.006   With effect from July 26, 2021, reg.2 of The Scotland Act 2016 (Social Security) (Consequential Provision) (Miscellaneous Amendment) Regulations 2021 (SI 2021/804) inserted after the definition of "child" the following definition:

> ""Child Disability Payment" means assistance under regulation 3 of the Disability Assistance for Children and Young People (Scotland) Regulations 2021;".

p.248, *amendment to the Social Security Contributions and Benefits Act 1992 s.148 (Entitlement of Pensioners to Christmas Bonus)*

2.007   With effect from December 3, 2021, reg.2 of the Social Security (Amendment) Regulations 2021 (SI 2021/1152) amended s.148 by substituting the words "or a member State" in subsection (1)(a) with "an EEA state or Switzerland".

p.319, *annotation to the Social Security Contributions and Benefits Act 1992 Sch.7 Pt V (Retirement Allowance)*

2.008   The appeal in *AR v SSWP (II)* [2021] UKUT 279 (AAC) was concerned with how the reduced earnings allowance legislation drafted in 1990 applies today to zero hours contracts. See further the note below to p.1621 of the main volume (annotation to the Social Security (Industrial Injuries) Regulations 1990 (SI 1990/256) reg.2 (Meaning of "regular employment")).

pp.339-341, *annotation to the New Style Jobseekers Act 1995 s.2 (The contribution-based conditions)*

NH v SSWP (JSA) [2021] UKUT 227 (AAC) contains a detailed and   2.009 helpful description of the working of the two contribution conditions in s.2(1) and in particular of how it may be the case that a claimant satisfies the second condition, but not the first, which can only be satisfied by Class 1 contributions that have actually been paid and has more restrictive rules about the calculation of relevant earnings that can go towards satisfying the condition. In *NH*, the claim for new style JSA was made on April 6, 2020, so that the "base years" in which the contribution conditions had to be satisfied were the tax years 2017/18 and 2018/19. The claimant accepted that she did not satisfy the first contribution condition in 2018/19, but disagreed with the DWP's view that she did not satisfy it in 2017/18. In that tax year she was only employed until June 6, 2017, when she was made redundant. She had received four weeks' wages (on which Class 1 contributions were paid) on each of April 14 and May 15 and three weeks' on June 9. But on that date she was also paid 13 weeks' wages in lieu of notice and two and a half weeks' holiday pay. She argued that she had been paid for 26 and a half weeks at a rate that worked out above the weekly lower earnings limit (LEL) in force at the time. Judge Wikeley upheld the First-tier Tribunal's rejection of that argument. Liability to Class 1 contributions under the SSCBA 1992 arises on the amounts received in particular weeks, not on a cumulative aggregation of earnings over a year. The claimant could therefore only rely on the contributions that had actually been made, not on contributions that would notionally have been made if the payment in lieu of notice and holiday pay was disaggregated and notionally regarded as paid for the future weeks involved. Although the earnings-related contribution due in the last week of employment would have been greatly increased by the inclusion of those payments in the claimant's earnings, reg.34 of the JSA Regulations 2013 prevented putting any earnings in that week above the amount of the LEL towards the amount of "relevant earnings" to be taken into account in applying the test in s.2(2)(b) (relevant earnings 26 times the LEL).

Although the claimant may have been mistaken in describing her situation on dismissal as effectively being on gardening leave (as she was no longer in employment, and so not "on leave"), it appears that the result would have been the same if her employment had not terminated until the expiry of her 13 weeks' notice and the employer had chosen to pay the 13 weeks' pay in advance in a lump sum. It would have been different if she had been paid as normal during the notice period, but that would not have allowed the weeks of holiday pay to be counted, so probably not different enough to affect the outcome.

pp.373-374, *annotation to the New Style Jobseekers Act 1995 s.6J (Higher-level sanctions)*

2.010   The minutes of the meeting of the Social Security Advisory Committee (SSAC) on September 8, 2021, relating to the proposal to make regulations amending reg.18 of the JSA Regulations 2013 to correct a drafting error (see the entry for pp.1151-3) reveal the extraordinary claim made by DWP officials that no sanctions had previously been imposed on any new style JSA or ESA claimant, apparently since 2013, the focus instead having been on engagement and encouragement by work coaches (para.2.2(b)). Such a claim is hard to accept in the light of the DWP's own regular issues of benefit sanctions statistics (and, if true, would be regarded by many as a dereliction of duty to the public). For instance, the January 2020 issue records 5,000 JSA sanction decisions as having been made in 2019. The statistics do not distinguish between old style and new style JSA, but some at least of the 5,000 must (even taking account of the effect of reg.5 of the JSA Regulations 2013) have been in new style JSA. What the statistics do show is a steady and heavy decline from 2013 in the number of JSA sanctions decisions. Could the officials have been referring only to sanctions particularly linked to "conditionality" in the sense of work-related requirements?

pp.761-763, *The Social Security and Family Allowances (Polygamous Marriages) Regulations 1975 (SI 1975/561), reg.2 (General rule as to the consequences of a polygamous marriage for the purpose of the Social Security Act and the Family Allowances Act)—General Note*

2.011   The Upper Tribunal's decision in *NA v SSWP (BB)* [2019] UKUT 144 (AAC) has been reversed by the Court of Appeal in *Secretary of State for Work and Pensions v Akhtar* [2021] EWCA Civ 1353. The Court of Appeal undertook a detailed review of the treatment of polygamous marriages for social security purposes. The Regulations applied only to polygamous marriages that were valid under English law and did not make sense if they applied to marriages that were void under English law, as was the respondent's marriage. The expression "in fact monogamous" had to mean that there were, as a matter of law, no other marriages. A polygamous marriage would only be "in fact monogamous" when both parties were spouses and neither had any spouse additional to the other. Neither the primary legislation in relation to bereavement payment and widowed parent's allowance could assist the claimant, as she was not validly married under the law of England and Wales, nor for the reasons above could the Polygamous Marriages Regulations. Her human rights case was no stronger than had already been decided by the Supreme Court in *Re McLaughlin's Application for Judicial Review* [2018] UKSC 48 (as to which, see Vol.3 and the corresponding entry in this Supplement); in particular, in relation to bereavement payment, people who have contracted a marriage which is valid under English law and those who have not are not in an analogous position, alternatively the difference in treatment created by the legislation is justified.

p.771, *amendment to the Social Security (Attendance Allowance) Regulations 1991 (SI 1991/2740) reg.2C (Refugees)*

With effect from September 15, 2021, reg.4 of the Social Security 2.012 (Habitual Residence and Past Presence) (Amendment) Regulations 2021 (SI 2021/1034) amended reg.2C as follows:

(1) For the title to reg.2C substitute "Refugees and certain persons with leave to enter or remain in the United Kingdom".

(2) In paragraph (1)

(a) At the end of sub-paragraph (a) omit the word "or"

(b) After sub-paragraph (b) insert—

"(c) leave to enter or remain in the United Kingdom granted under the immigration rules by virtue of—
  (i) the Afghan Relocations and Assistance Policy; or
  (ii) the previous scheme for locally-employed staff in Afghanistan (sometimes referred to as the ex-gratia scheme);

(d) been granted discretionary leave outside the immigration rules as a dependant of a person referred to in sub-paragraph (c); or

(e) leave granted under the Afghan Citizens Resettlement Scheme.".

(3) After paragraph (1) insert—

"(1A) Regulation 2(1)(a) shall not apply where paragraph (1)(c), (d) or (e) applies to the person.".

The amendments made by these regulations apply in respect of England and Wales only. The same amendments are made with effect from the same date in respect of Scotland only by reg.2 of the Social Security (Residence Requirements) (Afghanistan) (Scotland) Regulations 2021 (SI 2021/320) but in addition that regulation also substitutes for para.(2) of reg.2C the following—

"(2) For the purposes of this regulation—

(a) "immigration rules" means the rules laid before Parliament under section 3(2) of the Immigration Act 1971,

(b) "the Afghan Citizens Resettlement Scheme" means the scheme announced by the United Kingdom Government on 18 August 2021."

p.789, *amendment to the Social Security (Disability Living Allowance) Regulations 1991 (SI 1991/2890) reg.2C (Refugees)*

With effect from September 15, 2021, reg.4 of the Social Security 2.013 (Habitual Residence and Past Presence) (Amendment) Regulations 2021 (SI 2021/1034) amended reg.2C as follows:

(1) For the title to reg.2C substitute "Refugees and certain persons with leave to enter or remain in the United Kingdom".

(2) In paragraph (1)

(a) At the end of sub-paragraph (a) omit the word "or"
(b) After sub-paragraph (b) insert—
 "(c) leave to enter or remain in the United Kingdom granted under the immigration rules by virtue of—
 (i) the Afghan Relocations and Assistance Policy; or
 (ii) the previous scheme for locally-employed staff in Afghanistan (sometimes referred to as the ex-gratia scheme);
 (d) been granted discretionary leave outside the immigration rules as a dependant of a person referred to in sub-paragraph (c); or
 (e) leave granted under the Afghan Citizens Resettlement Scheme.".
(3) After paragraph (1) insert—

"(1A) Regulation 2(1)(a) shall not apply where paragraph (1)(c), (d) or (e) applies to the person.".

The amendments made by these regulations apply in respect of England and Wales only. The same amendments are made with effect from the same date in respect of Scotland only by reg.2 of the Social Security (Residence Requirements) (Afghanistan) (Scotland) Regulations 2021 (SI 2021/320) but in addition that regulation also substitutes for para.(2) of reg.2C the following—

"(2) For the purposes of this regulation—
 (a) "immigration rules" means the rules laid before Parliament under section 3(2) of the Immigration Act 1971,
 (b) "the Afghan Citizens Resettlement Scheme" means the scheme announced by the United Kingdom Government on 18 August 2021."

p.850, *annotation to the Social Security (Invalid Care Allowance) Regulations 1976 (SI 1976/409) reg.4 (Circumstances in which persons are or are not to be treated as engaged or regularly and substantially engaged in caring for severely disabled persons)*

2.014   The text of reg.9 on p.850 should appear in a smaller font as it is reg.9 of the Social Security (Coronavirus) (Further Measures) Regulations 2020 (SI 2020/371) and part of the commentary to reg.4 of the Social Security (Invalid Care Allowance) Regulations 1976 (SI 1976/409). It is not reg.9 of the 1976 Regulations. The latter appears in its correct position in the text at pp.856-858. The running header on p.851 should therefore read *(SI 1976/409 reg.4) (as amended)*.

p.860, *amendment to the Social Security (Invalid Care Allowance) Regulations 1976 (SI 1976/409) reg.9C (Refugees)*

2.015   With effect from September 15, 2021, reg.4 of the Social Security (Habitual Residence and Past Presence) (Amendment) Regulations 2021 (SI 2021/1034) amended reg.9C as follows:

(1) For the title to reg.9C substitute "Refugees and certain persons with leave to enter or remain in the United Kingdom".

(2) In paragraph (1)

(a) At the end of sub-paragraph (a) omit the word "or"

(b) After sub-paragraph (b) insert—

"(c) leave to enter or remain in the United Kingdom granted under the immigration rules by virtue of—

(i) the Afghan Relocations and Assistance Policy; or

(ii) the previous scheme for locally-employed staff in Afghanistan (sometimes referred to as the ex-gratia scheme);

(d) been granted discretionary leave outside the immigration rules as a dependant of a person referred to in sub-paragraph (c); or

(e) leave granted under the Afghan Citizens Resettlement Scheme.".

(3) After paragraph (1) insert—

"(1A) Regulation 9(1)(a) shall not apply where paragraph (1)(c), (d) or (e) applies to the person.".

The amendments made by these regulations apply in respect of England and Wales only. The same amendments are made with effect from the same date in respect of Scotland only by reg.2 of the Social Security (Residence Requirements) (Afghanistan) (Scotland) Regulations 2021 (SI 2021/320) but in addition that regulation also substitutes for para.(2) of reg.9C the following—

"(2) For the purposes of this regulation—

(a) "immigration rules" means the rules laid before Parliament under section 3(2) of the Immigration Act 1971,

(b) "the Afghan Citizens Resettlement Scheme" means the scheme announced by the United Kingdom Government on 18 August 2021."

p.869, *annotation to the Social Security (Personal Independence Payment) Regulations 2013 (SI 2013/377) reg.3 (Daily Living Activities and mobility activities)*

Where an appeal to the FTT is in respect of a transition decision (i.e. **2.016** moving the claimant from DLA to PIP) and a claimant who was previously awarded DLA is denied any entitlement to PIP at all, Judge Hemingway has decided, in *SM v SSWP (PIP)* [2021] UKUT 140 (AAC), that if the FTT is to dismiss that appeal, it must give reasons explaining why entitlement to benefit has stopped; failure to do so is an error of law. The judge suggests also, though not as part of his decision, that where the tribunal finds contradictions in the evidence before it, those contradictions should be put to the claimant if they are to be relied upon as a part of their decision. Further, he suggests too (though again not as a part of his decision) that there would be few statements of reasons for a decision that are adequate unless some reference is made to regulation 4(2A) in such a way as to demonstrate that the criteria set out there, have been applied in practice, even if not referred to specifically.

p.869, *annotation to the Social Security (Personal Independence Payment) Regulations 2013 (SI 2013/377) reg.3 (Daily Living Activities and mobility activities)*

2.017   Another innovation to the procedure that is followed within the DWP has been the introduction of a further reconsideration of entitlement following the making of an appeal by the claimant. Where the Secretary of State is minded to increase the award of points on than assessment the practice has developed of making an "offer" to the claimant but without the Secretary of State actually revising the decision. Where that offer would increase the claimant's entitlement, if accepted, the effect would be for the appeal to lapse. Initially it seems that such offers were made conditional on the claimant abandoning the appeal. Following judicial review proceedings in 2021 that condition was removed and such offers are now made with a statement telling the claimant that, although the current appeal would lapse, there will be a right to appeal against the new decision. The purpose of this process is obviously to avoid the need to continue with appeals in which the Secretary of State is likely to concede that there is a right to further entitlement. The reluctance of the Secretary of State to make a revision is possibly explained by not wishing to deprive the claimant of his appeal when the claimant may wish to argue for an even greater award and may not wish to lose time by having to enter a new appeal. This was effectively the situation that arose in *DO v SSWP (PIP)* [2021] UKUT 161 (AAC) (though, in that case, it seems that the claimant, who was autistic, may not have understood his right to make a new appeal and simply wanted to have a chance to explain to the tribunal how his condition affected him).

The question that arises in these cases is how the FTT should approach the information given to them about the Secretary of State's reconsidered view of the claimant's entitlement. In this case the FTT, having heard that view, nevertheless awarded a lesser amount than the Secretary of State would have been willing to concede (though a greater amount than the original award of benefit). Judge Wright held that it was an error of law to do so, though he does so for what may be two different reasons. On one hand, he takes the view (paras. 45 and 46) that the FTT did not have before it any issue relating to the claimant's entitlement to benefit at the rate for which the Secretary of State had conceded entitlement, and hence had no jurisdiction to decide on that matter. On the other, he went on (para. 47) to observe that if the FTT considered that there was an issue as to the claimant's entitlement to benefit even at the rate that had been conceded, and bearing in mind that the claimant was unrepresented and was autistic, fairness would require that the FTT should have at least given a warning, and possibly adjourned the proceedings for the claimant to be able to take advice. Perhaps the answer is that where (as the judge thought in this case) the Secretary of State has taken an unequivocal and conclusive view of the claimant's entitlement (see para.42) then the former will be the correct course for the FTT to take, but if the Secretary of State is thought to be offering a tentative view that is more of an evidential nature to the FTT, then the latter course should be followed. Now that the right to a fresh appeal has been made explicit these cases are less likely to arise.

p.873, *annotation to the Social Security (Personal Independence Payment) Regulations 2013 (SI 2013/377) reg.3 (Daily Living Activities and mobility activities)*

An example where reasons to explain the difference between a pre- 2.018 vious entitlement to DLA, but now no entitlement to PIP, were held to be adequate can be seen in the decision, again by Judge Hemingway, in *MM-C v SSWP (PIP)* UKUT [2021] UKUT 183 (AAC). The reasons given there by the FTT included passages drawn from the medical evidence that showed there had been an improvement in the claimant's medical condition and supported an inference that she was now more able to find her way about on her own and hence did not qualify for the mobility component.

p.897, *amendment to the Social Security (Personal Independence Payment) Regulations 2013 (2013/377) reg.23A (Refugees)*

With effect from September 15, 2021, reg.4 of the Social Security 2.019 (Habitual Residence and Past Presence) (Amendment) Regulations 2021 (SI 2021/1034) amended reg.23A as follows:

(1) For the title to reg.23A substitute "Refugees and certain persons with leave to enter or remain in the United Kingdom".
(2) In paragraph (1)
(a) At the end of sub-paragraph (a) omit the word "or"
(b) After sub-paragraph (b) insert—
    "(c) leave to enter or remain in the United Kingdom granted under the immigration rules by virtue of—
        (i) the Afghan Relocations and Assistance Policy; or
        (ii) the previous scheme for locally-employed staff in Afghanistan (sometimes referred to as the ex-gratia scheme);
    (d) been granted discretionary leave outside the immigration rules as a dependant of a person referred to in sub-paragraph (c); or
    (e) leave granted under the Afghan Citizens Resettlement Scheme.".
(3) After paragraph (1) insert—

"(1A) Regulation 2(1)(a) shall not apply where paragraph (1)(c), (d) or (e) applies to the person.".

The amendments made by these regulations apply in respect of England and Wales only. The same amendments are made with effect from the same date in respect of Scotland only by reg.2 of the Social Security (Residence Requirements) (Afghanistan) (Scotland) Regulations 2021

(SI 2021/320) but in addition that regulation also substitutes for para.(2) of reg.23A the following—

"(2) For the purposes of this regulation—
  (a) "immigration rules" means the rules laid before Parliament under section 3(2) of the Immigration Act 1971,
  (b) "the Afghan Citizens Resettlement Scheme" means the scheme announced by the United Kingdom Government on 18 August 2021."

p.914, *annotation to the Social Security (Personal Independence Payment) Regulations 2013 (SI 2013/377) Sch.1 (Personal Independence Assessment)*

2.020   The effect of an addiction to alcohol in a claimant has been considered again, at length, in *DE v SSWP (PIP)* [2021] UKUT 226 (AAC). The claimant was what was described as a functioning alcoholic who had made a succession of claims for PIP none of which had succeeded. In this latest claim the HCP had accepted that he was entitled to 2 points because he required an aid, in the form of a stool, to support him when cooking a meal. The claimant suffered from a number of physical conditions, as well as depression, all of which, he said, were "alcohol related". The FTT had rejected his appeal; they said that his disability was the result of a "lifestyle choice". In the UT Judge Clough allowed his appeal and returned the case for rehearing before a fresh tribunal. In doing so she gives extensive guidance to the new tribunal as to the correct approach for a tribunal dealing with addiction cases, advice which will be of benefit to all tribunals dealing with such issues. She begins by explaining the nature of addiction that will amount to an identifiable medical condition according to the latest Diagnostic and Statistical Manual of Mental Disorders of the American Psychiatric Association (DSM-5) which now uses the term Alcohol Use Disorder (AUD). As the judge explains AUD is:

"a discrete illness, characterised predominantly by a loss of self-control over alcohol use, typically rendering a person incapable of refraining from alcohol consumption despite any impacts it may be having on their health and ability to function (see *R(DLA) 6/06*, and the updated DSM-5)."

But that is not to say that the claimant must be totally incapable of exercising self-control. As the judge herself points out, the decision in *R (DLA) 6/06* shows that the condition need not be uncontrollable in the sense that it is absolutely impossible for a person to control the condition, it is a matter of degree.

Where the evidence before the tribunal includes a diagnosis of AUD (or of its predecessor, Alcohol Dependency Syndrome (ADS)) the way is clear for the tribunal to move to assessing its effect upon the claimant's ability to satisfy daily living activities, but there need not be such a diagnosis if the tribunal can satisfy themselves that, on the evidence before them, the claimant does indeed suffer from AUD—see *R (DLA) 3/06)*.

Thereafter the task of the FTT will be to make a careful, usually detailed, account of how the claimant's condition affects his ability to satisfy the PIP activities. That may vary according to the time of day and the extent to which the claimant has or has not consumed alcohol, because, especially in the case of a functioning alcoholic, the consumption of alcohol may improve that claimant's ability. The question is not whether the claimant is to be tested before or after he has consumed alcohol, but rather it is to establish the claimant's normal pattern of daily behaviour and to test his ability in the state that he then may be. Having done that the judge explains, in some detail, how the tribunal should then proceed to check that ability against all four of the criteria contained in reg.4(2A)—safely, to a reasonable standard, repeatedly and in a timely manner. Especially with regard to safety, careful fact finding and estimation of risk may be necessary. Finally, after all that the claimant's behaviour must be measured against the requirements of reg.7—the 50% rule. Any tribunal faced with one of these cases would do well to read the whole of this judgment.

p.943, *annotation to the Social Security (Personal Independence Payment) Regulations 2013 (SI 2013/377) (Activity 9—Engaging with other people face to face)*

A further example of where the claimant might be said to engage successfully but only with a limited range of people is found in *AC v SSWP (PIP)* [2021] UKUT 216 (AAC). The claimant had Asperger's syndrome and Prader Willi Syndrome. Evidence was given to the FTT that he was able to relate to others when he visited a shop selling wargames and that he could take part, in person, at wargaming competitions. Judge Church, in the UT, allowed an appeal on the ground that the tribunal had placed disproportionate emphasis on his ability to participate in wargaming and had drawn impermissible inferences from that about his ability to form social relationships for which they had allowed zero points. 2.021

pp.943-944, *correction to paragraph commencing at the bottom of p.943 (Activity 9—Engaging with other people face to face)*

This paragraph should be replaced by the following: 2.022

The meaning of "social support" in Descriptor 9c (for which 4 points are awarded) and the difference between that and "prompting" in 9b (only 2 points) has given rise to a number of cases. In the Scottish case of *SSWP v MMcK* [2017] CSIH 57 the Inner House of the Court of Session upheld a decision of Judge Agnew that had held the difference to depend mainly on the fact that social support could be given only by a person trained or experienced (in the wider sense that had been accepted by Judge Mark in the *PR.* case above). The Court of Session affirmed also that support given in advance of the occasion could qualify, though they did suggest that there must be some "temporal or causal" link between help given and the event to which it was related. In England, at the same time, a number of cases had been decided by the UT in which it was said that there must be something more than just the training and experience of the person giving support to justify the difference in the points awarded. There must be, it was said, some qualitative difference between the actions that were social support and those that amounted only to prompting. That was the view taken by Judge Humphrey in *AH v SSWP (PIP)* [2016] UKUT 147 (AAC). That case was appealed to the CA where it is reported as *Hickey v Secretary of State for Work and Pensions* [2018] EWCA Civ. 851, but in which the court found it unnecessary to reach a decision on the points raised above. Clarification has now been provided by the decision of the Supreme Court on the appeal from the Court of Session in the *MMcK* case reported as *Secretary of State for Work and Pensions v MM* [2019] UKSC 34. The appeal was allowed, but only because the unanimous decision of the court (given by Lady Black) was for slightly different reasons than those in the court below; the result remains the same.

p.1043, *annotation to the Social Security (Widow's Benefit and Retirement Pensions) Regulations 1979 reg.6 (SI 1979/642)*

2.023   The operation of reg.6 was explained by Upper Tribunal Judge Wikeley in *BB v Secretary of State for Work & Pensions (RP)* [2021] UKUT 141 (AAC) as follows:

> "19. Those persons who did not satisfy the second contribution condition [provided for by paragraph 5 of Part I to Schedule 3 to the Social Security Contributions and Benefits Act 1992] were nevertheless entitled to a reduced Category A retirement pension if they had either paid or been credited with sufficient contributions in at least 25% of the requisite number of years of their working lives (see regulation 6 of the Social Security (Widow's Benefit and Retirement Pensions) Regulations 1979 (SI 1979/642)). The Appellant fell into this category. His national insurance record showed that he had 36 qualifying years of insurance paid into the UK scheme (as against 44 years for the requisite number of years for the full rate pension). The Appellant was therefore entitled to a reduced Category A retirement pension representing 82% of the full rate pension (36/44, when rounded up, equates to 82%)."

p.1104, *amendment to the State Pension Regulations 2005 reg.37 (Credits for persons engaged in caring)*

2.024   With effect from November 17, 2021, reg.4 of the Social Security (Scotland) Act 2018 (Disability Assistance for Children and Young People) (Consequential Modifications) (No.2) Order 2021 (SI 2021/1301) reg.37 by inserting the following words at the end of reg.37(3):

"(h) the care component of child disability payment at the middle or highest rate in accordance with regulation 11 of the Disability Assistance for Children and Young People (Scotland) Regulations 2021."

pp.1126-1128, *annotation to the Jobseeker's Allowance Regulations 2013 (SI 2013/378) reg.5 (Application of regulations where there is dual entitlement)*

In the examination by the Social Security Advisory Committee (SSAC) of the proposal to amend reg.18 (see the entry for pp.1151-3) at its meeting of September 8, 2021, the anomalous results flowing from the prohibition on applying a sanction to new style JSA when the claimant is also entitled to universal credit were raised. See the notes to reg.5 in the main volume for details (and in what was then Vol.II from 2014/15 onwards). The DWP appeared initially not to consider the results problematic, but following the SSAC's expressions of concern, it said that it was starting to look at the issue of dual entitlement (para.1.2 of the minutes of the SSAC meeting of October 7, 2021, published with the minutes of the September meeting). The chair's letter of October 7 recorded the SSAC's strong view that the inconsistency be reviewed and addressed at the earliest opportunity. The Minister's reply of the same date committed to an investigation of whether the effect of reg.5 (and reg.42 of the ESA Regulations 2013) represented the policy intent and, if not, the extent of the issues, and to produce proposals addressing the SSAC's concerns.

2.025

pp.1151-1153, *amendment to the Jobseeker's Allowance Regulations 2013 (SI 2013/378) reg.18 (General principles for calculating reduction periods)*

With effect from November 1, 2021, reg.2 of the Jobseeker's Allowance and Employment and Support Allowance (Amendment) Regulations 2021 (SI 2021/1132) substituted "paragraph (3)" for "paragraphs (3) and (4)" in para.(1) and omitted para.(4).

2.026

This amendment corrects the fundamental error in the amendment to reg.18 (and to the equivalent new style ESA provision) carried out by SI 2016/678, as detailed in the note in the main volume and first identified in the 2017/18 edition of what was then Vol.II. The plain words of reg.18 as amended in 2016 prevented any "escalation" in the length of a sanction by reason of the existence of previous sanctionable failures, as provided for in regs 19-21. That obstacle has now been removed by the revocation of para.(4). But the correction only operates with effect from November 1, 2021. The Explanatory Note and Explanatory Memorandum to SI 2021/1132 describe the process as the correction of an error, which may possibly be taken as an endorsement of the argument in the note in the main volume that the rule of statutory interpretation allowing correction of drafting mistakes entails that the error should be regarded as not having existed from July 25, 2016. However, the Explanatory Memorandum does not spell that out and refers to the 2016 amendment having raised ambiguity and says that, as the words of the amendment had not been applied in practice, no claimant would be adversely affected by the removal of reg.18(4). That explanation appears on its face to be disingenuous at best, if claimants had in practice been made subject to escalating sanctions from July 25, 2016 when there was no clear legislative authority. However, the minutes of the meeting of the Social Security Advisory Committee (SSAC) on September 8, 2021 reveal the extraordinary (and hard to accept: see the entry for pp.373-4) claim made by DWP officials that no sanctions had been imposed on any new style JSA or ESA claimant since 2013, the focus instead having been on engagement and encouragement by work coaches (para.2.2(b)). There was, though, to be a process of applying sanctions for the future, so that the error (that was said to have been identified in 2018, but not corrected through lack of Parliamentary time) now needed to be corrected.

In a letter to the Minister for Employment dated October 7, 2021, the chairman of the SSAC said that it had decided, following its September meeting, not to take the amending regulations on formal reference. However, two areas of concern were raised: the inconsistent effect of the sanctions rules where there was dual entitlement to new style JSA or ESA and universal credit and the weakness of the DWP's equality analysis. The first concern goes much wider than the effect of this specific amendment, as was noted in the holding reply of October 7, 2021 by the Minister, Mims Davies. The difficulty arises from reg.5 of the JSA Regulations 2013 and reg.42 of the ESA Regulations 2013, as explained in the notes to reg.5 from the 2014/15 edition of what was then Vol.II onwards (now at 7.13 of the main volume). See further in the entry for pp.1126-8.

p.1156, *annotation to the Jobseeker's Allowance Regulations 2013 (SI 2013/378) reg.19 (Higher-level sanction)*

2.027   Note that reg.18(4) has been revoked with effect from November 1, 2021 (see the entry for pp.1151-3).

p.1159, *annotation to the Jobseeker's Allowance Regulations 2013 (SI 2013/378) reg.20 (Medium-level sanctions)*

2.028   Note that reg.18(4) has been revoked with effect from November 1, 2021 (see the entry for pp.1151-3).

p.1161, *annotation to the Jobseeker's Allowance Regulations 2013 (SI 2013/378) reg.21 (Low-level sanctions)*

2.029   Note that reg.18(4) has been revoked with effect from November 1, 2021 (see the entry for pp.1151-3).

p.1173, *annotation to the Jobseeker's Allowance Regulations 2013 (SI 2013/378) reg.34 (The conditions and relevant earnings)*

2.030   See *NH v SSWP (JSA)* [2021] UKUT 227 (AAC), detailed in the entry for pp.339-41, for an illustration of the effect of reg.34.

p.1241, *amendment to the Social Security (Coronavirus) (Further Measures) Regulations 2020 (SI 2020/371) reg.10(2B) (Expiry of regs 8 and 9)*

With effect from May 12, 2021, reg.3 of the Social Security (Coro-   2.031
navirus) (Miscellaneous Amendments) Regulations 2021 (SI 2021/476) substituted "31st August 2021" for "12th May 2021".

p.1296, *amendment to the Employment and Support Allowance Regulations 2013 (SI 2013/379) reg.51 (General principles for calculating reduction periods)*

With effect from November 1, 2021, reg.3 of the Jobseeker's Allow-   2.032
ance and Employment and Support Allowance (Amendment) Regulations 2021 (SI 2021/1132) amended reg.51 by substituting "paragraph (3)" for "paragraphs (3) and (4)" in para.(1) and omitting para.(4). See further the detailed analysis of the parallel amendments to the new-style JSA regulations at para.2.026 above.

p.1328, *amendment to the Employment and Support Allowance Regulations 2013 (SI 2013/379) reg.94 (Meaning of "person in hardship")*

With effect from July 26, 2021, art.23 of the Social Security (Scot-   2.033
land) Act 2018 (Disability Assistance for Children and Young People) (Consequential Modifications) Order 2021 (SI 2021/786) amended reg.94 by inserting ", child disability payment" after "disability living allowance" in paras (3)(b) and 3(c)(ii) and by substituting for the definition of "care component" in para.(7) the following new definitions:

""care component" means—
  (a) the care component of disability living allowance at the highest or middle rate prescribed under section 72(3) of the Contributions and Benefits Act; or
  (b) the care component of child disability payment at the highest or middle rate provided for in regulation 11(5) of the Disability Assistance for Children and Young People (Scotland) Regulations 2021;
"child disability payment" has the meaning given in regulation 2 of the Disability Assistance for Children and Young People (Scotland) Regulations 2021;".

p.1336, *correction to text of the Employment and Support Allowance Regulations 2013 (SI 2013/379) Sch.2 (Assessment of whether a claimant has limited capability for work: Activity 1—Mobilising unaided, etc)*

The points score for descriptor 1(d) is 6—the figure 6 has been   2.034
misplaced next to descriptor 1(c)(i).

pp.1406-1417, *annotation to the Employment and Support Allowance Regulations 2008 (SI 2008/794) reg.35 (Certain claimants to be treated as having limited capability for work-related activity)*

2.035   For further examples of the need for sufficient fact-finding and adequate reasons in appeals where reg.35 is in issue, see *MH v SSWP (ESA)* [2021] UKUT 90 (AAC) and *CT v SSWP (ESA)* [2021] UKUT 131 (AAC).

p.1408, *annotation to the Employment and Support Allowance Regulations 2008 (SI 2008/794) reg.35 (Certain claimants to be treated as having limited capability for work-related activity)*

2.036   Lest there be any doubt about the matter, the decision in *IM v SSWP (ESA)* [2014] UKUT 412 (AAC); [2015] AACR 10 is binding on First-tier Tribunals: *CT v SSWP (ESA)* [2021] UKUT 131 (AAC).

p.1412, *annotation to the Employment and Support Allowance Regulations 2008 (SI 008/794) reg.35 (Certain claimants to be treated as having limited capability for work-related activity)*

2.037   In the importance of tribunals in universal credit appeals (that turn on the equivalent provision to reg.35 in Schedule 9, paragraph 4) ensuring they have been provided with an accurate list of work-related activities, see *KS v SSWP (UC)* [2021] UKUT 132 (AAC). Secretary of State appeal responses on such appeals may not have included accurate lists of work-related activities until after July 2020.

p.1473, *annotation to the Employment and Support Allowance Regulations 2008 (SI 2008/794) Sch.2 activity 17 (Appropriateness of behaviour with other people, due to cognitive impairment or mental disorder)*

2.038   Consideration of activity 17 may require the disclosure of Unacceptable Customer Behaviour (UCB) forms as provided in confidence by the DWP to HMCTS: *MH v SSWP (ESA)* [2021] UKUT 90 (AAC).

p.1502, *annotation to the Social Security (General Benefit) Regulations 1982 (SI 1982/1408) reg.11(4) (Further definition of the principles of assessment of disablement and prescribed degrees of disablement)*

2.039   See further *PA v SSWP (II)* [2021] UKUT 257 (AAC), where the claimant injured his back in an industrial accident in 1981 and later had surgery to correct the effects of the accident. In 1986 he was awarded industrial injuries disablement benefit, based on an assessment of disablement at 7 per cent 'final' for life. In 2019 the claimant then appealed a refusal of his second attempt to supersede the award on the ground that his condition had deteriorated. The FTT dismissed the appeal, finding that some of the deterioration was due to general wear and tear. As the FTT acknowledged that at least some of the deterioration caused by the surgery resulted from the accident, Judge Poynter held that " . . . regulation 11(4) required it to perform a notional assessment as a building block towards the actual assessment. The tribunal should have assessed how disabled the claimant would have been 'during the period taken into account by the assessment' if the constitutional degenerative changes had not occurred'" (para. 14). Furthermore, " . . . Even if the notional assessment was less than 11 per cent, the claimant would nevertheless have been entitled to have the existing assessment of 7 per cent increased to reflect any additional disability caused by the deterioration attributable to the accident. The only exception to that would be if the additional disability was so trivial that it was insufficient to affect the 7 per cent assessment. If that was the case, the written statement of reasons should have explained why that it was the case" (paras 29 and 30).

pp.1599–1600, *annotation to the Social Security (Industrial Injuries) (Prescribed Diseases) Regulations 1985 (SI 1985/967) Sch.1 A15 (Dupuytren's contracture)*

The onset of the disease occurs not when the claimant first experiences Dupuytren's disease but only when the signs of the contracture stage, as contained in the statutory definition, manifest themselves: *DR v SSWP (II)* [2021] UKUT 191 (AAC).   2.040

pp.1599–1600, *annotation to the Social Security (Industrial Injuries) (Prescribed Diseases) Regulations 1985 (SI 1985/967) Sch.1 D1 (Pneumoconiosis)*

On the level of reasoning required to explain a negative diagnosis of D1, see *KH (deceased) (by his appointee AMH) v SSWP (II)* [2021] UKUT 189 (AAC) paras 15-18.   2.041

p.1605, *annotation to the Social Security (Industrial Injuries) (Prescribed Diseases) Regulations 1985 (SI 1985/967) Sch.1 D9 (Unilateral or bilateral diffuse pleural thickening)*

See *KH (deceased) (by his appointee AMH) v SSWP (II)* [2021] UKUT 189 (AAC) at para 13, where Judge Poynter, giving permission to appeal, observed that "The claimant must be suffering from thickening of the "pleura" (i.e., the membrane that forms the lining of the lungs). That thickening need only affect one lung ("unilateral")—although it may affect both ("bilateral")—but it must be "diffuse", which is another word for "widespread". Pleural thickening that is localised (which is often called "pleural plaques") does not meet the definition."   2.042

p.1621, *annotation to the Social Security (Industrial Injuries) Regulations 1990 (SI 1990/256) reg.2 (Meaning of "regular employment")*

The appeal in *AR v SSWP (II)* [2021] UKUT 279 (AAC) was concerned with how the reduced earnings allowance legislation drafted in 1990 applies today to zero hours contracts. The DWP decided that, as   2.043

the claimant had not worked at least an average of 10 hours p.w. over a nine-week period since reaching pensionable age, his REA had to be converted to retirement allowance. The claimant appealed on the ground that he had worked under a zero hours contract and his average hours should be calculated over a period of more than five (or indeed nine) weeks, as this would show that he had worked an average of around 24 hours p.w. (and without entitlement to sick leave or paid holiday) in the last year. The FTT dismissed his appeal, as did Judge Jacobs in the Upper Tribunal:

"12. Paragraph 13 of Schedule 7 to the 1992 Act provides that a claimant shall cease to be entitled 'as from the day on which he gives up regular employment.' Regulation 2 defines the expression 'regular employment'. The regulation provides what 'regular employment' means. That word conveys that the regulation contains an exhaustive definition of the expression. There is no scope for arguing that the claimant actually remained in regular employment as that expression might normally be understood. As Mr Commissioner Howell wrote in *CI/16202/96* at [5], regulation 2 contains: . . . an artificial test of when a person is to be regarded as having 'given up regular employment' and if the facts of his case are caught by the regulations it is no answer to say that he always intended to go on working regularly, or had in fact done so, in ways that for some reason or another failed to meet the prescribed conditions.

13. Regulation 2(a) does not apply to the claimant's circumstances. It only applies if a claimant is party to a contract of service (employment) that requires them to work. This applies to the traditional contract of employment in which a claimant contracts to work for a particular number of hours a week, barring periods of holiday or sickness. It does not apply to a zero hours contract under which: (a) the employer is not obliged to make any work available for the employee; and (b) the employee is not obliged to take up any work offered.

14. Regulation 2(b) does apply to the claimant's circumstances. It was almost certainly not drafted with zero hours contracts in mind. It was probably designed for claimants who were self-employed or working on a casual basis. But that does not matter. What matters is what it says. By its terms, it applies to work actually undertaken rather than work that the claimant is required to do under a contract. That is apt to cover zero hours contracts and exactly captures the claimant's circumstances. There is no equivalent provision to the qualification in regulation 2(a) for absences allowed by the contract. The reason is that, unlike regulation 2(a), regulation 2(b) is based on actual work outside the framework of a contract."

pp.1621–1623, *annotation to the Social Security (Industrial Injuries) Regulations 1990 (SI 1990/256) reg.3 (Circumstances in which a person over pensionable age is to be regarded as having given up regular employment)*

2.044   See note to reg.2.

p.1683, *amendments to the Vaccine Damage Payments (Specified Disease) Order 2015 (SI 2015/47)*

With effect from May 25, 2021, art. 2 of the Vaccine Damage Pay-   2.045
ments (Specified Disease) (Amendment) Order 2021 (SI 2021/508)
amended art.3 so it now reads as follows:

Modification of conditions of entitlement

3. The conditions of entitlement in section 2(1) of the Act have
effect subject to the following modifications—
- (a) in relation to vaccination against rotavirus, in sub-paragraph
  (ii) of section 2(1)(a), for "5th July 1948" substitute "1st July
  2013";
- [¹(b) in relation to vaccination against influenza, other than influenza caused by a pandemic influenza virus, in sub-paragraph
  (ii) of section 2(1)(a)—
    - (i) in relation to a vaccination carried out at a time when the
      person to whom it was given was under the age of eight-
      een, for "5th July 1948" substitute "1st September 2013";
      and
    - (ii) in relation to a vaccination carried out at a time when the
      person to whom it was given was aged eighteen or over, for
      "5th July 1948" substitute "24th May 2015"];
- (c) in relation to vaccination against rotavirus [¹ . . .], for paragraph (b) of section 2(1) substitute—
  "(b) that the vaccination was carried out at a time when the
  person to whom it was given was under the age of eighteen;
  and".
- [¹(d) The condition of entitlement in section 2(1)(b) of the Act (age
  or time at which vaccination was carried out) is omitted in
  relation to vaccination against influenza, other than influenza
  caused by a pandemic influenza virus.]

AMENDMENT

1. Vaccine Damage Payments (Specified Disease) (Amendment) Order
   2021 (SI 2021/508) art.2 (May 25, 2021).

PART III

UPDATING MATERIAL
VOLUME II

UNIVERSAL CREDIT, STATE PENSION CREDIT AND THE SOCIAL FUND

Commentary by

John Mesher

Tom Royston

Nick Wikeley

p.50, *Universal Credit—General Note: 'Incentivising work'*

The October 2021 Budget included a high profile announcement that **3.001** the universal credit work allowance and the earnings deduction rate, both specified in reg.22(1) of the 2013 Regulations, would each be made more generous to claimants: *Autumn Budget and Spending Review 2021* (HC 822, October 27, 2021), p.4.

Consequently, from November 24, 2021, higher and lower work allowance rates have each increased by £42 per assessment period, and the earnings deduction rate has reduced from 63 to 55 pence in the pound: Universal Credit (Work Allowance and Taper) (Amendment) Regulations 2021 (SI 2021/1283).

The extent to which these measures offset the equally high profile October 6, 2021 end of the coronavirus-related temporary uplift to the amount of the standard allowance will depend on a household's individual circumstances. (The temporary uplift had been provided by the Universal Credit (Extension of Coronavirus Measures) Regulations 2021 (SI 2021/313), reg.2).

p.52, *Universal Credit—General Note: 'Introduction of universal credit–existing claimants'*

The Secretary of State intends ultimately to move all legacy benefit **3.002** recipients onto universal credit. The Universal Credit (Managed Migration Pilot and Miscellaneous Amendments) Regulations 2019 (SI 2019/1152) allow for up to 10,000 people to experimentally undergo 'managed moves' onto universal credit from legacy benefit. The managed migration legislation itself is in Part 4 Universal Credit (Transitional Provisions) Regulations 2014; the 10,000 person limitation is imposed by reg.2 of SI 2019/1152.

A pilot scheme began in Harrogate in July 2019, but as of January 2020 only 13 people had actually moved to universal credit [HC Deb (January 27, 2020), vol 670 col 521], and operation of the scheme was suspended altogether upon the outbreak of coronavirus. On November 8, 2021, the Secretary of State announced that the Harrogate scheme would not be resumed, and that a plan was 'still in preparation, on resuming the managed move to universal credit' [HC Deb (November 8, 2021), vol 703 col 8].

The Department's most recent estimate is that all legacy benefit claimants will have migrated to UC by the end of 2024: House of Commons Work and Pensions Committee, *DWP's Annual Report and Accounts 20/21 and Spending Review settlement—Oral evidence* (HC 728, November 24, 2021), Q19.

pp.57-60, *Universal Credit—General Note: 'Calculation of income— earned income—employees'; Universal Credit—General Note: 'The benefit cap'*

In *Secretary of State for Work and Pensions v Pantellerisco* [2021] EWCA **3.003** Civ 1454 (October 8, 2021) the Court of Appeal allowed an appeal from a decision of the High Court, [2020] EWHC 1944 (Admin). Garnham J had declared that it was irrational in the case of 4-weekly paid workers to disapply the benefit cap based on earnings received in an assessment period.

The Court of Appeal decided that the provision was not irrational. It considered the 'earnings received' approach to be part of the 'fundamental' structure of UC, and that the Secretary of State was entitled not to disrupt that structure by making provision for people to be exempted from the benefit cap where in an assessment period they had done enough work but not received enough pay.

Ms Pantellerisco has applied for permission to appeal to the Supreme Court.

p.176, *ERRATUM—annotation to the Welfare Reform and Work Act 2016 s.18 (Loans for mortgage interest etc)*

3.004 The third paragraph of the General Note to this section is out of date, and should be replaced with the following:

> The Loans for Mortgage Interest Regulations 2017 (SI 2017/725) were made on July 5, 2017. They were fully in force, subject to limited transitional provision, by April 6, 2018. They make repayable loans available to eligible persons, and amend reg.25 and Sch.1 of the Universal Credit Regulations 2013 (SI 2013/376), as well as regulations relating to various legacy benefits, to remove provision for owner-occupier housing costs payments.

> SI 2017/725 is included in the main work (§§2.583-2.688), and the consequential amendments to secondary legislation are also included in the relevant volumes.

pp.207-208, *amendment to the Universal Credit Regulations 2013 (SI 2013/376), Reg 9 (Persons treated as in Great Britain)*

3.005 With effect from September 15, 2021, reg.3 of the Social Security (Habitual Residence and Past Presence) (Amendment) Regulations 2021 amended reg.9(4) (which prescribes persons who are exempt from the requirement to be habitually resident). The amendment inserted before sub-paragraph (a):

> "(za) a person granted leave in accordance with the immigration rules made under section 3(2) of the Immigration Act 1971, where such leave is granted by virtue of—
> (i) the Afghan Relocations and Assistance Policy; or
> (ii) the previous scheme for locally-employed staff in Afghanistan (sometimes referred to as the ex-gratia scheme);
> (zb) a person in Great Britain not coming within sub-paragraph (za) or (e)(iv) who left Afghanistan in connection with the collapse of the Afghan government that took place on 15th August 2021;"

From the same date the amendment also added a new reg.9(4)(e)(iv), so sub-paragraph (e) now reads:

"(e) a person who has been granted, or who is deemed to have been granted, leave outside the rules made under section 3(2) of the Immigration Act 1971 where that leave is—
  (i) discretionary leave to enter or remain in the United Kingdom,
  (ii) leave to remain under the Destitution Domestic Violence concession, [. . .]
  (iii) leave deemed to have been granted by virtue of regulation 3 of the Displaced Persons (Temporary Protection) Regulations 2005; [or
  [(iv) granted under the Afghan Citizens Resettlement Scheme;]"

pp.209–210, *annotation to the Universal Credit Regulations 2013 (SI 2013/376) reg.9 (Persons treated as in Great Britain)*

In *R (Fratila) v Secretary of State for Work and Pensions* [2021] UKSC   **3.006**
53 (December 1, 2021) the Supreme Court allowed the Secretary of State's appeal against the decision of the Court of Appeal, which had found reg.9(3)(c)(i) unlawfully discriminatory contrary to Art 18 TFEU for treating EU nationals with pre-settled status differently to UK nationals. The judgment of the Court of Appeal had become unsustainable following the decision of the CJEU, in *CG v Department for Communities* (C-709/20, July 15, 2021), that such a provision is not contrary to Art 18 TFEU or Directive 2004/38.

However, what the Supreme Court elected not to address (since it was a new point, which would have required new evidence) was the implications for the domestic Regulations of what had also been said in *CG* about the Charter of Fundamental Rights of the European Union ('the Charter'). The Court of Justice had stated:

"[93] . . . [Where] a Union citizen resides legally, on the basis of national law, in the territory of a Member State other than that of which he or she is a national, the national authorities empowered to grant social assistance are required to check that a refusal to grant such benefits based on that legislation does not expose that citizen, and the children for which he or she is responsible, to an actual and current risk of violation of their fundamental rights, as enshrined in Articles 1, 7 and 24 of the Charter. Where that citizen does not have any resources to provide for his or her own needs and those of his or her children and is isolated, those authorities must ensure that, in the event of a refusal to grant social assistance, that citizen may nevertheless live with his or her children in dignified conditions. In the context of that examination, those authorities may take into account all means of assistance provided for by national law, from which the citizen concerned and her children are actually entitled to benefit."

Important unanswered questions arising from *CG* are:

• whether the Charter has any ongoing application, since the end of the transition period in December 2020, for EU nationals resident in the UK on the basis of pre-settled status; and

- what if any substantive or procedural requirements are imposed on the Secretary of State by the obligation to 'check' that Charter rights will not be breached.

pp.221-222, *amendments to the Universal Credit Regulations 2013 (SI 2013/376) reg.14 (Exceptions to the requirement not to be receiving education)*

3.007   With effect from August 5, 2020, reg.2 of the Universal Credit (Exceptions to the Requirement not to be receiving education) (Amendment) Regulations 2020 (SI 2020/827) amended reg.14 so that it reads as follows:

"Exceptions to the requirement not to be receiving education

14.—[(1)] A person does not have to meet the basic condition in s.4(1)(d) of the Act (not receiving education) if—

(a)   the person—
    (i)   is undertaking a full- time course of study or training which is not a course of advanced education,
    (ii)   is under the age of 21, or is 21 and reached that age whilst undertaking the course, and
    (iii)   is without parental support (as defined in regulation 8(3));

[(b)   the person is entitled to attendance allowance, disability living allowance or personal independence payment and it has been determined—
    (i)   that the person has limited capability for work or limited capability for work and work-related activity on the basis of an assessment under Part 5 of these Regulations or Part 4 or 5 of the ESA Regulations;
    (ii)   that the person is to be treated as having limited capability for work under Schedule 8 or limited capability for work and work-related activity under Schedule 9;
    (iii)   that the person is to be treated as having limited capability for work or limited capability for work and work-related activity under regulation 19(2)(b) or (4)(b) of the Universal Credit (Transitional Provisions) Regulations 2014,
and that determination was made on or before the date of claim to universal credit, where the person is receiving education on the date the claim is made, or the date on which the person starts receiving education, where the person starts receiving education after the date of claim to universal credit;]

(c)   the person is responsible for a child or a qualifying young person;

(d)   the person is a single person and a foster parent with whom a child is placed;

(e) the person is a member of a couple, both of whom are receiving education, and the other member is—
    (i) responsible for a child or qualifying young person, or
    (ii) a foster parent with whom a child is placed; or
(f) the person—
    (i) has reached the qualifying age for state pension credit, and
    (ii) is a member of a couple the other member of which has not reached that age.

[(2) Where regulation 9(6)(a) or 9(10) of the Universal Credit, Personal Independence Payment, Jobseeker's Allowance and Employment and Support Allowance (Claims and Payments) Regulations 2013 (award of universal credit without a claim) applies to a person who is receiving education, paragraph (1)(b) is to be read as if each reference to "date of claim" was a reference to "date of award".]

These amendments were in response to the litigation in *R (Kauser and JL) v Secretary of State for Work and Pensions* CO/987/2020, in which the High Court (Fordham J) subsequently issued a declaration by consent that, under the previous law, the Secretary of State had breached reg.14(b) when read with regs 38 and 39(1)(a), in failing to determine whether the claimants had limited capability for work; and failing to conduct a Work Capability Assessment *before* deciding the claimants' entitlement to Universal Credit (emphasis added). The order making the declaration is available on Rightsnet *at https://www.rightsnet.org.uk/pdfs/ CO_987_2020.pdf.*

With effect from July 26, 2021, art.20 and Sch.11, para.3 of the Social Security (Scotland) Act 2018 (Disability Assistance for Children and Young People) (Consequential Modifications) Order 2021 (SI 2021/786) made an amendment to these amendments in turn by inserting ", child disability payment" after "disability living allowance" in reg.14(1)(b).

However, with effect from December 15, 2021, reg.2 of the Universal Credit (Exceptions to the Requirement not to be receiving Education) (Amendment) Regulations 2021 (SI 2021/1224) further amended reg.14 by omitting para.(2) and substituting a new para.(1)(b) as follows:

"(b) the person is entitled to attendance allowance, disability living allowance, child disability payment or personal independence payment and, on a date before the date on which the person starts receiving education—
    (i) it has been determined that the person has limited capability for work or limited capability for work and work-related activity on the basis of an assessment under Part 5 or under Part 4 or 5 of the ESA Regulations; or
    (ii) the person is treated as having limited capability for work under Schedule 8 or limited capability for work and work-related activity under Schedule 9;".

pp.234-235, *amendment to the Universal Credit Regulations 2013 (SI 2013/376) reg. 22 (Deduction of income and work allowance)*

3.008   With effect from November 24, 2021, the Universal Credit (Work Allowance and Taper) (Amendment) Regulations 2021 (SI 2021/1283) amended the earnings deduction rate and the work allowance:

- In regulation 22(1)(b)(i) and (ii) for "63%" substitute "55%".
- In the table of work allowances set out in regulation 22—
    (a) for "£515.00" substitute "£557.00"; and
    (b) for "£293.00" substitute "£335.00".

Regulation 1(2) of SI 2021/1283 makes clear that these amendments have effect for any assessment period ending on or after November 24, 2021.

pp.246-247, *ERRATUM—annotation to the Universal Credit Regulations 2013 (SI 2013/376) reg.25 (The housing costs condition)*

3.009   The General Note to this regulation is out of date. It does not reflect the amendment made by the Loans for Mortgage Interest Regulations 2017 (SI 2017/725) to reg.25(2), which means UC no longer provides housing costs support for "owner-occupier payments". Instead claimants can obtain repayable loans.

The amendment is shown correctly in the main work. SI 2017/725 is also included in the main work (pp.577-633, §§2.583-2.688).

pp.255-256, *annotation to the Universal Credit Regulations 2013 (SI 2013/376) reg.33 (The childcare costs condition)*

3.010   In *Secretary of State for Work And Pensions v Salvato* [2021] EWCA Civ 1482 (October 13, 2021) the Court of Appeal allowed the Secretary of State's appeal from a decision of the High Court ([2021] EWHC 102 (Admin) (Chamberlain J)) that the reg.33(1)(za) "Proof of Payment rule" (i.e. the requirement that the claimant should actually have paid childcare costs, as opposed to merely incurring a liability to do so, before the childcare costs element can be paid) was irrational and unlawfully discriminatory contrary to art.14, taken together with art.8 of, and with art.1 of the First Protocol to, the European Convention on Human Rights. The Court of Appeal decided that the "Proof of Payment rule" was rational and justified.

Ms Salvato has applied for permission to appeal to the Supreme Court.

p.311, *annotation to the Universal Credit Regulations 2013 (SI 2013/376) reg.50(1) (Notional capital–deprivation)*

3.011   The general principle as to the effect of the limitation of the application of reg.50(1) to circumstances in which the claimant's purpose was to secure entitlement to or an increased amount of universal credit was accepted in *DB v DfC (JSA)* [2021] NICom 43 (see the entry for pp.1029-30 of Vol.V).

pp.322-324, *annotation to the Universal Credit Regulations 2013 (SI 2013/376) reg.54 (Calculation of earned income—general principles)*

The Court of Appeal in *Pantellerisco v Secretary of State for Work and Pensions* [2021] EWCA Civ 1454; [2021] P.T.S.R. 1922 has overturned the decision of Garnham J in the Divisional Court, discussed in the main volume. Since the claimant's judicial review challenge was directed specifically against the operation of the earnings-related exception to the operation of the benefit cap for claimants paid four-weekly and working for 16 hours a work at national minimum wage level. In the closely reasoned judgment of Underhill LJ the Court concluded that it was not irrational for the Secretary of State not to have introduced some solution to the problem that, compared with a claimant in identical circumstances who was paid monthly, Ms Pantellerisco was some £500 a year worse off because she was excepted from the benefit cap in only one assessment period in the year, not all 12. Any suggested solution would involve deeming (at least for benefit cap purposes) some earnings accrued in an assessment period, but not actually received, as having been received. That, in the judges' view, would do unacceptable damage to the system of calculating earnings by reference to receipts in assessment periods of calendar months and seriously undermine the reliability and workability of the assessment of entitlement, because all elements of the system had to fit together. The confirmation by Lord Reed in para.146 of *R (SC) v Secretary of State for Work and Pensions* [2021] UKSC 26, [2021] 3 W.L.R. 428 that in the context of social and economic policy, covering social security benefits, the test of unreasonableness should be applied with considerable care and caution, especially where a statutory instrument had been reviewed by Parliament, also appears to have been influential. **3.012**

Ms Pantellerisco's application to the Supreme Court for permission to appeal is awaiting determination at the time of going to press.

Thus, subject to any possible further appeal, so far as the ordinary operation of regs 54 and 61, without the complication of the benefit cap exception, to claimants paid four-weekly or at any other weekly interval is concerned, there now appears no possibility of any conclusion of irrationality or unreasonableness. The effect of a downward fluctuation in universal credit entitlement in the one assessment period in a year (for the four-weekly paid) in which two payments are received is vastly less than that of the benefit cap rule, and might not arise, depending on the accident of how long a claimant was in receipt of universal credit and whether that period included a two-payment assessment period. Plus, there is Judge May's pertinent question from *LG v SSWP (UC)* [2021] UKUT 121 (AAC) of how, if one payment were to be taken out of such an assessment period, it could be attributed across any other assessment periods.

What did emerge from the evidence discussed by the Court of Appeal is that, following the report of March 12, 2019 by the House of Commons Work and Pensions Committee, the DWP is apparently considering whether some reform should be made to the rules on pay cycles.

pp.324-328, *amendment to the Universal Credit Regulations 2013 (SI 2013/376) reg.54A(6) (Surplus earnings) and annotations to reg.54A*

3.013   With effect from November 24, 2021 (or, for existing claimants, any assessment period ending on or after November 24, 2021), reg.2(2) of the Universal Credit (Work Allowance and Taper) (Amendment) Regulations 2021 (SI 2021/1283) substituted the following for the formula in the definition of "the nil UC threshold" in reg.54A(6) (the layout of the formula in the Queen's Printers version of SI 2021/1283 differs from that used previously):

"$(M - U) / 55 \times 100 + WA$"

Various examples given in the annotations using the previous taper percentage of 63% need to be adjusted accordingly.

It has been announced that the temporary increase to £2,500 of the "de minimis" figure is to be continued for a further year to March 31, 2023 (Autumn Budget and Spending Review 2021 (HC 822), para.5.12).

pp.336-340, *annotation to the Universal Credit Regulations 2013 (SI 2013/376) reg.55 (Employed earnings)*

3.014   *DfC v RM (UC)* [2021] NICom 36 confirms the basic principle that, subject to some exceptions, the definition of "employed earnings" is by reference to s.62(2) of the Income Tax (Earnings and Pensions) Act 2003 (ITEPA 2003). That was in the context of a gross sum of £5,228.42 received in December 2018 by the claimant in settlement, after conciliation, of Industrial Tribunal proceedings against his employer for non-payment of wages or of holiday pay entitlement. The employer described the payment as a gesture of goodwill rather than in fulfilment of a contractual liability, but the payment was apparently calculated to cover 1.5 hours of work a week over a period from 2005 to 2012. The DfC treated the net payment, after deduction of income tax and national insurance, and including regular monthly salary, of £5,221.45 notified by HMRC in the particular assessment period through the real time information system (see reg.61) as employed earnings in respect of that period. The appeal tribunal allowed the claimant's appeal, finding under the equivalent of reg.61(3)(b)(ii) as in force at the time that the information received from HMRC did not reflect the definition of employed earnings in reg.55, so that the amount attributable to the settlement was not to be taken into account in the assessment period in question. On further appeal by the DfC, the Northern Ireland Commissioner rightly rejected its argument that the tribunal must have regarded the payment as capital, contrary to the principles set out in *Minter v Kingston upon Hull CC* and *Potter v Secretary of State for Work and Pensions* [2011] EWCA Civ 1155, [2012] AACR 21 (for full details of those decisions see Vol.V of this series at 2.204-06). Those decisions were not in point because the essential question under reg.55 is how the payment would be treated under s.62(2) of ITEPA

2003. The Commissioner then declined to hold the tribunal in error of law for failing to deal with the question of what the outcome would be under s.62(2). He considered that the inquisitorial duty of the tribunal, and the Commissioner, could not extend to the exploration of income tax law, rather than the familiar social security issues, in the absence of structured submissions (and apparently his view that there was at least a good argument that the payment was made in consideration of the abandonment of the proceedings, rather than in return for the claimant's service in the period from 2005 to 2012). The onus was thus firmly on the DfC to establish its case to the tribunal and the Commissioner. It had not done so, because it had not referred the tribunal or the Commissioner to any case law relevant to the taxation of compensation settlement payments.

It is submitted that that decision is based on too limited a view of the scope of the proper inquisitorial approach of appeal tribunals, and in particular of the Commissioner and, in Great Britain, the Upper Tribunal. It is not as if direct reference to ITEPA 2003 was a new feature for universal credit. That is the technique used for working tax credit (see the definition of "earnings" in reg.2 of the Tax Credits (Definition and Calculation of Income) Regulations 2002 in Vol.IV of this series, which also sets out all the relevant provisions of ITEPA 2003). And there is the instructive decision in *AH v HMRC (TC)* [2019] UKUT 5 (AAC) on that definition, briefly mentioned in the notes to reg.55 (and dealt with in detail in Vol.IV at 2.222), where Judge Wikeley discussed and applied the income tax cases on the meaning of "emolument of employment" in s.62(2). In those circumstances and when the adoption of the ITEPA 2003 test is an express part of the legislation to be applied, it appears wrong for the Commissioner not to have addressed the issue, possibly after obtaining further submissions. As it is, the decision in *RM* gives no guidance as to how future cases should be decided in substance (although of course it would as a Northern Ireland decision technically only have had persuasive authority in Great Britain).

In *AH*, the claimant had reached a draft settlement agreement on his claim against his NHS employer that it had made unlawful deductions from salary, in the sum of £16,000. However, because the parties wanted to avoid HM Treasury restrictions on compensation payments of more than £10,000, payment was made in two lump sums of £3,000 in August 2016 and March 2017 and by way of giving the claimant a 20-month fixed term contract of employment at £500 per month. In the event, before end of the fixed term the employer offered to pay the claimant the balance of his salary entitlement in a lump sum and the contract was terminated by mutual consent. HMRC took all the payments into account as employment income on the WTC claim. In the Upper Tribunal Judge Wikeley agreed. His analysis of the income tax authorities included the point that older cases decided when the formula of "emolument from employment" was in effect were still instructive although s.62(2) refers to "emolument of the employment". In addition, *Kuehne and Nagel Drinks Logistics Ltd v Commissioner for HMRC* [2012] EWCA Civ 34, [2012] STC 840 showed that where a payment was made for a reason other than being or becoming an employee (there to compensate for loss of future pension rights on the transfer of a business) and for a reason that was so related (there to encourage the heading off of strike action), it was enough to make the payment "from the employment" that the latter reason was sufficiently substantial, despite the existence of some other substantial reason. The claimant could only escape the conclusion that the payments made to reimburse him for non-payment of salary were emoluments of his employment if the arrangements, especially the fixed-term contract, were a sham, which the judge rejected.

The current HMRC guidance in its *Employment Income Manual* (EIM 12965, up-dated in respect of that paragraph on January 27, 2020) applies the principle that compensation should derive its character from the nature of the payment it replaces. That principle is of course familiar in the related, but different, social security context of income or capital (see *Minter* and *Potter* above). The guidance relies specifically on the decision in *Pettigrew v Commissioners of HMRC* [2018] UKFTT 240 (TC). Although as a First-tier decision it can have no precedential authority, it is based on an exhaustive survey of the case-law and a detailed analysis of the application of the principles to the facts.

Mr Pettigrew was a part-time fee-paid chairman of Industrial Tribunals and then an Employment Judge from 1996 to 2016. He lodged a claim against the Ministry of Justice (MoJ) for underpayments of fees for training, sitting and other days of service on the basis of discrimination by comparison with salaried office-holders. The MoJ offered him £55,045.42, including interest, in full and final settlement of his claim, which he accepted. When the payment was made, some £22,000 was deducted under PAYE. When submitting his 2014-15 self-assessment tax return Mr Pettigrew challenged that deduction on the basis that the payment was not arrears of wages or salary, but compensation for breach of the Part-Time Workers Regulations. That challenge was rejected by HMRC and by the FtT on appeal. After the review of the authority (which incidentally confirmed the relevance of the pre-ITEPA 2003 authority, as had been accepted by Lord Hodge in *RFC 2012 plc (in liquidation) (formerly the Rangers Football Club Plc) v Advocate General for Scotland* [2017] UKSC 45, [2017] 1 W.L.R. 2767 at [35]), the judge distilled five principles (paras 75–79). Three in particular were (1) that a payment of compensation for loss of rights directly connected with an employment will generally be an emolument of that employment (para.76); (2) that the character for tax purposes of a payment of compensation for failure to make a payment due should be the same as that of the payment if it had been paid (para.78); and (3) that where there is more than one reason for the payment then the employment must be a sufficiently substantial reason for the payment to characterise it as an emolument of the employment (para.79). Applying those principles to the facts found, the lump sum payment, apart from the interest element, plainly constituted an emolument of Mr Pettigrew's employment, particularly as a result of principle (2). Although, as he had submitted, the prompt for the making of the payment was the settlement of the litigation of which he was part, the methodology and quantification of the payment was to remedy the underpayments under the contract of employment, so that the test in *Kuehne and Nagel* (principle (3)) was met.

Applying those principles to the facts of *RM* would seem to lead equally inevitably to the conclusion that the settlement payment constituted employed earnings within s.62(2) of ITEPA 2003 and reg.55 of the Universal Credit Regulations 2013.

A Northern Ireland Commissioner accepted in para.36 of *RMcE v DfC (UC)* [2021] NICom 59, without having had submissions on the point, that a payment that constituted post-employment notice pay (PENP) within s.402D of ITEPA 2003 (see 2.204 of the main volume) would count as employed earnings under reg.55. That appears correct in general, though not of relevance to the facts of *RMcE*, where the payment in question was received before the amendments to ITEPA 2003 containing the PENP provisions came into force on April 6, 2018. The Commissioner rightly stressed the need in reg.55 appeals for the official party to provide explanatory material, legislation and jurisprudence relating to income tax to enable tribunals to perform their role properly.

p.346, *annotation to the Universal Credit Regulations 2013 (SI 2013/376) reg.57 (Self-employed earnings)*

The two Business Interruption Loan Schemes and the Bounce Back Loan Scheme ceased to operate on March 31, 2021, to be replaced by the Recovery Loan Scheme. **3.015**

pp.361-371, *annotation to the Universal Credit Regulations 2013 (SI 2013/376) reg.61 (Information for calculating earned income—real time information etc.)*

The Court of Appeal in *Pantellerisco v Secretary of State for Work and Pensions* [2021] EWCA Civ 1454, [2021] P.T.S.R. 1922 has overturned the decision of Garnham J in the Divisional Court, mentioned in the main volume at 2.223, 2.226 and 2.227. Ms Pantellerisco's application to the Supreme Court for permission to appeal is awaiting determination at the time of going to press. See the entry for pp.322-24 (reg.54). **3.016**

pp.372-373, *annotation to the Universal Credit Regulations 2013 (SI 2013/376) reg.62 (Minimum income floor (temporary coronavirus provisions)*

With effect from July 31, 2021, reg.2(1) of the Universal Credit (Restoration of the Minimum Income Floor) Regulations 2021 (SI 2021/807) has, as briefly mentioned in the main volume, provided for the reintroduction of the minimum income floor (MIF) subject to some exceptions and qualifications. Those Regulations are set out in Part I of this Supplement. Their mechanism is not directly to amend reg.10(2A) of the Further Measures Regulations, which provided for reg.2 of those **3.017**

Regulations, which contained the temporary coronavirus provisions on the MIF, to cease to have effect on July 31, 2021. Nor do they set out directly the rules that are to apply from July 31, 2021. Instead, they provide separately for parts of reg.2 to continue to have effect down to the end of July 31, 2022 (reg.2(1) of the Restoration Regulations), but subject to qualifications. That appears likely to cause confusion: the technical interaction of the provisions is not easy to work out.

The Explanatory Memorandum states that as the economy had started to reopen and restrictions on business eased, there should be plans for the reintroduction of the gainful self-employment (GSE) test, start-up periods and the MIF in general, while allowing current "easements" to continue as appropriate, thus ensuring claimants have the support they need to restart their businesses (paras 7.1 and 7.2). Paragraph 7.3 notes that reg.2(1)(c) and (d) of the Further Measures Regulations (allowing a claimant found to be in GSE to be treated as not being and allowing an existing start-up period to be extended) are excluded from the continuing effect, but that the general discretion to reduce the MIF continues, subject to qualifications, explained as follows:

"7.4 Regulation 2(2) [of the Restoration Regulations] provides for the claimants who had been determined to be in gainful self-employment on 13th March 2020 when the general MIF suspension first came into force. For these claimants the MIF has been reduced to zero (either at the outset or, if they were in a 12-month start-up period, on the expiry of that 12 months). The Secretary of State is to restore the MIF, but only after determining that the claimant continues to be in gainful self-employment. Claimants must be given at least one full Assessment Period (AP) notice before the MIF is applied. If a claimant had been in a start-up period on 13th March 2020 a period equal to the balance of the start-up period outstanding on that date will be granted before restoring the MIF. This is subject to regulation 2(3), as explained below.

7.5 Regulation 2(3) allows for cases where the MIF may still be reduced to zero but only for those who are still financially impacted by COVID Government restrictions (and can demonstrate this). Work Coaches can award up to two-months discretionary suspension of the MIF, assessed on a case by case basis, reviewed at the end of the two months. Work Coaches can award up to a maximum of 3 suspensions, adding up to six months in total.

7.6 Under regulation 2(4) [the] Secretary of State can choose to withdraw this discretion should public economic conditions improve to such a point where it is no longer appropriate to suspend the MIF. Any MIF suspension awarded prior to withdrawal date will not be affected."

There is further information on the policy intention and the plans for practical application of these provisions in the minutes of the meeting of the Social Security Advisory Committee (SSAC) on July 7, 2021 (available on the SSAC website), including subsequent correspondence. The SSAC had some reservations, in particular about the length of the notice that individual claimants would receive of the imposition of the MIF, but decided not to take the proposed regulations on formal reference.

The most straightforward provision is the exclusion of sub-paras (c) and (d) of reg.2(1) of the Further Measures Regulations from the year's continuation of effect beyond July 31, 2021. Thus, there is now no power to treat any claimant who has already been determined to be in GSE as not being. Any existing claimant whose exemption from the operation of the MIF was based on that ground (rather than the more general deeming of a reduced or zero MIF threshold under sub-para.(a)), would appear to have the full MIF rules applied immediately, in the light of the restricted meaning of "the MIF easement" in reg.2(6) of the Restoration Regulations (see further below). Nor can an extension now be made to a start-up period (see reg.63 of the Universal Credit Regulations), although possibly if a period had been extended in advance for dates after July 30, 2021, that might not be affected.

Sub-paragraphs (b) and (e) appear to have unqualified further effect during the year's extension. Thus sub-para.(b) allows the making of a determination that a claimant is in GSE to be deferred, but only (as with all the reg.2 powers) where that appears expedient as a consequence of the outbreak of coronavirus disease. The operation of sub-para.(e) is more complicated. Under reg.90(5) of the Universal Credit Regulations the rule is that a claimant who is treated as having earned income under reg.62 cannot have any work-related requirements imposed. A claimant who in normal times would not fall into any other category of exemption from the default subjection to all work-related requirements under s.22 of the WRA 2012, and so would fall within reg.62(1)(b) and be made subject to the MIF (with the protection of reg.90(5)), but did not have the MIF actually applied as a result of the operation of any part of reg.2 of the Further Measures Regulations, would on the face of it lose the protection of reg.90. Sub-paragraph (e) as continued in effect allows the exemption of such a claimant from a work search or work availability requirement, but not the other work-related requirements or a connected requirement.

The consequence of those provisions is that, so far as new claims from July 31, 2021 onwards, and existing claimants becoming newly self-employed, are concerned it is very much, in the DWP's words (SSAC minutes, July 7, 2021, Annex B, para.16), "business as usual" in relation to the MIF. However, the MIF cannot bite and a start-up period cannot start until the Secretary of State has determined that a claimant is in GSE. The power to delay such a determination still exists until July 31, 2022, even for new claimants. There will no doubt be some administrative delay for new cases as officials work through the backlog of those who have not had the rule applied to them during the previous 15 months or so.

That leaves the general power under sub-para.(a) to reduce the amount of the individual or couple threshold under the MIF rules, including a reduction to nil, which remains in effect in general. There appear to be at least three alternative circumstances. The first is where such a reduction ("the MIF easement": reg.2(6) of the Restoration Regulations) was being applied on July 31, 2021. By definition, such a claimant cannot have been treated as not in GSE or had a GSE determination deferred (as appears to have been the case for all claimants who had not already been determined to be in GSE before March 20, 2020), or be in a start-up period, because such claimants would not have reached the stage of having the threshold applied. Where the "easement" is in operation, reg.2(2) of the Restoration Regulations requires it to cease after the end of the assessment period in which the Secretary of State determines that the claimant continues to be in GSE, plus (if the claimant was in a start-up period on March 13, 2020) however many whole months of that period remained to be served on that date. Thus it appears to be a pre-condition of the automatic removal of the "easement" that the Secretary of State has reconsidered the GSE question in current circumstances, but presumably the Secretary of State could at any time, within the terms of sub-para.(a), change their mind about the application of the discretion it contains. However, reg.2(2) is subject to reg.2(3), under which the "easement" may continue for not more than two assessment periods at a time, and no more than six in total, if the claimant's business remains adversely affected by the outbreak. Note that reg.2(3) does not specify any particular degree or kind of effect ("financial" is an invention of the Explanatory Memorandum) or what is needed to demonstrate the adverse effect, but such matters will be relevant to the exercise of the discretion ("may"). Regulation 2(3) is again subject to the power in reg.2(4) for the Secretary of State, "if economic conditions have sufficiently improved", to determine that the "easement" is no longer to apply. This is a power that must in principle (contrary to the DWP's suggestion in para.2.3(o) of the SSAC's minutes of July 7, 2021) operate according to the circumstances of individual cases, so must depend on economic conditions relevant to the particular nature and locality of the business, rather than a judgment relating to the nation as a whole.

The second category is of claimants who fall outside reg.2(2) because they have been treated as not in GSE or had such a determination deferred, or were still in a start-up period on July 31, 2021. Such a claimant, if already determined to be in GSE, can no longer be treated as not in GSE, because reg.2(1)(c) of the Further Measures Regulations no longer has effect. Then, unless the Secretary of State makes a new determination that the claimant is not now actually in GSE, the discretion given by reg.2(1)(a) continues to be available until July 31, 2022, subject to termination under reg.2(4) of the Restoration Regulations. If the GSE determination had been deferred, then the MIF cannot be applied until the Secretary of State gets round to making a determination, under the administrative constraints of dealing with the caseload involved. If the claimant was still in a start-up period on July 31, 2021, the MIF cannot be applied until that period expires.

The third category is of new claimants after July 26, 2021 or existing claimants who become newly self-employed after that date. The DWP's suggestion to the SSAC that it would be "business as usual" for such claimants appears right in practice for the vast majority, but not quite right technically. Although the GSE and start-up period rules would apply as usual, the general discretion in reg.2(1)(a) of the Further

Measures Regulations would continue to be potentially available until July 31, 2022 where a consequence of the coronavirus outbreak could be shown. However, the vast majority would never need that discretion because they would have a 12-month start-up period before the MIF began to bite. As recognised in para.16 of Annex B to the SSAC minutes of July 7, 2021, only the small minority who do not qualify for a start-up period could in practice benefit from an exercise of the discretion.

pp.398–401, *annotation to the Universal Credit Regulations 2013 (SI 2013/376) reg.66 (What is included in unearned income? Attribution of unearned income to assessment periods)*

A further problem area has emerged in the 2021 delays in making decisions on claims for retirement pension and putting payment into place. Until payment is put into place no actual unearned income (for an under-pension-age claimant's partner) from that source exists to be taken into account as retirement pension income for universal credit purposes under reg.66(1)(a) and there can be no notional unearned income under reg.74 because an "application" has been made for retirement pension. When payment is put into place there may be a large payment of arrears due. Following the principle put forward in the main volume, that payment constitutes unearned income and is to be attributed to the assessment periods covered by the weeks to which the arrears relate. That circumstance will, depending on the date from which universal credit had been awarded, constitute a ground of revision of the original award of universal credit from the outset, under reg.12 of the Decisions and Appeals Regulations 1999 and s.9(3) of the SSA 1998, or of supersession on the ground of relevant change of circumstances from the first day of the assessment period in which the entitlement to retirement pension arose, under reg.23(1) and para.31(2)(a)(i) of Sch.1. That will give rise to an overpayment of universal credit that is recoverable under s.71ZB of the SSAA 1992, possibly by deduction from the arrears of retirement pension otherwise payable. Whether there has been such a deduction or not, the amount of arrears remaining after the end of the assessment periods to which it has been attributed will then metamorphose into capital, whose value would not fall to be disregarded under para.18 of Sch.10 to the Universal Credit Regulations 2013 (see para.18(1)(c)). However, if a universal credit overpayment recoverability decision has been made but repayment has not yet occurred, it is arguable that to the extent of the amount determined to be recoverable the arrears have not metamorphosed into capital because that amount constitutes a "relevant liability" to be taken into account (*R(SB) 2/83* and see the discussion at 3.197 of the main volume in relation to the surplus earnings rule in reg.54A) even though different benefits are involved. 3.018

p.421, *annotation to the Universal Credit Regulations 2013 (SI 2013/376) Part 7 (The benefit cap)*

The Court of Appeal in *Pantellerisco v Secretary of State for Work and Pensions* [2021] EWCA Civ 1454; [2021] PTSR 1922 has reversed the 3.018.1

decision of Garnham J in the Divisional Court, discussed in the main volume. See further the discussion at para.3.012 above.

pp.493–494, *ERRATUM—annotation to the Universal Credit Regulations 2013 (SI 2013/376) Sch.1 (Meaning of payments in respect of accommodation)*

3.019   The General Note to this schedule is out of date. It does not reflect the amendment made by the Loans for Mortgage Interest Regulations 2017 (SI 2017/725) to reg.25(2), which means UC no longer provides housing costs support for "owner-occupier payments". Instead claimants can obtain repayable loans.

The amendment is shown correctly in the main work. SI 2017/725 is also included in the main work (§§2.583–2.688).

p.515, *amendment to the Universal Credit Regulations 2013 (SI 2013/376) Sch.4 (Housing costs element for renters)*

3.020   With effect from May 31, 2021, reg.3 of the Housing Benefit and Universal Credit (Care Leavers and Homeless) (Amendment) Regulations 2021 (SI 2021/546) amended sub-paragraphs 2 and 4 of paragraph 29, which prescribes circumstances where renters are excepted from the shared accommodation rate. It:

- increases from 22 to 25 years the upper age limit at which care leavers are exempted from the shared accommodation rate; and
- reduces the lower age limit for the exemption from 25 to 16 years for those who have spent at least 3 months in a homeless hostel whilst receiving support to assist with community resettlement or rehabilitation.

p.518, *amendment to the Universal Credit Regulations 2013 (SI 2013/376) Sch.4 (Housing costs element for renters)*

3.021   With effect from October 1, 2021, reg.4 of the Domestic Abuse Support (Relevant Accommodation and Housing Benefit and Universal Credit Sanctuary Schemes) (Amendment) Regulations 2021 (SI 991/2021) amended paragraph 36 of Schedule 4 (the under-occupancy deduction), by inserting after sub-paragraph (5)—

"(6) No deduction for under occupation is to be made in calculating the amount of a renter's housing cost element under this part where—
  (i) domestic violence has been inflicted upon or threatened against the claimant or a member of the claimant's extended benefit unit ("the victim") by that person's partner or former partner, or by a relative;
  (ii) the victim is not living at the same address as the person who inflicted or threatened the domestic violence, except where that person is a qualifying young person and is a

      dependant of a member of the claimant's extended benefit unit; and

(iii) the claimant provides evidence from a person acting in an official capacity which demonstrates that the claimant is living in a property adapted under a sanctuary scheme and—

    (aa) the victim's circumstances are consistent with those of a person who has had domestic violence inflicted upon or threatened against them; and

    (bb) the victim has made contact with the person acting in an official capacity in relation to such an incident;

(b) in this paragraph—

    "domestic violence" and "person acting in an official capacity" have the meaning given to them in regulation 98(4) of these Regulations;

    "relative" has the meaning given by section 63(1) of the Family Law Act 1996;

    "sanctuary scheme" means a scheme operated by a provider of social housing enabling victims of domestic violence to remain in their homes through the installation of additional security to the property or the perimeter of the property at which the victim resides.".

Transitional provision is made by reg.5 of SI 991/2021:

"(1) When an amendment made by regulation 4 applies in respect of an existing award of universal credit, that amendment has effect for the purpose of that award—

(a) on 1st October 2021, if there is an assessment period for the award that begins on that day; or

(b) if sub-paragraph (a) does not apply, on the first day of the next assessment period for the award beginning after 1st October 2021.

(2) In paragraph (1)—

"assessment period" has the meaning given by regulation 21 of the Universal Credit Regulations 2013;

"existing award of universal credit" means an award of universal credit that exists on 1st October 2021."

These amendments remedy the legislative incompatibility with Convention rights identified by the First Section of the ECtHR in *JD & A v United Kingdom (Apps 32949/17 and 34614/17)* [2019] ECHR 753. A victim of domestic violence living in "sanctuary scheme" accommodation was discriminated against, contrary to Art 14 ECHR read with Art 1 Protocol 1, by having an under-occupation deduction made from her benefit. The effect on her was disproportionately prejudicial [§91, §§103-105]: a major aim of the under-occupation deduction policy was encouraging tenants to move to smaller accommodation, but sanctuary schemes existed to allow tenants to stay where they were, and the UK provided no weighty reasons to justify prioritising the former aim over the latter.

The decision of the ECtHR conflicts directly with the decision of the Supreme Court in *R (Carmichael) v Secretary of State for Work and Pensions* [2016] UKSC 58, [2016] 1 W.L.R. 4550, where the same argument from the same litigant ('A') was rejected by a majority of the Court (Hale DPSC and Carnwath JSC dissenting). The UK's request for the case to be referred to the Grand Chamber has been rejected, so the ECtHR decision is final.

p.549, *annotation to the Universal Credit Regulations 2013 (SI 2013/376) Sch.10 para.6 (Capital to be disregarded–business assets)*

3.022   The two Business Interruption Loan Schemes and the Bounce Back Loan Scheme ceased to operate on March 31, 2021, to be replaced by the Recovery Loan Scheme.

p.577, *annotation to the Universal Credit (Surpluses and Self-employed Losses) (Digital Service) Amendment Regulations 2015 (SI 2015/345), reg.5 (Transitional provision–temporary de minimis period)*

3.023   The Autumn Budget and Spending Review 2021 (HC 822, 27 October 2021), 134 §16 announced that the temporary de minimis period will be extended for a further year (i.e. to March 31, 2023). However, this announcement will not have legal effect until the Secretary of State makes a formal Determination doing so.

p.642, *annotation to the Social Security (Coronavirus) (Further Measures) Regulations 2020 (SI 2020/371) reg.2 (Universal credit—minimum income floor)*

3.024   With effect from July 31, 2021, reg.2(1) of the Universal Credit (Restoration of the Minimum Income Floor) Regulations 2021 (SI 2021/807) has provided that reg.2 is (apart from sub-paras (c) and (d) of para.(1)) to continue to have effect down to and including July 31, 2022, but subject to the provisions of the rest of reg.2 of the Restoration Regulations. Those Regulations are set out in Part I of this Supplement and their effect is explained in the entry of pp.372-73 (reg.61 (Minimum income floor (temporary coronavirus provisions)).

p.661, *annotation to the Universal Credit (Transitional Provisions) Regulations 2014 (SI 2014/1230) reg.4A (Restriction on claims for universal credit by persons entitled to a severe disability premium)*

3.024.1   See also *R (On the application of TP) v Secretary of State for Work and Pensions* [2022] EWHC 123 (Admin), in which Holgate J held that Sch. 2 to the 2014 Regulations, as preserved by the Universal Credit (Transitional Provisions) (Claimants previously entitled to a severe disability premium) Amendment Regulations 2021 (SI 2021/4) reg.3), discriminated against certain severely disabled claimants and as such breached ECHR art.14. The High Court held the Secretary of State had not justified her decision to dispense with any element of transitional relief for the loss of the enhanced disability premium, payable with legacy benefits (and the disabled child element of child tax credit), for those claimants subject to natural migration to universal credit through a change of circumstances (rather than DWP-initiated managed migration).

p.687, *amendment to the Universal Credit (Transitional Provisions) Regulations 2014 (SI 2014/1230) reg.19 (Transition from old-style ESA)*

With effect from December 15, 2021, reg.3(a) of the Universal Credit 3.025 (Exceptions to the Requirement not to be receiving Education) (Amendment) Regulations 2021 (SI 2021/1224) amended reg.19 by omitting "the Act" at the end of para.(1)(b) and substituting:

"the Act; and
(c) the claimant is to be treated as if the determination that they have limited capability for work, for the purposes of regulation 14(1)(b) of the Universal Credit Regulations, was made before the date on which the claimant started receiving education (see regulations 12(2) and 13 of the Universal Credit Regulations).";

p.688, *amendment to the Universal Credit (Transitional Provisions) Regulations 2014 (SI 2014/1230) reg.19 (Transition from old-style ESA)*

With effect from December 15, 2021, reg.3(b) of the Universal Credit 3.026 (Exceptions to the Requirement not to be receiving Education) (Amendment) Regulations 2021 (SI 2021/1224) amended reg.19 by omitting "and" at the end of para.(4)(a), omitting "the Act" in para.(4)(b) and substituting:

"the Act; and
(c) the claimant is to be treated as if the determination that they have limited capability for work and work-related activity, for the purposes of regulation 14(1)(b) of those Regulations, was made before the date on which the claimant started receiving education.".

p.730, *annotation to the Universal Credit (Transitional Provisions) Regulations 2014 (SI 2014/1230) reg.54 (The transitional element— indicative UC amount)*

On the special rule noted in the final paragraph of the General Note, 3.027 see further reg.2(2) of the Universal Credit (Extension of Coronavirus Measures) Regulations 2021 (SI 2021/313).

p.731, *annotation to the Universal Credit (Transitional Provisions) Regulations 2014 (SI 2014/1230) reg.54 (The transitional element–initial amount and adjustment where other elements increase)*

On the special rule noted in the final paragraph of the General Note, 3.028 see further reg.2(2) of the Universal Credit (Extension of Coronavirus Measures) Regulations 2021 (SI 2021/313).

pp.741–742, *annotation to the Universal Credit (Transitional Provisions) Regulations 2014 (SI 2014/1230) Sch.2 (Claimants previously entitled to a severe disability premium)*

3.028.1   See entry to p.661 above.

p.761, *amendment to the State Pension Credit Regulations 2002 (SI 2002/1792) reg.2 (Persons not in Great Britain)*

3.029   With effect from September 15, 2021, reg.2 of the Social Security (Habitual Residence and Past Presence) (Amendment) Regulations 2021 (SI 2021/1034) inserted the following new sub-paragraphs before sub-para.(za):

"(zza) a person granted leave in accordance with the immigration rules made under section 3(2) of the Immigration Act 1971, where such leave is granted by virtue of—
    (i) the Afghan Relocations and Assistance Policy; or
    (ii) the previous scheme for locally-employed staff in Afghanistan (sometimes referred to as the ex-gratia scheme);
  (zzb) a person in Great Britain not coming within sub-paragraph (zza) or (h)(iv) who left Afghanistan in connection with the collapse of the Afghan government that took place on 15th August 2021;".

p.762, *amendment to the State Pension Credit Regulations 2002 (SI 2002/1792) reg.2 (Persons not in Great Britain)*

3.030   With effect from September 15, 2021, reg.2 of the Social Security (Habitual Residence and Past Presence) (Amendment) Regulations 2021 (SI 2021/1034) omitted "or" at the end of sub-para.(h)(ii) and inserted after sub-para.(h)(iii) the following:

"or
    (iv) granted under the Afghan Citizens Resettlement Scheme;".

p.789, *amendment to the State Pension Credit Regulations 2002 (SI 2002/1792) reg.15 (Income for the purposes of the Act)*

3.031   With effect from July 26, 2021, art.13(2) of the Social Security (Scotland) Act 2018 (Disability Assistance, Young Carer Grants, Short-term Assistance and Winter Heating Assistance) (Consequential Provision and Modifications) Order 2021 (SI 2021/886) inserted the following new disregard after sub-para.(rg):

"(rh) disability assistance given in accordance with regulations made under section 31 of the Social Security (Scotland) Act 2018;".

p.832, *amendments to the State Pension Credit Regulations 2002 (SI 2002/1792) Sch.IIA para 9 (Additional amount applicable for claimants responsible for a child or qualifying young person)*

3.032   With effect from July 26, 2021, art.10 of the Social Security (Scotland) Act 2018 (Disability Assistance for Children and Young People)

(Consequential Modifications) Order 2021 (SI 2021/786) amended para.9 (amount of additional payment) in two respects. First, in sub-para.(2), the phrase ", child disability payment (within the meaning given in regulation 2 of the Disability Assistance for Children and Young People (Scotland) Regulations 2021)" was inserted after "disability living allowance". Second, a new para.(aa) was inserted in sub-para.(3) after para.(a) as follows:

"(aa) entitled to the care component of child disability payment at the highest rate in accordance with regulation 11(5) of the Disability Assistance for Children and Young People (Scotland) Regulations 2021; or".

p.845, *ERRATUM: the State Pension Credit Regulations 2002 (SI 2002/1792) Sch.5 Part I para.20 (Capital disregarded for the purpose of calculating income)*

The items "(ba) personal independence payment" and "(bb) armed forces independence payment" appear in the list of items set out in sub-para.(1) of para.20. Footnotes correctly record these items as having been inserted by SIs 2013/388 and 2013/591 respectively. However, these items should have been inserted in sub-para. (2) of para.20, not sub-para.(1).   **3.033**

p.846, *amendment to the State Pension Credit Regulations 2002 (SI 2002/1792) Sch.5 Part I para.20 (Capital disregarded for the purpose of calculating income)*

With effect from July 26, 2021, art.13(3) of the Social Security (Scotland) Act 2018 (Disability Assistance, Young Carer Grants, Short-term Assistance and Winter Heating Assistance) (Consequential Provision and Modifications) Order 2021 (SI 2021/886) inserted the following new disregard after sub-para.(2)(x):   **3.034**

"(y) disability assistance given in accordance with regulations made under section 31 of the Social Security (Scotland) Act 2018.".

pp.906–908, *annotation to the Social Fund Maternity and Funeral Expenses (General) Regs 2005 (SI 2005/3061) reg.7 (Funeral payments: entitlement) Place of funeral*

In *JEC v Secretary of State for Work and Pensions (SF)* [2021] UKUT 243 (AAC) (June 23, 2021), UTJ Caldwell QC decides that in relation to the reg.7(9) requirement for a funeral to take place in the UK (or, in certain circumstances, an EU/EFTA state), "for the purposes of the 2005 Regulations a 'funeral' is one event that involves disposal of the deceased's body" [§37].   **3.035**

JEC does not address situations where there is no body, and the Secretary of State has subsequently issued guidance [ADM Memo 17/21, §6]: "In the case where there is no body or remains of the deceased, a payment may be made for a single commemorative event."

p.942, *amendment to the Social Security (Immigration and Asylum) Consequential Amendments Regulations 2000 (SI 2000/636) reg.2 (Persons not excluded from specified benefits under section 115 of the Immigration and Asylum Act 1999)*

3.036   With effect from May 13, 2021, reg.4 of the Social Security and Tax Credits (Miscellaneous and Coronavirus Amendments) Regulations 2021 (SI 2021/495) substitutes a new paragraph 3A of reg.2:

"(3A) For the purposes of entitlement to child benefit under the Contributions and Benefits Act, a person—
    (a) who is lawfully working in Great Britain; and
    (b) who is a national of a State with which the United Kingdom has concluded an agreement which replaces, in whole or in part, an agreement under Article 217 of the Treaty on the Functioning of the European Union which makes provision for the receipt of family allowances for members of their family who are legally resident in the United Kingdom,
is a person to whom section 115 of the Act does not apply."

PART IV

UPDATING MATERIAL
VOLUME III

ADMINISTRATION, ADJUDICATION AND THE EUROPEAN DIMENSION

Commentary by

Mark Rowland

Christopher Ward

p.85, *Social Security Administration Act 1992, s.71ZE (Court action etc.)*

With effect from April 22, 2014, the words "a county court" in subsection (1) were replaced by the words "the county court" by the Crime and Courts Act 2013, s.17(5) and Sch.9, para.52.   4.001

p.126, *Social Security Administration Act 1992, s.126 (Personal representatives to give information about the estate of a deceased person who was in receipt of income support or supplementary benefit)*

With effect from April 22, 2014, the words "a county court" in subsection (3) were replaced by the words "the county court" by the Crime and Courts Act 2013, s.17(5) and Sch.9, para.52.   4.002

pp.185-186, *annotation to the Social Security (Recovery of Benefits) Act 1997 s.6 (Liability to pay Secretary of State amount of benefits)*

Henshaw J's two judgments in *R. (Aviva Insurance Ltd) v Secretary of State for Work and Pensions* have been reported together at [2021] 1 W.L.R. 2187. However, the Court of Appeal has allowed an appeal by the Secretary of State and dismissed a cross-appeal by the insurers, holding that the 1997 Act and regulations made under it did not infringe the insurers' human rights under Article 1 of Protocol 1 to the European Convention on Human Rights. The legislation had a legitimate aim, there was a rational connection between that aim and the interference with the insurers' interests and the interference was no more than was necessary to meet the aim. Overall, the scheme of the legislation struck a fair balance (*R. (Aviva Insurance Ltd) v Secretary of State for Work and Pensions* [2022] EWCA Civ 15).   4.003

pp.223-224, *annotation to the Social Security Act 1998 s.8 (Decisions by Secretary of State)*

Regulations 6 and 16 of the Employment and Support Allowance (Transitional Provisions, Housing Benefit and Council Tax Benefit) (Existing Awards) (No.2) Regulations 2010 (SI 2010/1907) are not in Vol.I of the current edition, but are set out on pp.1423 and 1433 of Vol.I of the 2020/21 edition.   4.004

p.229, *annotation to the Social Security Act 1998 s.9 (Revision of decisions)*

See the supplemental annotation to s.8, above.   4.005

p.235, *annotation to the Social Security Act 1998 s.10 (Decisions superseding earlier decisions)*

See the supplemental annotation to s.8, above.   4.006

p.254, *annotation to the Social Security Act 1998 s.12 (Appeal to First-tier Tribunal)*

4.007   The meaning of the term "litigation capacity" as it applies in the Court of Protection was considered by Mostyn J in *An NHS Trust v P (by her litigation friend, the Official Solicitor* [2021] EWCOP 27, where he said—

> "26. It is trite law that a person can have capacity in relation to some matters but not in relation to others. In *Dunhill v Burgin* [2014] UKSC 18; [2014] 1 W.L.R 933 at [13] Baroness Hale of Richmond stated "capacity is to be judged in relation to the decision or activity in question and not globally". When judging a person's capacity to conduct litigation the question is whether the person can conduct the particular proceeding rather than litigation generally.
>
> 27. Conducting litigation is not simply a question of providing instructions to a lawyer and then sitting back and watching the case unfold. Litigation is a heavy-duty, dynamic transactional process, both prior to and in court, with information to be recalled, instructions to be given, advice to be received and decisions to be taken, on many occasions, on a number of issues, over the span of the proceedings as they develop: *TB and KB v LH (Capacity to Conduct Proceedings)* [2019] EWCOP 14 at [29] per MacDonald J.
>
> 28. In *Masterman-Lister v Brutton & Co (Nos 1 and 2)* [2002] EWCA Civ 1889; [2003] 1 W.L.T 1511, a case which pre-dated the Mental Capacity Act 2005, Kennedy LJ at [26] stated that litigation capacity required the ability to recognise a problem; to obtain and receive and understand relevant information about it, including advice; the ability to weigh the information (including that derived from advice) in the balance in reaching a decision; and the ability to communicate that decision. It is obvious that when the Act came to be written the draughtsman took those standards and restated them in very similar language in s.3.
>
> 29. Unlike certain other human activities discussed in the caselaw, where the level of capacity is set low, I am of no doubt that the level of capacity to conduct litigation is set relatively high. Litigation, even so-called simple litigation, is a complex business. For virtually every case the substantive law, to say nothing of the procedural rules, is a daunting challenge, and can be a minefield.
>
> 30. In *TB and KB v LH (Capacity to Conduct Proceedings)* MacDonald J at [25] went on to say:
>
> > " . . . where a litigant in person does not, in their own right, have capacity to conduct proceedings, the question remains whether they have the capacity to instruct others to conduct those proceedings on their behalf. This is consistent with the principle that an individual who, by themselves, lacks capacity on the subject matter in issue should be facilitated to make a capacitous decision on that subject matter by the taking of all practicable steps to help them to do so. Where a litigant in person lacks capacity to conduct proceedings absent advice and assistance and lacks capacity to instruct advisers,

he or she will lack capacity to conduct proceedings. A question remains as to the position where a litigant in person lacks capacity to conduct proceedings in his or her own right but has capacity to instruct advisers to conduct those proceedings and *chooses* not to do so. However, for the reasons set out below, that is not the situation in this case and it is not therefore necessary for me to consider that point."

31. For my part, I would respectfully disagree that if a person lacks capacity to conduct proceedings as a litigant in person she might, nevertheless, have capacity to instruct lawyers to represent her and that the latter capacity might constitute capacity to conduct the litigation in question. I differ because, as MacDonald J himself eloquently explained, conducting proceedings is a dynamic transactional exercise requiring continuous, shifting, reactive value judgments and strategic forensic decisions. This is the case even if the litigant has instructed the best solicitors and counsel in the business. In a proceeding such as this, a litigant has to be mentally equipped not only to be able to follow what is going on, but also to be able figuratively to tug counsel's gown and to pass her a stream of yellow post-it notes. In my opinion, a litigant needs the same capacity to conduct litigation whether she is represented or not.

32. As mentioned above, this case is most unusual in that the initial capacity assessment of Dr Kemp concluded that P lacked capacity to make decisions about the treatment of the HIV, but nonetheless had capacity to conduct litigation about that very treatment. The document of Mr Anderson referred to above cited *Sheffield City Council v E* [2004] EWHC 2808 (Fam); [2005] Fam 326. In that famous case Munby J stated at [49]:

"Whilst it is not difficult to think of situations where someone has subject-matter capacity whilst lacking litigation capacity, and such cases may not be that rare, I suspect that cases where someone has litigation capacity whilst lacking subject-matter capacity are likely to be very much more infrequent, indeed pretty rare. Indeed, I would go so far as to say that only in unusual circumstances will it be possible to conclude that someone who lacks subject-matter capacity can nonetheless have litigation capacity."

33. I would go further and say that it is virtually impossible to conceive of circumstances where someone lacks capacity to make a decision about medical treatment, but yet has capacity to make decisions about the manifold steps or stances needed to be addressed in litigation about that very same subject matter. It seems to me to be completely illogical to say that someone is incapable of making a decision about medical treatment, but is capable of making a decision about what to submit to a judge who is making that very determination."

Because the First-tier Tribunal has an inquisitorial role in social security cases and its procedures and processes are designed to make representation of any sort unnecessary in proceedings before it (see the annotation to s.3 of the Tribunals, Courts and Enforcement Act 2007 on pp.1061-1065 of the main work), it is arguable that anyone who has the capacity to claim a benefit (in the sense of being capable of understanding instructions on a claim form and instructions to report changes of circumstances) must be taken to have the capacity to conduct an appeal against a decision made on the claim, notwithstanding what was said in *Sheffield City Council v E.*

p.266, *annotation to the Social Security Act 1998 s.13 (Redetermination etc. of appeals by tribunal)*

4.008   One reason that it is not usually regarded as necessary to obtain the opposing parties' views before determining an application for permission to appeal on a point of law is that it is recognized that, where issues of law are concerned, there is generally little that a successful party can say in opposition to an application for permission to appeal (*Global Energy Horizons Corporation v Gray* [2020] EWCA Civ 1668; [2021] 1 W.L.R. 2264 at [495]).

pp.278-279, *annotation to the Social Security Act 1998 s.19(3) (Medical examination required by Secretary of State)*

4.009   Some claimants may have mental health problems that effectively prevent them from complying with a request to attend for, or submit to, a medical examination and from responding more generally to requests for information, but it is not unlawful for the Secretary of State to approach cases where claimants have severe mental health difficulties on the basis that, while obtaining evidence from other sources will be considered, ultimately the burden of proving "good cause" lies on the claimant (*R. (Turner) v Secretary of State for Work and Pensions* [2021] EWHC 465 (Admin)).

p.383, *amendment to the Social Security (Claims and Payments) Regulations 1987 (SI 1987/1968) reg.2 (Interpretation)*

4.010   With effect from July 26, 2021, reg.9 of The Scotland Act 2016 (Social Security) (Consequential Provision) (Miscellaneous Amendment) Regulations 2021 (SI 2021/804) inserted after the definition of "the 2013 Regulations" the following:

   ""the 2018 Scotland Act" means the Social Security (Scotland) Act 2018;"

p.472, *amendments to the Social Security (Claims and Payments) Regulations 1987 (SI 1987/1968) to provide for payment of arrears of benefit by instalments*

4.011   With effect from October 18, 2021, reg.2 of the Social Security Benefits (Claims and Payments) (Amendment) Regulations 2021 (SI 2021/1065) introduces before reg.21A the following:

"Payment of arrears of benefit by instalments

21ZA. Except where regulation 23 applies, the Secretary of State may pay arrears of benefit in instalments where—
- (a) the Secretary of State considers it is necessary for protecting the interests of the beneficiary; and
- (b) the beneficiary agrees that those arrears may be paid in instalments.".

GENERAL NOTE

Regulation 2 extends, so far as England and Wales are concerned, to all benefits to which the 1987 Regulations apply. In relation to such of those benefits as fall within the competence of the Scottish Ministers, see reg.21ZB below; otherwise, reg.2 applies.

For DWP internal guidance, see Decision Makers Guide Memo 13/21.

With effect from October 18, 2021, reg.3 of the Social Security (Claims and Payments) (Miscellaneous Amendments) (Scotland) Regulations 2021 SSI 2021/305) introduces the text below, to follow reg.21ZA:

"Payment of arrears of benefit by instalments

21ZB. (1) In relation to payments made under provisions related to devolved social security matters, the Scottish Ministers may pay arrears of benefit in instalments where—
- (a) the Scottish Ministers consider it is necessary for protecting the interests of the beneficiary, and
- (b) the beneficiary agrees that those arrears may be paid in instalments.

(2) For the purpose of paragraph (1), "devolved social security matters" means matters which are within the legislative competence of the Scottish Parliament by virtue of exceptions 1 to 10 in Section F1 of Part 2 of schedule 5 of the Scotland Act 1998.".

p.500, *amendment to the Social Security (Claims and Payments) Regulations 1987 (SI 1987/1968) reg.33 (Persons unable to act)*

With effect from July 26, 2021, reg.9 of The Scotland Act 2016 (Social Security) (Consequential Provision) (Miscellaneous Amendment) Regulations 2021 (SI 2021/804) inserted after reg.33(1A) the following: **4.012**

"(1B) Where a natural person over the age of 18 has been appointed by the Scottish Ministers under a qualifying appointment pursuant to the 2018 Scotland Act in connection with the determination of assistance under section 24 of that Act (whether or not including an appointment to receive assistance on behalf of the individual), the Secretary of State may, if the person agrees, treat that person as if she had appointed them under paragraph (1).

(1C) In paragraph (1B), a qualifying appointment means—

    (a) an appointment made under section 58(1) of the 2018 Scotland Act in a case where section 58(4) of that Act applies, or

    (b) an appointment made under section 85B(1)(4) of the 2018 Scotland Act in a case where section 85B(7) of that Act applies.".

p.510, *amendment to the Social Security (Claims and Payments) Regulations 1987 (SI 1987/1968) reg.43 (Children)*

4.013   With effect from July 26, 2021, reg.9(4) of The Scotland Act 2016 (Social Security) (Consequential Provision) (Miscellaneous Amendment) Regulations 2021 (SI 2021/804) inserted after paragraph (1) the following:

"(1A) Subject to paragraph (1B), where a person has been appointed by the Scottish Ministers under section 85A(1) of the 2018 Scotland Act in connection with the determination of assistance under section 24 of that Act (whether or not including an appointment to receive assistance on behalf of the child), the Secretary of State may, if the person agrees, treat that person as if she had appointed them under paragraph (1).

(1B) Paragraph (1A) does not apply if the person appointed by the Scottish Ministers does not satisfy the conditions in paragraph (2).".

pp.527-542, *amendments to the Social Security (Claims and Payments) Regulations 1987 (SI 1987/1968) Sch.9 (Deductions from Benefit and Direct Payment to Third Parties)*

4.014   With effect from May 4, 2021, reg. 2 of the Social Security (Claims and Payments) (Amendment) Regulations (SI 2021/456) made the following amendments:

In paragraph 1(1) (interpretation), after the definition of "miscellaneous accommodation costs" the following words are inserted:

""*moratorium debt*" has the same meaning as in regulation 6 of the Debt Respite Scheme (Breathing Space Moratorium and Mental Health Crisis Moratorium) (England and Wales) Regulations 2020;".

In each of paragraphs 3(2) (housing costs), 6(4)(b) (fuel costs) and 7(6) (water charges) are inserted after "discharged" the words "or is a moratorium debt".

pp.579-580, *amendment to the Universal Credit, Personal Independence Payment, Jobseeker's Allowance and Employment and Support Allowance (Claims and Payments) Regulations 2013 reg.47 (Payment of universal credit)*

4.015   With effect from October 18, 2021, reg.3 of the Social Security Benefits (Claims and Payments) (Amendment) Regulations 2021 (SI 2021/1065) inserted after paragraph (6) the following:

"(6A) The Secretary of State may pay arrears of universal credit in instalments where—
  (a) the Secretary of State considers it is necessary for protecting the interests of the claimant, or, in the case of joint claimants, either of the claimants; and
  (b) the claimant agrees, or in the case of joint claimants, both claimants agree, that those arrears may be paid in instalments.".

GENERAL NOTE

For DWP internal guidance, see Advice to Decision Makers Memo 18/21.

p.581, *amendment to the Universal Credit, Personal Independence Payment, Jobseeker's Allowance and Employment and Support Allowance (Claims and Payments) Regulations 2013 reg.48 (Payment of personal independence payment)*

With effect from October 18, 2021, reg.3 of the Social Security   4.016
Benefits (Claims and Payments) (Amendment) Regulations 2021 (SI 2021/1065) inserted after paragraph (3) the following:

"(4) The Secretary of State may pay arrears of personal independence payment in instalments where—
  (a) the Secretary of State considers it is necessary for protecting the interests of the claimant; and
  (b) the claimant agrees that those arrears may be paid in instalments.".

GENERAL NOTE

For DWP internal guidance, see Advice to Decision Makers Memo 18/21

pp.582–583, *amendment to the Universal Credit, Personal Independence Payment, Jobseeker's Allowance and Employment and Support Allowance (Claims and Payments) Regulations 2013 reg.51 (Payment of an employment and support allowance)*

With effect from October 18, 2021, reg.3 of the Social Security   4.017
Benefits (Claims and Payments) (Amendment) Regulations 2021 (SI 2021/1065) inserted after paragraph (4) the following:

"(4A) The Secretary of State may pay arrears of employment and support allowance in instalments where—
  (a) the Secretary of State considers it is necessary for protecting the interests of the claimant; and
  (b) the claimant agrees that those arrears may be paid in instalments.".

GENERAL NOTE

For DWP internal guidance, see Advice to Decision Makers Memo 18/21.

pp.583-584, *amendment to the Universal Credit, Personal Independence Payment, Jobseeker's Allowance and Employment and Support Allowance (Claims and Payments) Regulations 2013 reg.52 (Payment of a jobseeker's allowance)*

4.018   With effect from October 18, 2021, reg.3 of the Social Security Benefits (Claims and Payments) (Amendment) Regulations 2021 (SI 2021/1065) inserted after paragraph (2) the following:

"(2A) The Secretary of State may pay arrears of jobseeker's allowance in instalments where—
(a) the Secretary of State considers it is necessary for protecting the interests of the claimant; and
(b) the claimant agrees that those arrears may be paid in instalments.".

GENERAL NOTE

For DWP internal guidance, see Advice to Decision Makers Memo 18/21.

p.586, *amendment to the Universal Credit, Personal Independence Payment, Jobseeker's Allowance and Employment and Support Allowance (Claims and Payments) Regulations 2013 reg.57 (Persons unable to act)*

4.019   With effect from July 26, 2021, reg.10 of The Scotland Act 2016 (Social Security) (Consequential Provision) (Miscellaneous Amendment) Regulations 2021 (SI 2021/804) inserted after paragraph (1) the following:

"(1A) Where a natural person over the age of 18 has been appointed by the Scottish Ministers under a qualifying appointment pursuant to the 2018 Scotland Act in connection with the determination of assistance under section 24 of that Act (whether or not including an appointment to receive assistance on behalf of the individual), the Secretary of State may, if the person agrees, treat that person as if the Secretary of State had appointed that person under paragraph (1).
(1B) In paragraph (1A) a qualifying appointment means—
(a) an appointment made under section 58(1) of the 2018 Scotland Act in a case where section 58(4) of that Act applies, or
(b) an appointment made under section 85B(1) of the 2018 Scotland Act in a case where section 85B(7) of that Act applies.
(1C) In this regulation "the 2018 Scotland Act" means the Social Security (Scotland) Act 2018.".

pp.599-600, *amendment to the Universal Credit, Personal Independence Payment, Jobseeker's Allowance and Employment and Support Allowance (Claims and Payments) Regulations 2013 Sch.6 (Deductions from benefit and direct payment to third parties)*

4.020   With effect from October 29, 2021, reg.3 of the Fines (Deductions from Income Support) (Miscellaneous Amendments) Regulations 2021 (SI 2021/1077) omitted from paragraph 5(2)(e) the words "where the amount of the deduction equals 5% of the standard allowance" and omitted paragraph 5(2)(q) altogether.

pp.609-613, *amendment to the Social Security and Child Support (Decisions and Appeals) Regulations 1999 (SI 1999/991) reg.1 (Citation, commencement, application and interpretation)*

With effect from July 26, 2021, reg.6(1) and (2) of the Social Security   4.021
(Scotland) Act 2018 (Disability Assistance for Children and Young People) (Consequential Modifications) Order 2021 (SI 2021/786) amends reg.1(3) of the 1999 Regulations by inserting after the definition of "Board"—

""child disability payment" has the meaning given in regulation 2 of the Disability Assistance for Children and Young People (Scotland) Regulations 2021;"

The Disability Assistance for Children and Young People (Scotland) Regulations 2021 are set out in Part I of this Supplement.

p.625, *amendment to the Social Security and Child Support (Decisions and Appeals) Regulations 1999 (SI 1999/991) reg.3(7)(b) (Revision of decisions)*

With effect from July 26, 2021, reg.6(1) and (3) of the Social Security   4.022
(Scotland) Act 2018 (Disability Assistance for Children and Young People) (Consequential Modifications) Order 2021 (SI 2021/786) amends reg.3(7)(b) of the 1999 Regulations by inserting after both occurrences of "benefit" the words "or child disability payment". See the annotation to reg.1, above.

p.634, *annotation to the Social Security and Child Support (Decisions and Appeals) Regulations 1999 (SI 1999/991) reg.3 (Revision of decisions)*

Regulations 6 and 16 of the Employment and Support Allowance   4.023
(Transitional Provisions, Housing Benefit and Council Tax Benefit) (Existing Awards) (No.2) Regulations 2010 (SI 2010/1907) are not in Vol.I of the current edition, but are set out on pp.1423 and 1433 of Vol.I of the 2020/21 edition.

p.650, *amendment to the Social Security and Child Support (Decisions and Appeals) Regulations 1999 (SI 1999/991) reg.6(2)(e)(ii) (Supersession of decisions)*

With effect from July 26, 2021, reg.6(1) and (4) of the Social Security   4.024
(Scotland) Act 2018 (Disability Assistance for Children and Young People) (Consequential Modifications) Order 2021 (SI 2021/786) amends reg.6(2)(e)(ii) of the 1999 Regulations by inserting after both occurrences of "benefit" the words "or child disability payment". See the annotation to reg.1, above.

p.669, *amendment to the Social Security and Child Support (Decisions and Appeals) Regulations 1999 (SI 1999/991) reg.7(7)(a) (Date from which a decision superseded under section 10 takes effect)*

4.025   With effect from July 26, 2021, reg.6(1) and (5) of the Social Security (Scotland) Act 2018 (Disability Assistance for Children and Young People) (Consequential Modifications) Order 2021 (SI 2021/786) amends reg.7(7)(a) of the 1999 Regulations by inserting after both occurrences of "benefit" the words "or child disability payment". See the annotation to reg.1, above.

pp.705-706, *annotation to the Social Security and Child Support (Decisions and Appeals) Regulations 1999 (SI 1999/991) reg.19 (Suspension and termination for failure to submit to medical examination)*

4.026   Some claimants may have mental health problems that effectively prevent them from complying with a requirement to submit to a medical examination or from responding more generally to requests for information, but it is not unlawful for the Secretary of State to approach cases where claimants have severe mental health difficulties on the basis that, while obtaining evidence from other sources will be considered, ultimately the burden of proving "good cause" lies on the claimant (*R. (Turner) v Secretary of State for Work and Pensions* [2021] EWHC 465 (Admin)).

pp.738-741, *amendment to the Universal Credit, Personal Independence Payment, Jobseeker's Allowance and Employment and Support Allowance (Decisions and Appeals) Regulations 2013 (SI 2013/381) reg.2 (Interpretation)*

4.027   With effect from July 26, 2021, reg.21(1) and (2) of the Social Security (Scotland) Act 2018 (Disability Assistance for Children and Young People) (Consequential Modifications) Order 2021 (SI 2021/786) amends reg.2 of the 2013 Regulations by inserting after the definition of "child"—

""child disability payment" has the meaning given in regulation 2 of the Disability Assistance for Children and Young People (Scotland) Regulations 2021;"

The Disability Assistance for Children and Young People (Scotland) Regulations 2021 are set out in Part I of this Supplement.

p.746, *amendment to the Universal Credit, Personal Independence Payment, Jobseeker's Allowance and Employment and Support Allowance (Decisions and Appeals) Regulations 2013 (SI 2013/381) reg.12 (Award of another benefit)*

4.028   With effect from July 26, 2021, reg.21(1) and (3) of the Social Security (Scotland) Act 2018 (Disability Assistance for Children and Young People) (Consequential Modifications) Order 2021 (SI 2021/786) amends reg.12(b) of the 2013 Regulations by inserting after both occurrences of "benefit" the words "or child disability payment". See the annotation to reg.1, above.

p.784, *amendment to the Universal Credit, Personal Independence Payment, Jobseeker's Allowance and Employment and Support Allowance (Decisions and Appeals) Regulations 2013 (SI 2013/381) Sch.1 (Effective dates for superseding decisions made on the ground of a change of circumstances)*

With effect from July 26, 2021, reg.21(1) and (4) of the Social Security (Scotland) Act 2018 (Disability Assistance for Children and Young People) (Consequential Modifications) Order 2021 (SI 2021/786) amends each of sub-paras. (1), (2)(a)(i), (2)(a)(ii) and (2)(a)(iii) of para.31 of Sch.1 to the 2013 Regulations by inserting after each occurrence of "benefit" the words "or child disability payment". See the annotation to reg.1, above. **4.029**

p.795, *ERRATUM in relation to heading of Part 3 of the Social Security (Information-sharing) Regulations 2012 (SI 2012/1483)*

With effect from February 11, 2013, "ETC." was omitted from the title of the Part. **4.030**

p.795, *amendment to heading of Part 3 of the Social Security (Information-sharing) Regulations 2012 (SI 2012/1483)*

With effect from November 8, 2021, reg.2 of the Social Security (Information-sharing in relation to Welfare Services etc.) (Amendment) Regulations 2021 (SI 2021/1129) inserted after the words "in relation to welfare services" the words "or housing benefit". **4.031**

p.800, *amendment to heading of Part 3 of the Social Security (Information-sharing) Regulations 2012 (SI 2012/1483)*

With effect from November 8, 2021, reg.2 of the Social Security (Information-sharing in relation to Welfare Services etc.) (Amendment) Regulations 2021 (SI 2021/1129) inserted after the words "IN RELATION TO WELFARE SERVICES" the words "OR HOUSING BENEFIT". **4.032**

p.802, *ERRATUM in relation to reg.6 of the Social Security (Information-sharing) Regulations 2012 (SI 2012/1483) (Holding purposes)*

With effect from February 11, 2013, reg.2 of the Social Security (Information-sharing in relation to Welfare Services etc.) (Amendment) **4.033**

Regulations 2013 (SI 2013/41) inserted after the words "the 2012 Act" the words "in relation to welfare services".

p.802, *amendment to reg. 6 of the Social Security (Information-sharing) Regulations 2012 (SI 2012/1483) (Holding purposes)*

4.034   With effect from November 8, 2021, reg.2 of the Social Security (Information-sharing in relation to Welfare Services etc.) (Amendment) Regulations 2021 (SI 2021/1129) inserted after the words "in relation to welfare services" (as to which, see the Erratum note above) the words "or housing benefit".

pp.1059-1086, *annotation to the Tribunals, Courts and Enforcement Act 2007 s.3 (The First-tier Tribunal and the Upper Tribunal)*

4.035   The Upper Tribunal referred to *Aria Technology Ltd v HMRC* [2018] UKUT 111 (TCC); [2018] 1 W.L.R. 4377 (mentioned on p.1059 of the main work) and applied a similar approach when deciding in *DVLA v IC (Rule 14 Order)* [2020] UKUT 310 (AAC) that a party to proceedings before the First-tier Tribunal required the permission of the tribunal before publishing the tribunal bundle on the internet. Noting that, in the High Court, disclosure of documents was ordered on the basis of an implied undertaking by other parties not to use them for collateral purposes and that there would be practical difficulties in ensuring that personal details contained in bundles were redacted, the Upper Tribunal not only refused permission but also made an order under reg.14(1)(a) of the Tribunal Procedure (Upper Tribunal) Rules 2008, prohibiting the party from publishing "the electronic documents and bundles (including the skeleton arguments) provided in accordance with the case management directions for the purposes of these proceedings". See also *Williams v IC* [2021] UKUT 110 (AAC); [2022] 1 W.L.R. 259, where the same approach was taken and the applicant was refused permission to publish tribunal bundles on the internet for the purpose of obtaining representation, on the basis that such publication was not necessary to enable the applicant to obtain representation. In that case, an order under r.14(1) was made prohibiting the publication of the bundles "on the internet or elsewhere by any method" but the applicant was given permission to provide a copy of the bundle to a representative or a person considering whether to be a representative, although it was made clear that the terms of the r.14 order also bound any such person from publishing the documents.

Unlike decisions of the Upper Tribunal, decisions of the First-tier Tribunal do not create precedents that must be followed in other cases. Nonetheless, its decisions, are binding on the parties to the proceedings in which they are made and those parties, including the Secretary of State, must give effect to them and obey any directions that are given. In *R (Majera) v Secretary of State for the Home Department* [2021] UKSC 46; [2021] 3 W.L.R. 1075 at [44], the Supreme Court reiterated the "well established principle of our constitutional law that a court order must be obeyed unless and until it has been set aside or varied by the court (or, conceivably, overruled by legislation)" when deciding that the Secretary of State could not rely on an error in a decision of the First-tier Tribunal's as a defence to a judicial review of her decision not to give effect to it. Her remedy would have been to appeal or otherwise apply for the decision to be set aside. The Court referred to Lord Radcliffe's statement in *Smith v East Elloe Rural District Council* [1956] A.C. 736, 769 that—

> "An order, even if not made in good faith, is still an act capable of legal consequences. It bears no brand of invalidity upon on its forehead. Unless the necessary proceedings are taken at law to establish the cause of invalidity and to get it quashed or otherwise upset, it will remain as effective for its ostensible purpose as the most impeccable of orders."

Evidence

Questions of foreign law are treated as questions of fact, in respect of which expert evidence may be adduced, rather than as questions of law. In the absence of expert evidence, there is a presumption in England and Wales that foreign law is the same as the law of England and Wales. However, that presumption applies only if it is a fair and reasonable assumption to make in a particular case (*Brownlie v FS Cairo (Nile Plaza) LLC* [2021] UKSC 45; [2021 3 W.L.R. 1011). Otherwise, evidence is required and the question may arise in social security cases —where, say, there is a question as to the ownership of foreign property that turns on a point of law—as to which party should be expected to provide it and will bear the consequence of failing to do so.

The possibility of a tribunal hearing evidence by video link from a witness who is in another country has raised some complicated issues. In *Agbabiaka (evidence from abroad, Nare guidance) Nigeria* [2021] UKUT 286 (IAC), the Upper Tribunal said—

"B. TAKING EVIDENCE FROM ABROAD

12. There has long been an understanding among Nation States that one State should not seek to exercise the powers of its courts within the territory of another, without having the permission of that other State to do so. Any breach of that understanding by a court or tribunal in the United Kingdom risks damaging this country's diplomatic relations with other States and is, thus, contrary to the public interest. The potential damage includes harm to the interests of justice since, if a court or tribunal acts in such a way as to damage international relations with another State, this risks permission being refused in subsequent cases, where evidence needs to be taken from within that State.

13. As that last point indicates, it has long been accepted between Nation States that a court in one State may have a legitimate need to undertake the examination of a witness who is present in another State, or to inspect documents or other property in that State.

The Hague Convention

14. The Convention on the Taking of Evidence Abroad in Civil or Commercial Matters (18 March 1970), hereafter referred to as the Hague Convention, established a uniform framework of co-operation mechanisms in order to facilitate and streamline the taking of evidence, etc abroad. The Hague Convention operates by means of Letters of Request, containing specified information, sent by the judicial authority of a contracting State, to the Central Authority of the other State.

15. Article 1 provides as follows:—

"In civil or commercial matters a judicial authority of a Contracting State may, in accordance with the provisions of the law of that State, request the competent authority of another Contracting State, by means of a Letter of Request, to obtain evidence, or to perform some other judicial act.

A Letter shall not be used to obtain evidence which is not intended for use in judicial proceedings, commenced or contemplated.

The expression "other judicial act" does not cover the service of judicial documents or the issuance of any process by which judgments or orders are executed or enforced, or orders for provisional or protective measures."

16. There is no definition of "civil or commercial matters" in Article 1 of the Hague Convention. Mr Holborn [counsel for the appellant Secretary of State] points out that some assistance in discovering its meaning is to be found in the Explanatory Report on the Convention by Ph W Amram, the Rapporteur of the Commission of the Hague Conference on International Law, which drafted the Convention.

17. Mr Amran states that "any potential disagreement on the meaning of [the words 'civil or commercial matters'] is to be settled through diplomatic channels . . . No further discussion is needed". Interpretation of this provision is, therefore, a matter that is ultimately settled by diplomacy rather than legal process.

18. The position of the Secretary of State is that the Hague Convention does not apply to immigration proceedings in the United Kingdom, as these are administrative, rather than civil, proceedings. Both Mr Holborn and Mr Bazini [counsel for the respondent] are, however, agreed that, for present purposes, it is unnecessary for us to express any view on the correctness of that stance.

19. We agree. Not all States are signatories to the Hague Convention. Whenever the issue arises in a tribunal about the taking of evidence from outside the United Kingdom, the question of whether it would be lawful to do so is a question of law for that country, whether or not that country is a signatory to the Hague Convention: *Interdigital Technology Corporation & Ors v Lenovo Group Ltd & Ors* [2021] EWHC 255 (Pat). In all cases, therefore, what the Tribunal needs to know is whether it may take such evidence without damaging

the United Kingdom's diplomatic relationship with the other country.

C. THE KEY ISSUES

20. The key issues are, first, the circumstances in which the need for
such an answer arises; and, secondly, the steps that are to be taken
where they do.

21. It will be noted that Article 1 of the Hague Convention refers
not only to obtaining evidence but also to the performing of "some
other judicial act". That expression is restricted by the last paragraph
of Article 1. It is also partly explained by the reference in Article 3 to
the inspection of documents or other property.

Submissions and written evidence

22. The third recital to the Upper Tribunal's directions of 11 June
2021 referred to "the issue of evidence/submissions given from
abroad". Both Mr Holborn and Mr Bazini addressed us on whether
the giving of oral submissions to the Tribunal by a person outside the
United Kingdom falls to be regarded in the same way as the giving of
oral evidence. Mr Bazini considered that the making of submissions
on the law or on the evidence that has been adduced in a case was
likely to be regarded by the foreign State as of at least equal significance to the giving of oral evidence. Mr Holborn, however,
informed us that the FCDO does not regard the making of oral
submissions as akin to the giving of oral evidence. The FCDO's
position is that it is taking of oral evidence, without the requisite
permission, that is problematic.

23. On this issue, we find that the view of the FCDO is determinative. At least in the present context, it is not for this (or any other)
tribunal to form its own view of what may, or may not, damage the
United Kingdom's relations with a foreign State. Accordingly, the
steps which we describe later do not need to be taken where the
Tribunal is satisfied that the person who will be speaking to it by video
from abroad will be making submissions and not giving evidence.

24. However, as we were at pains to emphasise to Mr Holborn at the
hearing, the dividing line between submissions and evidence may in
practice not be an easy one to hold. In particular, if the person
concerned is not a professional representative but the appellant, the
Tribunal may need to treat with circumspection any assertion that the
appellant will confine him or herself to submissions and not stray into
the giving of evidence. For that reason, we believe that a tribunal is
likely, in such cases, to conclude that the steps we describe will need
to be taken.

25. It is also necessary to clarify the position of written evidence. As
with submissions, Mr Holborn's instructions were that a written statement of evidence can be provided to the tribunal by a person outside
the United Kingdom, without risk to diplomatic relations.

The proposed FCDO process

26. Sarah Broughton of the Consular Directorate, FCDO has filed a witness statement dated 1 October 2021. She confirms that the FCDO's current role in checking that overseas governments have no diplomatic or other objections to the provision of evidence by video-link from countries overseas covers only civil and commercial proceedings, as interpreted above. Such proceedings do not, therefore, include what she describes as administrative tribunals. Nor do they include criminal proceedings.

27. In June 2021, the FCDO's Consular Document Policy Team learned that there was no process within the United Kingdom government for checking that overseas governments had no diplomatic or other objections to provision of evidence by video-link from countries overseas, where the evidence was to be given to an administrative tribunal, such as in asylum and immigration appeal hearings. The Team had previously been unaware of the decision in *Nare*.

28. At the same time, it became apparent that a small number of previous enquiries had been replied to inaccurately, as the official dealing with Service of Process (SOP) requests made by courts pursuant to Practice Direction 32 of the Civil Procedure Rules had not appreciated that the enquiries from tribunals were not considered to be within the scope of civil or commercial proceedings. Ms Broughton says that the FCDO have "put measures in place to ensure that this mistake is not repeated". Any previous advice that specific countries do not object to their citizens or residents providing evidence by video-link to administrative tribunals in the United Kingdom should not be considered as authoritative "as administrative tribunals would not have been specified in the request to the relevant host government".

29. The FCDO has, however, now "considered how to address the identified gap and have internal agreement to set up a process to expand the checks it provides to include checking that overseas governments have no diplomatic or other objections to provision of evidence by video-link from countries overseas to Administrative Tribunals". The Senior Master at the Royal Courts of Justice who supervises the International Process Section is said to have no objection to the proposed solution.

30. Ms Broughton says it is anticipated that from November 2021 (precise date to be determined), a new "Taking of Evidence" (ToE) Unit will be established in order to cover the "likely increase from 15-20 requests per year for civil and commercial cases to several hundred for Administrative Tribunals". Ms Broughton states that the process is likely to be akin to that for civil and commercial proceedings."

The position has therefore been that there are no difficulties about a person providing written evidence from abroad or, subject to the point made by the Upper Tribunal at [24], about a person making submissions from abroad. However, the consent of the relevant country has been required in relation to the provision of oral evidence and most tribunals and courts rely on the Foreign, Commonwealth and Development Office

(FCDO) for information as to whether the relevant consent had been given. What emerged as a result of the case before the Upper Tribunal is that some tribunals had been using a list of countries where the FCDO was satisfied that their governments did not have diplomatic or other objections to the provision of evidence by video-link from that country to a court in the United Kingdom, but that the FCDO's checks had covered only civil and commercial proceedings, which they interpreted as not including either administrative proceedings before tribunals or criminal proceedings. Steps are being taken to "address the identified gap" but, meanwhile, most tribunals are not receiving oral evidence from abroad.

Precedent

Although decisions of the First-tier Tribunal on points of law do not carry any formal precedential value, it would be wrong for the Secretary of State to ignore a consistent line of them when considering other cases and so refuse claims that would be very likely to succeed on appeal, even if she considered that the decisions were wrong in law. The proper course to take would be to bring an appeal to the Upper Tribunal in order to have the point of law authoritatively established one way or the other, so that all claimants would in future be treated alike (see *R. (Secretary of State for the Home Department) v First-tier Tribunal* [2021] EWHC 1690 (Admin); [2022] 1 W.L.R. 22 at [69]).

pp.1087-1088, *annotation to the Tribunals, Courts and Enforcement Act 2007 s.7 (Chambers: jurisdiction and Presidents)*

There was a period after the Childcare (Early Years Provision Free of Charge) (Extended Entitlement) Regulations 2016 came into force but before art.6(eb) of the First-tier Tribunal and Upper Tribunal (Chambers) Order 2010 (which is set out in the annotation in the main work) was introduced with effect from 6 March 2020, during which a number of appeals under the 2016 Regulations were heard in the Social Entitlement Chamber of the First-tier Tribunal. In *HMRC v JS* [2021] UKUT 264 (AAC), that was held to have been wrong because, in the absence of provision in art.6, appeals to the First-tier Tribunal against decisions of HMRC fall to be heard in the Tax Chamber by virtue of art.7(a) of the 2010 Order. 4.035.1

p.1093, *annotation to the Tribunals, Courts and Enforcement Act 2007 s.9(5)(b), (6) and (7) (Review of decision of the First-tier Tribunal)*

In *HMRC v RS (TC)* [2021] UKUT 310 (AAC), the Upper Tribunal again made the point that a case cannot be referred to the Upper Tribunal under s.9(5)(b) when permission to appeal to the Upper Tribunal is being given in respect of the same matter. That is simply because a case can be referred under s.9(5)(b) only when the decision of the First-tier Tribunal has been set aside, whereas permission to appeal cannot be given against a decision that has been set aside (see s.11(5)(e)). 4.035.2

pp.1097-1114, *annotation to the Tribunals, Courts and Enforcement Act 2007 s.11(1) (Right to appeal to Upper Tribunal)*

4.036   A decision of the First-tier Tribunal is not invalid or wrong in law merely because it was made under procedural rules that have been held to be invalid on the ground that they were unfair; the decision of the First-tier Tribunal will be wrong in law only if the process by which it was reached was unfair in the particular circumstances of the case (*R. (TN (Vietnam)) v Secretary of State for the Home Department* [2021] UKSC 41; [2021] 1 W.L.R. 4902).

pp.1097-1114, *annotation to the Tribunals, Courts and Enforcement Act 2007 s.12 (Proceedings on appeal to Upper Tribunal)*

4.037   In *JG v SSWP (BB)* [2021] UKUT 194 (AAC), the claimant had appealed to the Upper Tribunal following a decision of the High Court in Northern Ireland in which a declaration of incompatibility had been made under s.4 of the Human Rights Act 1998 in respect of legislation equivalent to that applicable in the claimant's case. By the time the claimant's case reached the First-tier Tribunal, the Supreme Court had also made a declaration of incompatibility, but no remedial order under s.10 of the 1998 Act had been made and the First-tier Tribunal dismissed her appeal, applying the unamended legislation. The claimant appealed to the Upper Tribunal and her case was considered at a time when a draft remedial order had been prepared but not approved. The Upper Tribunal said that it was arguable that the First-tier Tribunal should have postponed giving a final decision because a decision on a new claim under legislation as amended by a remedial order that had retrospective effect might be effective from a much later date than a decision made on the original appeal in the light of such an order.

> "Whether that is really necessary in any particular case will depend on the circumstances of the case and it will often not be apparent when the First-tier Tribunal makes its initial decision because it will also depend not only on the remedial action (if any) to be taken but also on what incidental, supplemental or consequential provision is made to make that action effective. It is unlikely that the First-tier Tribunal will be able to anticipate exactly what action will be taken. This case provides a useful illustration."

The Upper Tribunal itself deferred giving a decision until the remedial order had come into force.

pp.1125–1134, *annotation to the Tribunals, Courts and Enforcement Act 2007 s.13 (Right to appeal to Court of Appeal etc.)*

4.038   In *MOC v Secretary of State for Work and Pensions* [2022] EWCA Civ 1, the Upper Tribunal had given permission to appeal on the basis that, as the appeal concerned the application of the law to a vulnerable group, it raised "an important point of principle or practice" justifying a "second appeal". However, the case ultimately failed on its facts and Singh LJ commented at [74] that—

"In those circumstances it is difficult to see how the test for an appeal to this Court could be satisfied, let alone the test for a second appeal. With respect to the UT, this case provides a salutary reminder that, although it has the power to grant permission to appeal, it may be better to leave that question to this Court, which is very familiar with the type of case that will satisfy the second appeal test."

That is perhaps a reminder that the "second appeal" test is additional to the test for first appeals, which is that an appeal should "have a reasonable prospect of success", as well as suggesting that lower tribunals should generally be more cautious about giving permission to appeal than the tribunal or court that is to hear the appeal might be.

In *Khurshid v Secretary of State for the Home Department* [2021] EWCA Civ 1515, the Court of Appeal held that it had no jurisdiction to hear an appeal where both the hearing before the First-tier Tribunal and the hearing before the Upper Tribunal had been in Scotland (where the appellant had been living since before bringing his appeal to the First-tier Tribunal) and the Upper Tribunal had expressly stated that the Court of Session, rather than the Court of Appeal was the "relevant appellate court". The Court of Appeal accepted, referring to *Tehrani v Secretary of State for the Home Department* [2006] UKHL 47; [2007] 1 AC 521, that, had there been exceptional circumstances, it would have been able to reconstitute itself as an administrative court for the purpose of considering an application for judicial review of the Upper Tribunal's decision. However, in *Tehrani*, where the decisions being challenged had been made in England, the House of Lords had held that the Court of Session had jurisdiction only because the appellant had been misled by the Court of Session's own previous practice into making an application to it rather than to the Court of Appeal, which would otherwise have been more appropriate in the circumstances of that case. In Mr Khurshid's case, his English solicitors had not been under a similar misapprehension and his desire to be represented by them did not justify an application to the Courts in England and Wales to exercise a supervisory jurisdiction over the Upper Tribunal sitting in Scotland when the Court of Session was obviously the relevant appellate court and the Upper Tribunal had specified it as such.

p.1222, *annotation to the Tribunal Procedure (First-tier Tribunal) (Social Entitlement Chamber) Rules 2008 (SI 2008/2685) r.8 (Striking out a party's case)*

In *R (Majera) v Secretary of State for the Home Department* [2021] UKSC 46; [2021] 3 WLR 1075, the Supreme Court has reiterated at [44] the fundamental point that the Secretary of State is not entitled to disregard a decision of the First-tier Tribunal even if he or she considers it to be wrong in law. His or her remedy was to apply for permission to appeal. **4.039**

"It is a well established principle of our constitutional law that a court order must be obeyed unless and until it has been set aside or varied by the court (or, conceivably, overruled by legislation)."

pp.1222-1224, *annotation to the Tribunal Procedure (First-tier Tribunal) (Social Entitlement Chamber) Rules 2008 (SI 2008/2685) r.9 (Substitution and addition of parties)*

4.040   A person from whom an overpayment might be recoverable instead of the appellant should be added as a party if he or she is not already one (*DBH v West Lindsey DC (HB)* [2021] UKUT 256 (AAC)). This will be necessary where the Secretary of State has not made a decision in respect of all those from whom an overpayment might be recoverable, which would automatically have made them all parties to any appeal.

pp.1231-1232, *annotation to the Tribunal Procedure (First-tier Tribunal) (Social Entitlement Chamber) Rules 2008 (SI 2008/2685) r.14(1) (Use of documents and information))*

4.041   In *DVLA v IC (Rule 14 Order)* [2020] UKUT 310 (AAC), it was held that, in principle, a party to tribunal proceedings required permission to publish documents disclosed to him or her in the proceedings under compulsion and that, indeed, an order could be made under r.14(1) prohibiting the party from publishing those documents. This is unlikely to be much of an issue in most social security cases but there are cases where personal or other confidential details relating to a third party need to be disclosed to the appellant in the interests of justice and so the question of making a r.14 order may occasionally arise. See, further, the supplemental annotation to s.3 of the Tribunals, Courts and Enforcement Act 2007, above.

pp.1251-1258, *annotation to the Tribunal Procedure (First-tier Tribunal) (Social Entitlement Chamber) Rules 2008 (SI 2008/2685) r.24(1) to (5) (Responses and replies)*

4.042   In *SE v SSWP (PIP) (Final decision)* [2021] UKUT 79 (AAC), it was said—

> "Bearing in mind that ESA (and the equivalent provisions in relation to universal credit) examine a number of activities testing mental, cognitive and intellectual function (and accordingly, simple cognitive tests generally form part of the assessment), it is entirely possible that an assessment carried out for the purposes of the work capability assessment will yield useful evidence in the context of assessing whether people with learning disabilities can score points under activities 8 and/or 10 for PIP, even though the activities under the two benefits are different. Both claimant representatives and the Secretary of State in the exercise of her responsibilities under rule 24(4) of the FtT rules to provide 'all documents relevant to the case in the decision maker's possession' may need to bear this in mind."

In *DVLA v IC (Rule 14 Order)* [2020] UKUT 310 (AAC), it was held that, in principle, a party to tribunal proceedings required permission to publish documents disclosed to him or her in the proceedings under compulsion and that, indeed, an order could be made under r.14 prohibiting the party from publishing those documents. This is unlikely to be much of an issue in most social security cases because documents revealed to a claimant are usually concerned with that claimant rather than anyone else, but there are cases where personal or other confidential details relating to one person need to be disclosed to another in the interests of justice and so the question of making an order 14 order may occasionally arise.

pp.1262-1273, *annotation to the Tribunal Procedure (First-tier Tribunal) (Social Entitlement Chamber) Rules 2008 (SI 2008/2685) r.27(1) and (2) (Decision with or without a hearing)*

FY v SSWP (RP) [2018] UKUT 146 (AAC) is wrongly cited on p.1268. The "flag" is (RP), not (PIP).　　4.043

Remote hearings, in which at least some of, and usually all of, the parties, witnesses and members of the First-tier Tribunal participated by telephone or video link, became common from mid-2020 as a result of the Covid-19 pandemic but, from October 2021, there was a general move back towards having face-to-face hearings. Nonetheless, now that the First-tier Tribunal has been provided with the technology and has become experienced in using it, it has become recognised that remote hearings may often be a more suitable way of conducting proceedings than face-to-face hearings, particularly when parties would prefer a remote hearing or find it more convenient. Thus, a significant proportion of cases are still listed on the basis that at least some of the parties or witnesses will participate by telephone or video link. However, even when that is so, the general rule since October 2021 has been that hearings are conducted from a tribunal venue, with panels sitting together, save in exceptional or unavoidable circumstances including where to do so would pose an unacceptable risk to a person's health or wellbeing or where there is not a suitable hearing room or adequate equipment at a venue for use by the judge or panel.

A number of decisions of the Upper Tribunal over the past several months have been made on issues arising out of remote hearings.

In *JS v Wirral MBC (HB)* [2021] UKUT 219 (AAC), an appeal was listed for a determination on the papers because the appellant had said on his listing enquiry form that he did not want a hearing. Given the background to the case and the obvious importance of the appellant giving oral evidence if he was serious about pursuing his appeal, the First-tier Tribunal drew the inference that the appellant had something to hide. However, the listing enquiry form had been sent to the tribunal in April 2020, during the first national lockdown to combat the Covid-19 pandemic, and it emerged during the appellant's appeal to the Upper Tribunal that he had been "shielding" at the time. Moreover, the form did not at that time offer appellants a remote hearing in which they could participate by telephone or video link, rather than a face-to-face hearing. In those circumstances, the Upper Tribunal held that it had been unfair to decide the appeal on the papers.

In one First-tier Tribunal decision, the point has been made that, if, during a remote hearing, the Tribunal mutes an appellant because he or she interrupts other witnesses, fairness may demand that the appellant be asked after each other witness has given evidence whether he or she has heard the evidence properly, particularly in a hearing in which some participants have had technical difficulties.

On the other hand, in *TC and BW v Islington LBC (SEN)* [2021] UKUT 196 (AAC), the Upper Tribunal rejected an appeal brought on the ground that one of the appellants and another witness had been unable to participate properly in a remote hearing due to their hearing disabilities. The decision turned on the particular facts of the case. The Upper Tribunal was satisfied that the First-tier Tribunal had properly considered how the giving of their evidence could be facilitated and neither of them had indicated during the hearing that they were having difficulty. Moreover, on analysis, there was very little objective evidence to suggest that the presentation of the appellants' case was materially impeded by the relevant appellant's hearing impairment. On the contrary, their dissatisfaction with the way the hearing had unfolded reflected choices that they had made during the hearing rather than failures of communication due to hearing disabilities. "That they chose to focus on certain, strongly-held, key points to the exclusion of others was a decision in the admittedly difficult context for litigants in person of a tribunal hearing. That, having received the FtT's reasons for its decision, they wished they had argued it differently is an experience that will be shared by many litigants, whether or not they have a hearing impairment."

In *Agbabiaka (evidence from abroad, Nare guidance) Nigeria* [2021] UKUT 286 (IAC), considered in detail in the supplemental annotation to s.3 of the Tribunals, Courts and Enforcement Act 2007, above, the Upper Tribunal considered the circumstances in which it is permissible to receive evidence from abroad and, in particular, oral evidence from abroad provided by telephone or video link.

pp.1280-1284, *annotation to the Tribunal Procedure (First-tier Tribunal) (Social Entitlement Chamber) Rules 2008 (SI 2008/2685) r.31 (Hearings in a party's absence)*

4.044   It is not always unfair for the Tribunal to take a new point when deciding a case in a party's absence. In *AB v SSWP (CSM)* [2021] UKUT 129 (AAC), it should have been apparent to the absent party from directions previously issued by the First-tier Tribunal that it did not regard its jurisdiction to be limited to the points raised in the grounds of appeal. Moreover, the absent party had not given details of the commitment that he had said prevented him from attending the hearing. The Upper Tribunal said—

"92. In any event, it is always in the interests of the parties to attend hearings before the First-tier Tribunal because appeals are on both fact and law and informal. One cannot always know from the papers that are circulated in advance quite how the other parent's case will be put and what evidence will be given. Absenting oneself from the hearing always runs the risk that of depriving oneself of the opportunity to answer any unexpected evidence or address additional issues.

93. It is striking that, so far as I can discern, the First-tier Tribunal was not given particulars of the allegedly pressing commitment which prevented the Father's attendance. Neither have I, even though I expressly raised the issue when I gave permission to appeal.

94. That is not satisfactory. Whether a commitment is sufficiently pressing to justify non-attendance at a judicial hearing is an issue on which, during my years as a District Tribunal Judge, the views of non-resident parents did not always coincide with my own. I suspect other judges of the Social Entitlement Chamber who hear child support appeals would say the same. But that issue does not fall to be decided by any individual party but by the Tribunal. If proper particulars of conflicting commitments are not given, it becomes difficult for the Tribunal to make that decision because it will not know where the case comes on what I have described elsewhere as "the hairdressing/cancer treatment spectrum" (*BV v SSWP (PIP)* [2019] 1 W.L.R. 3185, [2018] UKUT 444 (AAC) at [12] and [37]).

95. I acknowledge that the appellant in *BV* had applied for an adjournment and that— at least at the start of the hearing on 8 May 2019—the Father had not. I do not, however, regard that as a relevant distinction. Whether or not the Father wished for an adjournment, he was absent from the hearing and rule 31 of the SEC Rules prevents a tribunal from proceeding with a hearing in a party's absence unless (among other things) it considers that it is in the interests of justice to do so. The Tribunal was therefore required to address that issue.

96. The reason for a party's absence will always be a relevant factor when deciding what is in the interests of justice and the fact that a party is content for the hearing to proceed, though also relevant, will not always be determinative. The evidence relevant to the calculation of a non-resident parent's gross weekly income and the potential existence of an "additional income" ground for variation will usually be in that parent's sole knowledge. And even where some of it is known to the person with care, it will often require further explanation that only the non-resident parent can give. The interests of justice may therefore be furthered by the presence of the non-resident parent to answer questions, even if—and sometimes, especially if—he does not wish to attend. However, it is also in the interests of justice to avoid delay. Rule 31 therefore requires tribunals to strike what can be a delicate balance. The reason for the absence of a non-resident parent will often determine the side on which that balance comes down.

97. While I stand by my observation that non-attendance at hearings by non-resident parents is a familiar and illegitimate delaying tactic, I accept that that is not true of every such non-attendance. In this case, it is unnecessary for me to make any finding that the Father's absence from the hearing of 8 May 2019 either was, or was not, tactical.

98. When judging whether the procedure adopted by the Tribunal was fair, however, I can, and do, take into account that the Father took a deliberate decision not to attend the hearing—and therefore

assumed the risk identified in the final sentence of paragraph 92 above—and that, in the absence of a more detailed explanation, he has not established any circumstances that might suggest it would be unfair for him to bear the consequences of the eventuation of that risk."

pp.1291-1298, *annotation to the Tribunal Procedure (First-tier Tribunal) (Social Entitlement Chamber) Rules 2008 (SI 2008/2685) r.34 (Reasons for decisions—detailed guidance)*

4.045   In *SM v SSWP (PIP)* [2021] UKUT 140 (AAC), the Upper Tribunal considered the extent to which the First-tier Tribunal needed to make clear that it had had regard to reg.4(2A) of the Social Security (Personal Independence Payment) Regulations 2013 which provides that a claimant satisfies a descriptor only if he or she can carry out the relevant activity safely, to an acceptable standard, repeatedly and within a reasonable time period. The judge said—

"16. [. . .], I do not wish to seek to lay down any hard and fast rules at all as to what specific findings might be required of the F-tT or as to what it should say, if anything, about the criteria before a statement of reasons which it produces will properly be regarded as at least adequate. But I do think that since the criteria is, generally speaking, of importance and often of real significance in at least some PIP cases, an awareness of the criteria and a statement to the effect that it has been applied, is likely to be good practice in virtually all cases. Most F-tT's do, in my experience, have passages which demonstrate that the criteria is being applied. But a failure to mention the regulation or the criteria at all is not necessarily fatal. The important thing is not that the criteria is mentioned in terms but that the reasoning shows it has been applied in practice. If, for example, an F-tT is finding that a claimant does not have any difficulty of significance in managing the tasks relevant to a specific PIP activity, then there would be little point in it adding, with respect to such activity, that it had asked itself whether such tasks can be accompanied safely, within a reasonable time period, repeatedly, or to an acceptable standard. The finding that there are no difficulties or no difficulties of significance with respect to a particular activity will be comfortably sufficient. Where there is clear evidence of substance that performing tasks relevant to a specific PIP activity might, for example, be dangerous or might only be capable of being accomplished with a significant degree of slowness, then it may be that a specific evaluation as to how the criteria has relevance to the specific activity in issue, might be required. But it seems to me that any such obligation will not be triggered by vague and unpersuasive references to, for example, slowness or risk. In many cases I suspect that where an F-tT has said, in general terms, that it has borne the criteria in mind, it can be taken to have applied it throughout its assessment even if it does not refer to it, once again, with respect to each and every activity which is in issue before it."

The same judge emphasized in *MM-C v SSWP (PIP)* [2021] UKUT 183 (AAC) that the duty to give reasons for an apparent divergence from a previous decision held to exist in *R(M) 1/96* was "a simple, straightforward and undemanding one". It was satisfied in that case because it was clear from the First-tier Tribunal's statement of reasons that it was satisfied that there had been an improvement in the claimant's mental health condition which it considered significant.

In *KH (dec'd) by AMH v SSWP (IIDB)* [2021] UKUT 189 (AAC), the claimant's response to the decision of the First-tier Tribunal was to submit a medical report contradicting its key finding. When writing the statement of reasons for the tribunal's decision, the judge included a paragraph in which he said that that evidence was unlikely to have affected the tribunal's findings. The Upper Tribunal criticised that paragraph, both because the judge had apparently not consulted the medically-qualified member of the tribunal before expressing his view of the new evidence and because "it is not the function of a statement of reasons to discuss and dismiss evidence that the Tribunal did not take into account when reaching its decision". What, on the other hand, the First-tier Tribunal should have done was treat the submission of the medical report as an application for the setting aside of the decision.

pp.1301-1304, *annotation to the Tribunal Procedure (First-tier Tribunal) (Social Entitlement Chamber) Rules 2008 (SI 2008/2685) r.37 (Setting aside a decision which disposes of proceedings)*

In *KH (dec'd) by AMH v SSWP (IIDB)* [2021] UKUT 189 (AAC), the judge expressed some doubt about the correctness of *MA v SSWP (PIP)* [2000] UKUT 172 (AAC) (mentioned in the main work) but said that it in any event applied only where the applicant had made an unequivocal application for something and r.41 did not empower the First-tier Tribunal to treat that application as being also, or instead, an application for the setting aside of a decision. Where, as in *KH*, the applicant had sent a document to the First-tier Tribunal but had not made a clear application, the issue was simply whether the document should be interpreted as an application for the setting aside of a decision. In that case, the claimant had provided medical evidence dating from before the First-tier Tribunal's decision that directly contradicted a crucial finding of the First-tier Tribunal, and it was held that the First-tier Tribunal should have treated the submission of that document as an application for the setting aside of the decision on the ground that "a document relating to the proceedings was not sent to the Tribunal at an appropriate time". **4.046**

p.1308, *annotation to the Tribunal Procedure (First-tier Tribunal) (Social Entitlement Chamber) Rules 2008 (SI 2008/2685) r.39 (Tribunal's consideration of application for permission to appeal)*

One reason that it is not usually regarded as necessary to obtain the opposing party's view before determining an application for permission to appeal on a point of law is that it is recognized that, where issues of law **4.047** are concerned, generally "there may be little that the successful party can say in opposition to an application for permission to appeal" *Global Energy Horizons Corporation v Gray* [2020] EWCA Civ 1668; [2021] 1 W.L.R. 2264 at [495].

p.1320, *amendment of the Tribunal Procedure (Upper Tribunal) Rules 2008 (SI 2008/2698) r.1 (Citation, commencement, application and interpretation)*

4.048   With effect from December 31, 2020, reg.33 of the Immigration and Social Security Co-ordination (EU Withdrawal) Act 2020 (Consequential, Saving, Transitional and Transitory Provisions) (EU Exit) Regulations 2020 (SI 2020/1309) amended reg.1 of the 2008 Rules by omitting from the definition of "immigration case" the words "regulation 26 of the Immigration (European Economic Area) Regulations 2006", subject to a saving. This was in addition to the amendment already recorded in the main work.

p.1357, *annotation to the Tribunal Procedure (Upper Tribunal) Rules 2008 (SI 2008/2698) r.22 (Decision in relation to permission to appeal)*

4.049   It is not usually necessary to obtain the views of opposing parties to an application for permission to appeal on a point of law, but it is more often necessary in other cases. In *Global Energy Horizons Corporation v Gray* [2020] EWCA Civ 1668; [2021] 1 W.L.R. 2264 at [495], the Court of Appeal observed that—

> "While on many matters, including generally issues of law, there may be little that the successful party can say in opposition to an application for permission to appeal, we do not share the view that the same applies where detailed findings of fact in a complex case are challenged, and that goes as much for applications to this court as to the court below."

pp.1362-1364, *annotation to the Tribunal Procedure (Upper Tribunal) Rules 2008 (SI 2008/2698) r.24 (Response to the notice of appeal)*

4.050   Following the consultation mentioned at the end of the annotation in the main work, the Tribunal Procedure Committee has indicated that it is minded to amend r.24 so as to require a respondent to an appeal against a decision of the First-tier Tribunal to submit a response if they wish the Upper Tribunal to uphold the decision of the First-tier Tribunal for reasons other than those given by that tribunal or they rely on any grounds on which they were unsuccessful before that tribunal. The Committee also intends to amend the rule so as to require the response to include an application for permission to appeal where such an application is required in order to allow the respondent to advance their arguments—r.21 would be disapplied in such cases. It is anticipated that the Upper Tribunal would waive the new requirements where that would be in the interests of justice. Nonetheless, in the light of *HMRC v SSE Generation Ltd* [2021] EWCA Civ 105 (mentioned in the main work), it seems clear that the Upper Tribunal must consider whether or not to give permission to appeal if such permission is required.

p.1370, *annotation to the Tribunal Procedure (Upper Tribunal) Rules 2008, r.29 (Acknowledgment of service)*

In *R. (KA) v Secretary of State for the Home Department* [2021] EWCA **4.050.1** Civ 1040; [2021] 1 W.L.R. 6018, the Court of Appeal considered the way r.29 operates. Lewis LJ, with whom the other members of the Court agreed, said—

"32. . . . First, if a defendant wishes to take part in judicial review proceedings, he or she must provide the Upper Tribunal with an acknowledgment of service so that it is received by it no later than 21 days after the date on which the claim form was sent or provided to him. The clear implication in the Rules is that the Upper Tribunal will not determine the application for permission before the expiry of that 21 day period.

33. Secondly, rule 29(3) applies where a defendant fails to provide an acknowledgment of service either within 21 days or at all. In either of those situations, a defendant can only take part in an application for permission (whether at the stage of consideration of permission on the papers, or where permission is considered at an oral hearing) if allowed to do so by the Upper Tribunal.

34. Thirdly, a defendant who does not provide an acknowledgment of service within the prescribed 21 day period runs the risk that the Upper Tribunal will consider the application for permission, and reach a decision, without the benefit of an acknowledgment of service and without knowing if the defendant opposes the grant of permission and if so, the grounds for doing do. If a defendant knows that he or she is not going to be in a position to provide an acknowledgment of service within 21 days, but wishes to be sure that the Upper Tribunal will not consider the application for permission without the defendant first providing an acknowledgment of service, then the defendant will have to make an application for an extension of time to provide the acknowledgment of service. If that extension is granted, the Upper Tribunal would not consider the application for permission until the period, as extended, has expired.

. . .

46. On a proper interpretation . . . rule 29(3) of the Rules applies where a defendant has failed to provide an acknowledgment of service at all or has failed do so within the 21 day period prescribed by rule 29(1). The Upper Tribunal may allow a defendant to take part in the application for permission, and may thus consider an acknowledgment of service provided outside the 21 day time limit but before it takes a decision on whether to grant permission to apply for judicial review."

p.1389, *annotation to the Tribunal Procedure (Upper Tribunal) Rules 2008 (SI 2008/2698) r.45 (Upper Tribunal's consideration of application for permission to appeal)*

4.051   It is not usually necessary to obtain the views of opposing parties to an application for permission to appeal on a point of law, but the Upper Tribunal should consider doing so if a ground is raised that was not advanced on the appeal before it (*RH v South London and Maudsley NHS Foundation Trust* [2010] EWCA Civ 1273; [2011] AACR 14). Moreover, in *Global Energy Horizons Corporation v Gray* [2020] EWCA Civ 1668; [2021] 1 W.L.R. 2264 at [495], the Court of Appeal observed that—

> "While on many matters, including generally issues of law, there may be little that the successful party can say in opposition to an application for permission to appeal, we do not share the view that the same applies where detailed findings of fact in a complex case are challenged, and that goes as much for applications to this court as to the court below."

pp.1398-1399, *annotation to the Amended General Pilot Practice Direction: Contingency Arrangements in the First-tier Tribunal and the Upper Tribunal*

4.052   This Practice Direction expired on September 18, 2021 and has not been replaced.

p.1400, *annotation to the Amended General Pilot Practice Direction: Contingency Arrangements in the First-tier Tribunal and the Upper Tribunal*

4.053   This Practice Direction expired on September 18, 2021 and has not been replaced.

p.1408, *The post-1998 system of protection*

4.054   Protocol No. 15 entered into force on August 1, 2021. It amends the Preamble to the Convention, which now includes a reference to the subsidiarity principle and to the margin of appreciation doctrine. The 6-month time-limit for submitting an application to the Court after the final national decision will be reduced to four months, starting from 1 February 2022. Among other changes, when considering the admissibility criterion of "significant disadvantage", the second condition, namely that a case which has not been duly considered by a domestic tribunal cannot be rejected, has been deleted.

p.1409, *Admissibility*

4.055   Note the change to the admissibility criteria effected by Protocol No.15 (above).

p.1409, *The European Court of Human Rights–Composition and jurisdiction*

With effect from October 18, 2021, the Court amended its Rules of 4.056
Court, in particular with regard to the composition of, and organisation
of the proceedings of, the Grand Chamber. The Rules as amended may
be found at *Rules of Court - 18 October 2021 (coe.int)* (accessed December
6, 2021).

p.1438, *annotation to Human Rights Act 1998 Sch.1 Part 1 Article 2
(Right to life)*

For an (unsuccessful) attempt to rely on breach of art.2 where the 4.057
claimant had committed suicide having experienced benefit problems
resulting in the withdrawal of her ESA award, see *Dove v HM Assistant
Coroner for Teesside and Hartlepool, Rahman and SSWP* [2021] EWHC
2511 (Admin), discussed in Part VI below in the note to p.1260 (annotation to the Employment and Support Allowance Regulations 2008 (SI
2008/794) reg.24 (Matters to be taken into account in determining good
cause in relation to regulations 22 or 23)).

pp.1471-1473, *National authorities on art.14 read with A1P1—
bereavement—paras 4.152–4.153*

The Upper Tribunal's decision in *NA v SSWP (BB)* [2019] UKUT 4.058
144 (AAC) has been reversed by the Court of Appeal in *Secretary of State
for Work and Pensions v Akhtar* [2021] EWCA Civ 1353. Following a
detailed review of the treatment of polygamous marriages for social
security purposes, concluding that the Social Security and Family Allowances (Polygamous Marriages) Regulations 1975 (SI 1975/561) applied
only to polygamous marriages that were valid under English law, the
Court of Appeal held that in relation to bereavement payment, people
who have contracted a marriage which is valid under English law and
those who have not are not in an analogous position, alternatively the
difference in treatment created by the legislation is justified. Consequently, save to the extent already identified by the Supreme Court in
relation to widowed parent's allowance in *Re McLaughlin's Application for
Judicial Review* [2018] UKSC 48, the claimant's case on human rights
grounds likewise failed.

pp.1474-1475, *National authorities on art.14 read with A1P1—disability
—para.4.157*

The Court of Appeal in Northern Ireland has reversed the decision in 4.059
Re Cox's Judicial Review: see [2021] NICA 45.

p.1480, *National authorities on art.14 read with A1P1–universal credit*

The Court of Appeal has allowed the appeal in *SSWP v Salvato* [2021] 4.060
EWCA Civ 1482, holding that the discrimination which was involved

could be justified and that the route adopted was not irrational. In the Court's view, the case might more appropriately be regarded as falling within art.14 with art.8, but nothing turned on that.

p.1482, *Article 14 in conjunction with art.8*

4.061   For a further example of this type of case, see *SSWP v Salvato* (annotated under p.1480 above).

p.1489, *Human Rights Act 1998, Sch.2—General Note*

4.062   For an interim decision examining the draft Bereavement Benefits (Remedial) Order and its interplay with social security decision-taking processes, see *JG v SSWP (BB)* [2021] UKUT 194 (AAC).

pp.1526-8, *ERRATUM: European Union (Withdrawal) Act 2018, Sch.8—Consequential, Transitional, Transitory and Saving Provision*

4.063   With effect from December 31, 2020, the text of para.(1) was amended by the European Union Withdrawal (Consequential Modifications) (EU Exit) Regulations 2020/1447 Pt 2 reg.3(2)(a) and by the European Union (Withdrawal Agreement) Act 2020 Sch.5(2) para.54(2) so as to read:

"(1) Any reference so far as it, immediately before IP completion day—
  (a) exists in—
      (i) any enactment,
      (ii) any EU regulation, EU decision, EU tertiary legislation or provision of the EEA agreement which is to form part of domestic law by virtue of section 3, or
      (iii) any document relating to anything falling within sub-paragraph (i) or (ii), and
  (b) is a reference to (as it has effect from time to time) any EU regulation, EU decision, EU tertiary legislation or provision of the EEA agreement which is to form part of domestic law by virtue of section 3,
is to be read, on or after IP completion day, as a reference to the EU regulation, EU decision, EU tertiary legislation or provision of the EEA agreement as it forms part of domestic law by virtue of section 3 and, unless the contrary intention appears, as modified by domestic law from time to time.
  (2) Sub-paragraph (1) does not apply to any reference so far as it forms part of a power to make, confirm or approve subordinate legislation so far as the power to make the subordinate legislation—
  (a) continues to be part of domestic law by virtue of section 2, and
  (b) is subject to a procedure before Parliament, the Scottish Parliament, the National Assembly for Wales or the Northern Ireland Assembly.
  (3) Sub-paragraphs (1) and (2) are subject to any other provision made by or under this Act or any other enactment.

GENERAL NOTE

See also:
(a) the modifications of the effect of provisions within paras 1-2A contained in European Union (Withdrawal) Act 2018 and European Union (Withdrawal

Agreement) Act 2020 (Commencement, Transitional and Savings Provisions) Regulations 2020/1622, reg.19; and

(b) Interpretation Act 1978, s.20 (as amended with effect from December 31, 2020) which materially provides:

(2A) Where—

(a) an Act passed on or after IP completion day refers to any treaty relating to the EU or any instrument or other document of an EU entity, and

(b) the treaty, instrument or document has effect by virtue of section 7A or 7B of the European Union (Withdrawal) Act 2018 (general implementation of remainder of EU withdrawal agreement etc.),

the reference, unless the contrary intention appears and so far as required for the purposes of relevant separation agreement law, is a reference to the treaty, instrument or document as it so has effect (including, so far as so required, as it has effect from time to time).

(3) Subject to subsection (2A), where an Act passed on or after IP completion day refers to any EU regulation, EU decision, EU tertiary legislation or provision of the EEA agreement, the reference, unless the contrary intention appears, is a reference to the EU regulation, EU decision, EU tertiary legislation or provision of the EEA agreement as it forms part of domestic law by virtue of section 3 of the European Union (Withdrawal) Act 2018 or section 1 of the Direct Payments to Farmers (Legislative Continuity) Act 2020.

(4) Subsection (3) does not determine any question as to whether the reference is to be read as a reference to the EU regulation, EU decision, EU tertiary legislation or provision of the EEA agreement as modified by domestic law (and, accordingly, is without prejudice to subsection (2)).

(5) Any expression in subsection (3) or (4) which is defined in the European Union (Withdrawal) Act 2018 has the same meaning in the subsection concerned as in that Act.

p.1529, *ERRATA: Schedule 8 to the European Union (Withdrawal Act) 2018 (Consequential, Transitional, Transitory and Saving Provision)*

Paragraphs 36A and 37 were included in last year's Supplement but omitted in error from the selection from Schedule 8 in this year's main volume. They are set out below. In the case of para.37 the amendments in square brackets are made by the European Union (Withdrawal Agreement) Act 2020 Sch.5, para.55.   **4.064**

36A

(1) Anything done—

(a) in connection with anything which continues to be domestic law by virtue of section 1A(2) or 1B(2), or

(b) for a purpose mentioned in section 2(2)(a) or (b) of the European Communities Act 1972 or otherwise related to the EU or the EEA,

if in force or effective immediately before exit day, continues to be in force or effective on and after exit day.

(2) Anything done—

(a) in connection with anything which continues to be domestic law by virtue of section 1A(2) or 1B(2), or

(b) for a purpose mentioned in section 2(2)(a) or (b) of the European Communities Act 1972 or otherwise related to the EU or the EEA, which, immediately before exit day, is in the process of being done continues to be done on and after exit day.

(3) Sub-paragraphs (1) and (2) are subject to—

(a) sections 1 to 1B and the withdrawal of the United Kingdom from the EU,

(b) any provision made under section 23(6) of this Act or section 41(5) of the European Union (Withdrawal Agreement) Act 2020, and

(c) any other provision made by or under this Act, the European Union (Withdrawal Agreement) Act 2020 or any other enactment.

(4) References in this paragraph to anything done include references to anything omitted to be done.

37 Continuation of existing acts etc.

(1) Anything done—

(a) in connection with anything which continues to be, or forms part of, domestic law by virtue of section 2, 3, 4 or 6(3) or (6), or

(b) for a purpose mentioned in section 2(2)(a) or (b) of the European Communities Act 1972 or otherwise related to the EU or the EEA,

if in force or effective immediately before [IP completion day], continues to be in force or effective on and after [IP completion day].

(2) Anything done—

(a) in connection with anything which continues to be, or forms part of, domestic law by virtue of section 2, 3, 4 or 6(3) or (6), or

(b) for a purpose mentioned in section 2(2)(a) or (b) of the European Communities Act 1972 or otherwise related to the EU or the EEA,

which, immediately before [IP completion day], is in the process of being done continues to be done on and after [IP completion day].

(3) Sub-paragraphs (1) and (2) are subject to—

(a) [sections 1 to 1B] and the withdrawal of the United Kingdom from the EU,

(b) sections 2 to [7B] and Schedule 1,

(c) any provision made under section 23(6) [of this Act or section 41(5) of the European Union (Withdrawal Agreement) Act 2020], and

(d) any other provision made by or under this Act [, the European Union (Withdrawal Agreement) Act 2020] or any other enactment.

(4) References in this paragraph to anything done include references to anything omitted to be done.

With effect from December 31, 2020, the European Union (Withdrawal Agreement) Act, Sch.5, para.56 amended the italicised crossheading now appearing before para 37A to read *'Saved EU law at end of implementation period'*.

p.1541, *amendment to the European Union (Future Relationship) Act 2020, s.26 (Social security co-ordination)*

With effect from July 24, 2021, reg.2 of, and the Schedule to, the   4.065
European Union (Future Relationship) Act 2020 (References to the
Trade and Cooperation Agreement) Regulations 2021 SI 2021/884
amend subsection (1)(b) so as to read "Title I of Heading 4 of Part 2
(Trade, Transport, Fisheries and Other Arrangements)" and subsection
(1)(c) is amended to read "Articles 6 and 775, so far as applying to the
SSC Protocol."

pp.1550-1552, *Agreement on the Withdrawal of the United Kingdom—
Art.10 (Personal scope)*

GENERAL NOTE

ADM Memo 19/21 and DMG Memo 14/21 emphasise that, those claimants   4.066
who fall within the scope of art.10, will retain their entitlement to benefits if they
have made a claim before the end of the "grace period" of 30 June 2021 for
applying for settled status which has not yet been determined (or is under
appeal).

pp.1554-1558, *Agreement on the Withdrawal of the United Kingdom—
Art.18 (Issuance of residence documents)*

GENERAL NOTE

ADM Memo 19/21 and DMG Memo 14/21 emphasise that claimants who fall   4.067
within the scope of art.10 who have failed to submit their application for settled
status before the end of the "grace period" on 30 June 2021 may be protected by
Article 18 if they have reasonable grounds (as determined by the Home Office by
the issue of a "certificate of application") for submitting their application for
settled status late.

p.1576, *Treaty on the Functioning of the European Union–updating
commentary on Art.18 TFEU*

In *SSWP v Fratila and Tanase* [2021] UKSC 53, the Supreme Court   4.068
has allowed the Secretary of State's appeal, following the decision of the
CJEU in *CG v Department for Communities* in holding that as the claimants did not have a right to reside under Directive 2004/38, they could
not rely on the EU principle of non-discrimination on the ground of
nationality. The CJEU had also held (at [84]–[92]) that arts 1, 7 and 24
of the EU Charter provided a baseline below which a Member State
could not allow a person's circumstances to fall: Fratila and Tanase were
not permitted by the Supreme Court to run that argument, as it had not

been taken earlier in the case. It may still therefore be available in other cases which are still at a lower level.

p.1578, *Directive 2004/38/EC of the European Parliament and of the Council of 29 April 2004 on the right of citizens of the Union and their family members to move and reside freely within the territory of the Member States—updating commentary on art.7*

4.069 In an Opinion of September 30, 2021, Advocate General Hogan referred to the express wording within art.16(1) and proposed that the first of the three questions be answered in the negative. As regards the second question, he noted that VI had not claimed the case fell within art.10 of Regulation 492/2011, which was the successor of the provision which had been in issue in *Teixeira* and suggested that art.7 of the Directive had to be taken as it stood. At [56]-[64] the Advocate General included some remarks on whether reliance on a publicly funded health system could amount to comprehensive sickness insurance cover, although this was not the question put by the referring court. Having raised the point, he recognised that this was not the case in which to attempt to answer it definitively.

p.1578, *Directive 2004/38/EC of the European Parliament and of the Council of 29 April 2004 on the right of citizens of the Union and their family members to move and reside freely within the territory of the Member States—addition to commentary on art.13*

4.070

Para. in 2020/21 edition	
3.290	In its decision of September 2, 2021, the CJEU held that none of the matters raised by the referring court in *X v Belgian State* (C-930-19) called into question the validity of art.13(2).

p.1579, *Directive 2004/38/EC of the European Parliament and of the Council of 29 April 2004 on the right of citizens of the Union and their family members to move and reside freely within the territory of the Member State—addition to updating commentary, to address art.16*

4.071

Para. in 2020/21 edition	
3.296	In *VI v HMRC* (C-247/20), Advocate General Hogan in an Opinion of September 30, 2021 reiterated the notion that, as the wording of art.16 provides, a right of permanent residence once obtained is not subject to complying with the conditions of art.7.

p.1579, *Directive 2004/38/EC of the European Parliament and of the Council of 29 April 2004 on the right of citizens of the Union and their family members to move and reside freely within the territory of the Member States—updating commentary on art.24*

In *CG v Department for Communities,* the CJEU ruled that in a case   4.072
such as the one before them where art.24 was unavailable to the claimant, the claimant might nonetheless have a degree of protection from
arts. 1, 7 and 24 of the EU Charter. The claimants in *SSWP v Fratila and
Tanase* [2021] UKSC 53 were not permitted by the Supreme Court to
argue that point, thus its implications remain untested.

pp.1580-1581, *Regulation (EC) No.883/2004 of the European
Parliament and of the Council of 29 April 2004 on the coordination of
social security systems–updating commentary on Art.7 and Art.68*

The Court of Appeal, having permitted HMRC to raise arguments not   4.073
raised below, has reversed the decision of the Upper Tribunal in *WC v
HMRC (CHB)* [2019] UKUT 289 (AAC): see *HMRC v Carrington*
[2021] EWCA Civ 1724.

PART V

UPDATING MATERIAL
VOLUME IV

HMRC-ADMINISTERED
SOCIAL SECURITY
BENEFITS AND SCOTLAND

Commentary by

Ian Hooker

Edward Mitchell

Mark Rowland

Nick Wikeley

p.xv, *Contents (Part I)*

The paragraph cross-reference for the Childcare Act 2016 should read 1.1061.

5.001

p.xix, *Contents (Part X and Part XI)*

The heading for Part X should read 'TAX-FREE CHILDCARE' while the heading for Part XI should read 'THE 30 HOURS SCHEME'.

5.002

p.193, *annotation to the Tax Credits Act 2002 s.18 (Decisions after final notice)*

In *HMRC v ED (TC)* [2021] UKUT 195 (AAC), Upper Tribunal Judge Rowland expressed doubt as to whether HMRC had power to make a section 18 decision that would effectively negate a live appeal made against an earlier tax credits decision:

5.003

"14 . . . It seems to me to be arguable that it is improper for HMRC to make a section 18 decision in circumstances where a properly-made challenge to an earlier decision is under active consideration and the effect of making a section 18 decision is to force the claimant to go back to square one. If everything that had been done in relation to the earlier decision, including any application for mandatory reconsideration or any decision on mandatory reconsideration, were to be treated as having been done in relation to the section 18 decision, that would be one thing, but for the process to have be repeated in its entirety is likely to be unfair to the claimant and a waste of HMRC's resources in any case where the section 18 decision is to the same effect as the decision that is being challenged."

p.291, *amendment to the Income Tax (Earnings and Pensions) Act 2003 s.318B (Childcare: meaning of "care", "child" and "parental responsibility")*

With effect from 26 July 2021, art.4 of the Social Security (Scotland) Act 2018 (Disability Assistance, Young Carer Grants, Short-term Assistance and Winter Heating Assistance) (Consequential Provision and Modifications) Order 2021 (SI 2021/886) amended s.318BB by inserting the following paragraph after subsection (3)(a):

5.004

"(aa) disability assistance is given in respect of the child in accordance with regulations made under section 31 of the Social Security (Scotland) Act 2018,"

p.293, *amendment to the Income Tax (Earnings and Pensions) Act 2003 s.318C (Childcare: meaning of "qualifying child care")*

With effect from December 12, 2021, reg.2(a) of the Income Tax (Qualifying Child Care) (Wales) Regulations 2021 (SI 2021/1344) amended subs.(3) of s.318C by inserting in paragraphs (f) and (g)(ii) the words "or the Approval of Home Childcare Providers (Wales) Scheme

5.005

2021" after "Tax Credits (Approval of Child Care Providers) (Wales) Scheme 2007".

p.294, *ERRATUM: the Income Tax (Earnings and Pensions) Act 2003 s.318C (Childcare: meaning of "qualifying child care")*

5.006 Sub-sections (10) and (11) were omitted in error from the text in Vol IV. They were added with effect from November 21, 2009 by the Income Tax (Qualifying Child Care) (No. 2) Regulations 2009 (S.I. 2009/2888) but subs.(11) was subsequently repealed with effect from April 6, 2011 by the Income Tax (Qualifying Child Care) Regulations 2011 (S.I. 2011/775). So the text immediately before the sub-heading 'PART 5' should now read as follows:

"(10) In this section "foster parent" in relation to a child—
   (a) in relation to England, means a person with whom the child is placed under the Fostering Services Regulations 2002;
   (b) in relation to Wales, means a person with whom the child is placed under the Fostering Services (Wales) Regulations 2003; and
   (c) in relation to Northern Ireland, means a person with whom the child is placed under the Foster Placement (Children) Regulations (Northern Ireland) 1996."

p.317, *modification of the Income Tax (Earnings and Pensions) Act 2003 s.677 (UK social security benefits wholly exempt from tax: Table B)*

5.007 With effect from December 22, 2021, reg.6(a) of the Income Tax (Exemption of Social Security Benefits) Regulations 2021 (2021/1341) modified Table B-Part 1 in subs.(1) so that it has effect as if the following entries were inserted at the appropriate alphabetical place:

Payments made pursuant to the Covid Winter Grant Scheme or the Covid Local Support Grant	LGA 2003	Section 31
Payments made pursuant to any scheme or grant in Scotland, Wales or Northern Ireland corresponding to the Covid Winter Grant Scheme or the Covid Local Support Grant		

p.317, *amendment to the Income Tax (Earnings and Pensions) Act 2003 s.677 (UK social security benefits wholly exempt from tax: Table B)*

5.008 With effect from December 22, 2021, reg.2(a) of the Income Tax (Exemption of Social Security Benefits) Regulations 2021 (2021/1341) amended Table B-Part 1 in subs.(1) by inserting at the appropriate alphabetical place, so as to have effect for the tax year 2021/22 and subsequent years, the following entry:

Short-term assistance	SS(S)A 2018	Section 36

p.318, *amendment to the Income Tax (Earnings and Pensions) Act 2003 s.677 (UK social security benefits wholly exempt from tax: Table B)*

With effect from December 22, 2021, reg.2(b) of the Income Tax (Exemption of Social Security Benefits) Regulations 2021 (2021/1341) amended Table B-Part 1 in subs.(1) by inserting at the appropriate alphabetical place, so as to have effect for the tax year 2020/21 and subsequent years, the following entry: 5.009

Winter heating assistance	SS(S)A 2018	Section 30

p.318, *modification of the Income Tax (Earnings and Pensions) Act 2003 s.677 (UK social security benefits wholly exempt from tax: Table B)*

With effect from December 22, 2021, reg.6(b) of the Income Tax (Exemption of Social Security Benefits) Regulations 2021 (2021/1341) modified s.677 so that it has effect as if the following words were inserted after subs.(1):   5.010

"(1A) In this section—
    (a) "the Covid Winter Grant Scheme" means the scheme that was the subject of guidance published by the Department for Work and Pensions on 23 November 2020; and
    (b) "the Covid Local Support Grant" means the grant that was the subject of guidance published by that Department on 17 April 2021 and further guidance published by that Department on 21 June 2021.
(1B) References in this section to payments made pursuant to—
    (a) the Covid Winter Grant Scheme or the Covid Local Support Grant; or
    (b) any scheme or grant in Scotland, Wales or Northern Ireland corresponding to the scheme or grant in sub-paragraph (a),
are references only to payments made pursuant to such a scheme or grant for the tax year 2020-21 and subsequent tax years."

p.393, *amendment to the Income Tax (Trading and Other Income) Act 2005 s.369 (Charge to tax on interest)*

With effect from June 1, 2021, s.34(4)(a) of the Finance Act 2021 amended s.369 by repealing subsection (3)(f).   5.011

p.520, *annotation to the Childcare Act 2016*

5.012   On the jurisdictional issues raised, see further *HMRC v JS, EL and LG* [2021] UKUT 264 (AAC). This decision concerned three cases, each involving a claim to 30 hours free childcare, where the appeals were lodged before the Chambers amending Order came into force in 2020. HMRC had forwarded each of the three appeals to the Social Entitlement Chamber (SEC) of the FTT. Upper Tribunal Judge Gray held that the decisions of the FTT (SEC) were made without jurisdiction as they predated the amending Order. However, she expressed the view that any cases heard before the amendment which had not been appealed from the FTT remained valid unless or until they were set aside.

p.528, *expiry of Coronavirus Act 2020 s.77 (Up-rating of working tax credit etc)*

5.013   With effect from December 9, 2021, regs 2 and 3 of the Coronavirus Act 2020 (Early Expiry) (No.2) Regulations 2021 (SI 2021/1399) provided for the expiry of s.77.

pp.556-557, *amendment to the Universal Credit (Transitional Provisions) Regulations 2014 (SI 2014/1230) reg.2 (Interpretation)*

5.014   With effect from November 25, 2020, reg.6(2) of the Universal Credit (Persons who have attained state pension credit qualifying age) (Amendment) Regulations 2020 (SI 2020/655) added several new definitions to reg.2 which are not relevant to tax credits. The up-to-date version of reg.2 can be found as set out in Vol II of this series.

p.562, *annotation to the Universal Credit (Transitional Provisions) Regulations 2014 (SI 2014/1230) reg.8 (Termination of awards of certain existing benefits: other claimants)*

5.015   In *HMRC v AB* [2021] UKUT 209 (AAC), Upper Tribunal Judge Mitchell held that where a Universal Credit claim had been withdrawn before the Secretary of State had determined that she was satisfied that the basic conditions referred to in reg.8(1)(b) were met, reg.8(2) did not apply. Accordingly, reg.8(2) did not operate so as to terminate the claimant's entitlement to a tax credit. Judge Mitchell's decision proceeded on the assumption that the giving of what HMRC have termed a 'stop notice' amounted to a Secretary of State determination under reg.8(1)(b). Since the Universal Credit claim had been withdrawn before the stop notice was given, reg.8(2) did not apply. The decision in *AB* is distinguishable from Upper Tribunal Judge Jacobs' decision in *HMRC v LH* [2018] UKUT 306 (AAC) because, in that case, the claimant did not seek to withdraw a Universal Credit claim until *after* the Secretary of State had given a 'stop notice' for the purposes of reg.8(1). In *AB*, HMRC accepted that the claimant withdrew her Universal Credit claim before the 'stop notice' was given.

p.574, *amendment to the Universal Credit (Transitional Provisions) Regulations 2014 (SI 2014/1230) reg.46 (Termination of existing benefits if no claim before the deadline)*

With effect from July 22, 2020, reg.4(5) of the Universal Credit 5.016 (Managed Migration Pilot and Miscellaneous Amendments) Regulations 2019 (SI 2019/1152) amended reg.46(1) to read as follows:

"**46.**—(1) Where a notified person has not made a claim for universal credit on or before the deadline day, all awards of any existing benefits to which the person is entitled terminate—

(a) in the case of housing benefit, income support, income-based jobseeker's allowance or income-related employment and support allowance, on the last day of the period of two weeks beginning with the deadline day; and

(b) in the case of a tax credit, on the day before the deadline day."

p.574, *amendment to the Universal Credit (Transitional Provisions) Regulations 2014 (SI 2014/1230) reg.47 (Notified persons who claim as a different benefit unit)*

With effect from July 22, 2020, reg.4(6) of the Universal Credit 5.017 (Managed Migration Pilot and Miscellaneous Amendments) Regulations 2019 (SI 2019/1152) amended reg.47(2) to read as follows:

"(2) If any of those notified persons makes a claim for universal credit on or before the deadline day then, notwithstanding anything in regulation 8 (termination of awards of certain existing benefits: other claimants), all awards of any existing benefits to which any of those persons is entitled terminate—

(a) in the case of housing benefit, income support, income-based jobseeker's allowance or income-related employment and support allowance, on the last day of the period of two weeks beginning with the earliest day on which any of those persons is entitled to universal credit in connection with a claim (or, in a case where the person is not entitled to universal credit, on the day they would have been entitled if all the basic and financial conditions had been met); or

(b) in the case of a tax credit, on the day before the "earliest day" referred to in sub-paragraph (a)."

p.585, *repeal of the Universal Credit (Transitional Provisions) Regulations 2014 (SI 2014/1230) reg.59*

With effect from September 23, 2020, reg.6(2) of the Universal Credit 5.018 (Managed Migration Pilot and Miscellaneous Amendments) Regulations 2019 (SI 2019/1152) repealed reg.59–see further the commentary in Vol II at para.2.863.

p.594, *amendment to the Working Tax Credit (Entitlement and Maximum Rate) Regulations 2002 (SI 2002/2005) reg.2 (Interpretation)*

5.019 With effect from December 9, 2021, reg.2(2) of the Tax Credits and Child Benefit (Miscellaneous Amendments) Regulations 2021 (SI 2021/1286) inserted after the definition of "relevant child care charges" the following new definition:

""Scottish disability assistance" means a payment made by the Scottish ministers under section 31 of the Social Security (Scotland) Act 2018;".

p.621, *amendment to the Working Tax Credit (Entitlement and Maximum Rate) Regulations 2002 (SI 2002/2005) reg.9 (Disability element and workers who are to be treated as at a disadvantage in getting a job)*

5.020 With effect from December 9, 2021, reg.2(3) of the Tax Credits and Child Benefit (Miscellaneous Amendments) Regulations 2021 (SI 2021/1286) inserted after para.(4)(e) the following:

"(f) Scottish disability assistance."

p.624, *annotation to the Working Tax Credit (Entitlement and Maximum Rate) Regulations 2002 (SI 2002/2005 reg.9 (Disability element and workers who are to be treated as at a disadvantage in getting a job)*

5.021 Case C of the second disability condition provided for by reg.9 is met by virtue of a person's entitlement to Scottish disability assistance under s.31 of the Social Security (Scotland) Act 2018.

p.630, *amendment to the Working Tax Credit (Entitlement and Maximum Rate) Regulations 2002 (SI 2002/2005) reg.13 (Entitlement to childcare element of working tax credit)*

5.022 With effect from December 9, 2021, reg.2(4) of the Tax Credits and Child Benefit (Miscellaneous Amendments) Regulations 2021 (SI 2021/1286) inserted after para. (6)(k) the following:

"(l) Scottish disability assistance."

pp.634-635, *amendment to the Working Tax Credit (Entitlement and Maximum Rate) Regulations 2002 (SI 2002/2005) reg.14 (Entitlement to childcare element of working tax credit)*

5.023 With effect from December 9, 2021, reg.2(5) of the Tax Credits and Child Benefit (Miscellaneous Amendments) Regulations 2021 (SI 2021/1286) inserted at the end of para.(2)(f)(vii), but before the semicolon, the phrase "or The Approval of Home Childcare Providers (Wales) Scheme 2021", and at the end of para.(2D), but before the full stop, the phrase "or The Approval of Home Childcare Providers (Wales) Scheme 2021".

p.641, *amendment to the Working Tax Credit (Entitlement and Maximum Rate) Regulations 2002 (SI 2002/2005) reg.17 (Severe disability element)*

With effect from December 9, 2021, reg.2(6) of the Tax Credits and Child Benefit (Miscellaneous Amendments) Regulations 2021 (SI 2021/1286) inserted "or (5)" at the end of the para.(1), but before the full stop, and inserted after para.(4) the following new para.(5):   5.024

"(5) A person satisfies this paragraph if the higher rate daily living component of Scottish disability assistance is payable in respect of that person."

p.705, *amendment to the Tax Credits (Definition and Calculation of Income) Regulations 2002 (SI 2002/2006) reg.19 (General disregards in the calculation of income) Table 6*

With effect from July 29, 2021, reg.2 of the Tax Credits and Child Benefit (Miscellaneous and Coronavirus Amendments) Regulations 2021 (SI 2021/810) amended Table 6 by substituting for item 40 the following: 5.025

"**40.** Any payment made under the scheme known as the Covid Winter Grant Scheme. or the Covid Local Support Grant established under section 31 of the Local Government Act 2003 in respect of England or any corresponding schemes established by the Northern Ireland Executive, the Scottish Government or the Welsh Government for the purpose of providing financial support to families and vulnerable individuals to assist with the cost of food and utilities."

With effect from May 13, 2021, reg. 4 of the Social Security and Tax Credits (Miscellaneous and Coronavirus Amendments) Regulations 2021 (SI 2021/495) inserted after item 40 the following new entry:

"**41.** A payment made under the Covid-19 support scheme: working households receiving tax credits."

The relevant support scheme was established under a direction made under section 76 of the Coronavirus Act 2020. A copy of the direction can be found at *https://www.gov.uk/government/publications/treasury-direction-made-under-section-76-of-the-coronavirus-act-2020.*

With effect from December 9, 2021, reg.3 of the Tax Credits and Child Benefit (Miscellaneous Amendments) Regulations 2021 (SI 2021/1286) inserted after item 41 the following new entry:

"**42.** Any payment made under the scheme known as the "Household Support Fund" in respect of England or any corresponding schemes established by the Northern Ireland Executive, the Scottish Government or the Welsh Government.".

---

p.711, *annotation to the Tax Credits (Definition and Calculation of Income) Regulations 2002 (SI 2002/2006) reg.19 (General disregards in the calculation of income)*

5.026 The income disregards provided for by Table 6 in reg.19 include payments under the Household Support Fund or any corresponding fund established by the Northern Ireland Executive, the Scottish Government or the Welsh Government.

p.731, *amendment to the Child Tax Credit Regulations 2002 (SI 2002/2007) reg.8 (Prescribed conditions for a disabled or severely disabled child or qualifying young person)*

5.027 With effect from December 9, 2021, reg.4 of the Tax Credits and Child Benefit (Miscellaneous Amendments) Regulations 2021 (SI 2021/1286) amended reg.8(6) by inserting after the words "requirements of this paragraph if" the phrase "the care component of".

p.772, *annotation to the Tax Credits (Claims and Notifications) Regulations 2002 (SI 2002/2014) reg.5 (Manner in which claims to be made)*

5.028 In *HMRC v ED (TC)* [2021] UKUT 195 (AAC), Upper Tribunal Judge Rowland followed the finding in *MK v HMRC (TC)* [2018] UKUT 238 (AAC) that there is no right of appeal against decisions made by HMRC under reg.5(2)(b). However, the judge went on to express the view *obiter* that arguably a distinction ought to be drawn between the question whether, if information was provided, it should be treated as a claim and whether the information was in fact provided. Judge Rowland considered it at least arguable that the First-tier Tribunal has jurisdiction to determine an appeal on the question whether information has been provided. Judge Rowland considered that the First-tier Tribunal might have jurisdiction because such questions raise matters of pure fact rather than the exercise by HMRC of their discretion under reg.5(2)(b) whether to permit a claim to be made other than in writing on a form authorised or approved for the purposes of claiming a tax credit. To deny a right of appeal in such circumstances would arguably be a breach of the European Convention on Human Rights (see *ZM and AB v HMRC (TC)* [2013] UKUT 547 (AAC); [2014] AACR 17).

p.879, *amendment to the Child Benefit (General) Regulations 2006 (SI 2006/223) reg.1 (Citation, commencement and interpretation)*

5.029 With effect from December 9, 2021, reg.5 of the Tax Credits and Child Benefit (Miscellaneous Amendments) Regulations 2021 (SI 2021/1286) amended the definition of "approved training" in reg.1(3) by deleting paragraph (c) and substituting:

"(c) in relation to Scotland, known as "Employability Fund activity" or "No One Left Behind"; or".

With effect from July 29, 2021, reg.3(2) of the Tax Credits and Child Benefit (Miscellaneous and Coronavirus Amendments) Regulations 2021 (SI 2021/810) amended para.(d) of the definition of "approved training" by deleting the words "Training for Success" and substituting the words ""Training for Success" or "Skills for Life and Work"".

p.886, *amendments to the Child Benefit (General) Regulations 2006 (SI 2006/223) reg.7 (Qualifying young person: terminal dates)*

With effect from May 31, 2021, reg.2(2)(a) of the Child Benefit (General) (Coronavirus) (Amendment) Regulations 2021 (SI 2021/630) amended reg.7(2) in two ways. First, the words "in accordance with Cases 1 and 2 has not expired in his case" were repealed and replaced by: **5.030**

"in accordance with—
   (a) Cases 1 and 2, or,
   (b) for Summer Term 2021 where a person has been entered as a 2021 candidate for external examinations in connection with relevant education that person was receiving and those examinations have been cancelled due to coronavirus, Cases 1 and 3,
has not expired in his case."

Second, after Case 2, but before the words "this paragraph is subject to the following qualification", the following new case was inserted:

"*Case 3*
3.1. Where external examinations have been cancelled due to coronavirus, in the case of a person whose name had been entered as a 2021 candidate for any external examination in connection with relevant education which that person was receiving at that time, the period is from the date on which that person ceases to receive relevant education up to and including—
   (a) whichever of the dates in paragraph 1.2 of Case 1 (as modified by paragraph 1.3 where appropriate) first occurs after the scheduled date of conclusion of the examination, or the last of those examinations where the person was entered for more than one, or
   (b) if that person attains the age of 20 on or before that date, the week including the last Monday before that person attains that age."

With effect from May 31, 2021, reg. 2(2)(b) of the Child Benefit (General) (Coronavirus) (Amendment) Regulations 2021 (SI 2021/630) further amended reg.7(2) by inserting after para.(3) the following new paragraph:

"(4) In this regulation—
   "coronavirus" means severe acute respiratory syndrome coronavirus 2,

145

"entered as a 2021 candidate" includes a person who would have been entered as a candidate for one or more external examinations in Summer Term 2021 if the external examinations had not been cancelled before that person was entered as a candidate for such examinations,

"scheduled date" means the date on which the examination board setting the relevant examination had scheduled that examination to take place, and

"Summer Term 2021" means the period beginning with 1st June 2021 and ending with 31st August 2021.".

p.896, *amendments to the Child Benefit (General) Regulations 2006 (SI 2006/223) reg.23 (Circumstances in which person treated as not being in Great Britain)*

5.031   With effect from September 15, 2021, reg.2(2) of the Child Benefit (General) (Amendment) Regulations 2021 (SI 2021/1039) inserted after sub-para.(o) of para.(6) the following new entries:

"(p) has been granted leave to enter, or remain in, the United Kingdom under the Immigration Rules made under section 3(2) of the Immigration Act 1971 by virtue of—
    (i) the Afghan Relocations and Assistance Policy, or
    (ii) the previous scheme for locally employed staff in Afghanistan (sometimes referred to as the ex-gratia scheme);
(q) has been granted leave to enter, or remain in, the United Kingdom—
    (i) under the Immigration Rules made under section 3(2) of the Immigration Act 1971, or
    (ii) outside the Immigration Rules,
by virtue of the Afghan Citizens Resettlement Scheme;
    (r) left Afghanistan in connection with the collapse of the Afghan government that took place on 15th August 2021."

p.904, *amendments to the Child Benefit (General) Regulations 2006 (SI 2006/223) reg.27 (Circumstances in which person treated as not being in Northern Ireland)*

5.032   With effect from September 15, 2021, reg.2(3) of the Child Benefit (General) (Amendment) Regulations 2021 (SI 2021/1039) inserted after sub-para.(o) of para.(5) the following new entries:

"(p) has been granted leave to enter, or remain in, the United Kingdom under the Immigration Rules made under section 3(2) of the Immigration Act 1971 by virtue of—
    (i) the Afghan Relocations and Assistance Policy, or
    (ii) the previous scheme for locally employed staff in Afghanistan (sometimes referred to as the ex-gratia scheme);
(q) has been granted leave to enter, or remain in, the United Kingdom—
    (i) under the Immigration Rules made under section 3(2) of the Immigration Act 1971, or

    (ii) outside the Immigration Rules,
by virtue of the Afghan Citizens Resettlement Scheme;
    (r) left Afghanistan in connection with the collapse of the Afghan government that took place on 15th August 2021."

p.974, *amendments to the Statutory Sick Pay (Coronavirus) (Funding of Employers' Liabilities) Regulations 2020 (SI 2020/512) reg.3 (Funding of eligible employers' liabilities by HMRC)*

With effect from September 30, 2021, reg.3 of the Statutory Sick Pay   **5.033** (Coronavirus) (Funding of Employers' Liabilities) (Closure) Regulations and the Statutory Sick Pay (Coronavirus) (Funding of Employers' Liabilities) (Northern Ireland) (Closure) Regulations 2021(SI 2021/1013) amended para.(1)(b) by inserting "and no later than 30th September 2021" after "13th March 2020" and amended para.(1) by inserting ", (2A)" after "subject to paragraphs (2)". In addition, a new paragraph (2A) was inserted after para.(2) as follows:

"(2A) A reimbursement amount does not include any amount paid to an employee in respect of a qualifying day which falls after 30th September 2021.".

pp.977-978, *amendment to the Statutory Sick Pay (Coronavirus) (Funding of Employers' Liabilities) Regulations 2020 (SI 2020/512) reg.7 (Time limit for making a claim)*

With effect from September 30, 2021, reg.4 of the Statutory Sick Pay   **5.034** (Coronavirus) (Funding of Employers' Liabilities) (Closure) Regulations and the Statutory Sick Pay (Coronavirus) (Funding of Employers' Liabilities) (Northern Ireland) (Closure) Regulations 2021 (SI 2021/1013) amended reg.7 by substituting a new provision as follows:

"7. A claim may not be made after the earlier of—
    (a) 31st December 2021; or
    (b) the end of the period of 1 year beginning with the last qualifying day in the period of incapacity for work to which the reimbursement amount claimed relates.".

p.1289, *amendments to the Child Trust Funds Regulations 2004 (SI 2004/1450) reg.18A (Permitted withdrawals from an account where the child is terminally ill)*

With effect from July 26, 2021, art.5(2) of the Social Security (Scot-   **5.035** land) Act 2018 (Disability Assistance, Young Carer Grants, Short-term Assistance and Winter Heating Assistance) (Consequential Provision and Modifications) Order 2021 (SI 2021/886) amended Case 1 in reg.18A(2)(b) so as to omit both "or Scotland" in para.(i) and the "or" at the end of para.(i), while inserting a new para.(iii) as follows:

"; or

> (iii) in Scotland, falls within either of the provisions mentioned in paragraph (i), or is to be regarded as having a terminal illness, in accordance with regulations for disability assistance for children and young people made under section 31 of the Social Security (Scotland) Act 2018."

With effect from July 26, 2021, art.5(2) of the Social Security (Scotland) Act 2018 (Disability Assistance, Young Carer Grants, Short-term Assistance and Winter Heating Assistance) (Consequential Provision and Modifications) Order 2021 (SI 2021/886) amended reg.18A(6) by substituting "England and Wales" for "England, Wales and Scotland" in sub-para.(a), omitting "or" at the end of that sub-paragraph and inserting after sub-para.(b) the following:

"; or

> (c) for Scotland, as set out in regulations made under section 31 of the Social Security (Scotland) Act 2018."

p.1323, *Part X*

5.036   The heading for Part X should read 'TAX-FREE CHILDCARE' and not 'CHILDCARE PAYMENTS'.

pp.1325-1326, *amendments to the Childcare Payments (Eligibility) Regulations 2015 (SI 2015/448) reg.2 (Interpretation)*

5.037   With effect from July 22, 2021, reg.2(2) of the Childcare Payments (Miscellaneous Amendment) Regulations 2021 (SI 2021/781) amended reg.1 by omitting the definition of "another EEA State" and inserting, after the definition of "personal independence payment", the following new definition: "prescribed state" means any EEA state or Switzerland;".

p.1329, *amendment to the Childcare Payments (Eligibility) Regulations 2015 (SI 2015/448) reg.5 (Meaning of qualifying child)*

5.038   With effect from July 22, 2021, reg.2(3) of the Childcare Payments (Miscellaneous Amendment) Regulations 2021 (SI 2021/781) amended reg.5(5)(a)(iv) by substituting "a prescribed" for "another EEA".

p.1330, *amendments to the Childcare Payments (Eligibility) Regulations 2015 (SI 2015/448) reg.6 (Temporary absence from the United Kingdom)*

5.039   With effect from July 22, 2021, reg.2(4) of the Childcare Payments (Miscellaneous Amendment) Regulations 2021 (SI 2021/781) amended reg.6(6) by inserting "of the EEA" after "any member State" and omitting "(other than the United Kingdom) in the definition of "prescribed area.

p.1331, *amendments to the Childcare Payments (Eligibility) Regulations 2015 (SI 2015/448) reg.7 (Persons treated as being, or not being, in the United Kingdom)*

With effect from July 22, 2021, reg.2(5) of the Childcare Payments (Miscellaneous Amendment) Regulations 2021 (SI 2021/781) amended reg.7(1)(d) by substituting "a prescribed" for "another EEA" and inserting "who is not a person subject to immigration control and" after "state", as well as substituting "a prescribed" for "another EEA" in para.(3)(b)(ii).

5.040

pp.1332–1333, *amendments to the Childcare Payments (Eligibility) Regulations 2015 (SI 2015/448) reg.9 (The requirement to be in qualifying paid work)*

With effect from July 22, 2021, reg.2(6) of the Childcare Payments (Miscellaneous Amendment) Regulations 2021 (SI 2021/781) amended reg.9 by omitting what are displayed in the text as paras (1)(c) and (1)(ca) (see the General Note on p.1334 as to the drafting error) and replacing them with the following new paragraphs after para.(1)(b):

5.041

"(c) the person is in paid work as an employed person or as a self-employed person and the person's expected income from the work in the period specified in paragraph (4) is greater than or equal to the relevant threshold; or

(d) the person is in paid work as an employed person or as a self-employed person, the person's expected income does not meet the requirements of sub-paragraphs (a) or (b) due to coronavirus, and the person—
  (i) is receiving payments under a coronavirus support scheme; or
  (ii) has made a claim for and is reasonably expecting to receive payments under a coronavirus support scheme; or
  (iii) is intending to make a claim under a coronavirus support scheme, with the reasonable expectation of the claim being agreed; or
  (iv) is employed by an employer who is claiming a grant under a coronavirus support scheme to cover a proportion of the person's normal earnings."

Regulation 2(6) also substitute "a prescribed" for "another EEA" in para.(1A).

pp.1336–1337, *amendments to the Childcare Payments (Eligibility) Regulations 2015 (SI 2015/448) reg.12 (Qualifying paid work: time off in connection with sickness or parenting)*

With effect from July 22, 2021, reg.2(7) of the Childcare Payments (Miscellaneous Amendment) Regulations 2021 (SI 2021/781) amended reg.12(1)(n) and (o) by inserting "in relation to England, Wales and Scotland only," after "(n)" and "o" respectively and by substituting "a prescribed" for "another EEA" in para.(7).

5.042

p.1338, *amendment to the Childcare Payments (Eligibility) Regulations 2015 (SI 2015/448) reg.13 (Qualifying paid work: caring, incapacity for work or limited capability for work)*

5.043   With effect from July 22, 2021, reg.2(8) of the Childcare Payments (Miscellaneous Amendment) Regulations 2021 (SI 2021/781) amended para.(5) by substituting "a prescribed" for "another EEA".

p.1339, *amendment to the Childcare Payments (Eligibility) Regulations 2015 (SI 2015/448) reg.15 (Income not to exceed a certain level)*

5.044   With effect from July 22, 2021, reg.2(9) of the Childcare Payments (Miscellaneous Amendment) Regulations 2021 (SI 2021/781) amended para.(2) by substituting "a prescribed" for "another EEA".

p.1340, *amendments to the Childcare Payments (Eligibility) Regulations 2015 (SI 2015/448) reg.16 (Application of section 11 to EEA residents)*

5.045   With effect from July 22, 2021, reg.2(10) of the Childcare Payments (Miscellaneous Amendment) Regulations 2021 (SI 2021/781) amended the heading to reg.16 by substituting "residents of prescribed states" for "EEA residents" and amended para.(1) by substituting "a prescribed" for "another EEA".

p.1341, *amendments to the Childcare Payments (Eligibility) Regulations 2015 (SI 2015/448) reg.17 (Application of sections 12 and 13 to EEA residents)*

5.046   With effect from July 22, 2021, reg.2(10) of the Childcare Payments (Miscellaneous Amendment) Regulations 2021 (SI 2021/781) amended the heading to reg.17 by substituting "residents of prescribed states" for "EEA residents" and amended each of paras (1), (2)(a)(i) and (2)(b) by substituting "a prescribed" for "another EEA".

p.1343, *amendments to the Childcare Payments Regulations 2015 (SI 2015/522) reg.2 (Interpretation)*

5.047   With effect from July 22, 2021, reg.3(2) of the Childcare Payments (Miscellaneous Amendment) Regulations 2021 (SI 2021/781) amended reg.2 by omitting the definition of "another EEA state" and inserting after the definition of "personal independence payment" the following new definition: ""prescribed state" means any EEA state or Switzerland;".

p.1345, *amendment to the Childcare Payments Regulations 2015 (SI 2015/522) reg.3 (Qualifying childcare: registered or approved childcare)*

5.048   With effect from July 22, 2021, reg.3(3) of the Childcare Payments (Miscellaneous Amendment) Regulations 2021 (SI 2021/781) amended reg.3(6)(b) by substituting "a prescribed" for "an EEA".

p.1348, *amendment to the Childcare Payments Regulations 2015 (SI 2015/522) reg.6 (Declarations of eligibility)*

With effect from July 22, 2021, reg.3(4) of the Childcare Payments (Miscellaneous Amendment) Regulations 2021 (SI 2021/781) amended reg.6(6) by substituting "a prescribed" for "another EEA" and substituting "prescribed" for "other EEA". **5.049**

p.1348, *amendment to the Childcare Payments Regulations 2015 (SI 2015/522) reg.7 (Late declarations of eligibility)*

With effect from July 22, 2021, reg.3(5) of the Childcare Payments (Miscellaneous Amendment) Regulations 2021 (SI 2021/781) amended reg.7(4) by substituting "a prescribed" for "another EEA". **5.050**

p.1353, *amendment to the Childcare Payments Regulations 2015 (SI 2015/522) reg.14 (Variation of relevant maximum: delay in payment of allowances)*

With effect from July 22, 2021, reg.3(6) of the Childcare Payments (Miscellaneous Amendment) Regulations 2021 (SI 2021/781) amended reg.14(4) by substituting "a prescribed" for "another EEA". **5.051**

p.1354, *amendments to the Childcare Payments Regulations 2015 (SI 2015/522) reg.17 (Compensatory payments)*

With effect from July 22, 2021, reg.3(6)(a) and (b) of the Childcare Payments (Miscellaneous Amendment) Regulations 2021 (SI 2021/781) amended reg.17 by omitting "or" after para. (2)(b), omitting "." at the end of para.(2)(c) and inserting: **5.052**

"; or
   (d) a person has applied for leave to enter or remain under the EU Settlement Scheme, and the application has not been determined or there is an outstanding appeal."

p.1355, *amendments to the Childcare Payments Regulations 2015 (SI 2015/522) reg.17 (Compensatory payments)*

With effect from July 22, 2021, reg.3(6)(c) and (d) of the Childcare Payments (Miscellaneous Amendment) Regulations 2021 (SI 2021/781) amended reg.17 by substituting "a prescribed" for "another EEA" in para.(8) and by inserting after para.(8) the following new paragraph: **5.053**

"(9) In this regulation—
  "EU Settlement Scheme" means—
   (i) the residence scheme immigration rules in Appendix EU to the immigration rules except those rules or changes to that appendix which are identified in the immigration rules as not having effect in the residence scheme that operates in connection with the withdrawal of the United Kingdom from the EU; and

   (ii) any other rules which are identified in the immigration rules as having effect in connection with the withdrawal of the United Kingdom from the EU."

p.1358, *amendment to the Childcare Payments Regulations 2015 (SI 2015/522) reg.21 (Disqualification orders: meaning of "relevant benefit")*

5.054 With effect from July 22, 2021, reg.3(8) of the Childcare Payments (Miscellaneous Amendment) Regulations 2021 (SI 2021/781) amended reg.21(b) by substituting "a prescribed" for "another EEA".

p.1363, *Part XI*

5.055 The heading for Part XI should read 'THE 30 HOURS SCHEME' and not 'TAX-FREE CHILDCARE'.

p.1367, *amendment to the Childcare (Early Years Provision Free of Charge) (Extended Entitlement) Regulations 2016 (SI 2016/1257) reg.1 (Citation and commencement)*

5.056 On the jurisdictional issues raised by appeals relating to the Regulations, see the note to p.520 and the discussion of the decision in *HMRC v JS, EL and LG* [2021] UKUT 264 (AAC).

p.1369, *amendment to the Childcare (Early Years Provision Free of Charge) (Extended Entitlement) Regulations 2016 (SI 2016/1257) reg.2 (Interpretation)*

5.057 With effect from July 1, 2021, reg.5 of the Childcare (Early Years Provision Free of Charge) (Extended Entitlement) (Amendment) Regulations 2021 (SI 2021/674) amended reg.2 by inserting after the definition of "paid work" the following new definition: ""prescribed state" means an EEA state or Switzerland;".

pp.1373-1374, *amendments to the Childcare (Early Years Provision Free of Charge) (Extended Entitlement) Regulations 2016 (SI 2016/1257) reg.5 (The requirement to be in qualifying paid work)*

5.058 With effect from July 1, 2021, reg.6 of the Childcare (Early Years Provision Free of Charge) (Extended Entitlement) (Amendment) Regulations 2021 (SI 2021/674) amended reg.5 as follows:
  (a) deleting "," at the end of para.(1)(b)(ii);
  (b) inserting "a" after "an employed or" and "—" after "and the person" in para.(1)(c);
  (c) substituting "expecting to receive" for "anticipating receiving" and "; or" for ", or" in para.(1)(c)(ii);
  (d) substituting "is employed by an employer who" for "where the person is employed, their employer" in para.(iv); and
  (e) substituting "a prescribed" for "another EEA" in para.(1A).

pp.1373-1374, *annotation to the Childcare (Early Years Provision Free of Charge) (Extended Entitlement) Regulations 2016 (SI 2016/1257) reg.5 (The requirement to be in qualifying paid work)*

In *HMRC v JS, EL and LG* [2021] UKUT 264 (AAC) Upper Tribu-   5.059
nal Judge Gray expressed the view (strictly obiter) that "the concept of expected income must reference the level of earnings that relate to the contractual obligations, or the work expected to be carried out (for the self-employed) during the period of the declaration, the period for which childcare is being claimed." As such the Judge rejected HMRC's inter-pretation of reg.6(1), namely "that the expected income under regula-tion 6(1) is the amount the person expects to receive during the 13-week period, and not the amount that the person has earned during that period." Rather, the calculation should be related to the amount of work to be performed in the period covered by the declaration irrespective of the arrangements made for payment for it. This may result (e.g. for a term-time only worker) in three periods each year of entitlement to childcare, and one where there was no (or little) income, and therefore no entitlement.

p.1377, *amendment to the Childcare (Early Years Provision Free of Charge) (Extended Entitlement) Regulations 2016 (SI 2016/1257) reg.8 (Qualifying paid work and work outside role as a foster parent: time off in connection with sickness or parenting)*

With effect from July 1, 2021, reg.7 of the Childcare (Early Years   5.060
Provision Free of Charge) (Extended Entitlement) (Amendment) Reg-ulations 2021 (SI 2021/674) amended reg.8(6) by substituting "a pre-scribed" for "another EEA".

p.1378, *amendment to the Childcare (Early Years Provision Free of Charge) (Extended Entitlement) Regulations 2016 (SI 2016/1257) reg.9 (Qualifying paid work and work outside role as a foster parent: caring, incapacity for work or limited capability for work)*

With effect from July 1, 2021, reg.8 of the Childcare (Early Years   5.061
Provision Free of Charge) (Extended Entitlement) (Amendment) Reg-ulations 2021 (SI 2021/674) amended reg.8(6) by substituting "a pre-scribed" for "another EEA".

p.1380, *amendments to the Childcare (Early Years Provision Free of Charge) (Extended Entitlement) Regulations 2016 (SI 2016/1257) reg.12 (Being in the United Kingdom)*

With effect from July 1, 2021, reg.9 of the Childcare (Early Years   5.062
Provision Free of Charge) (Extended Entitlement) (Amendment) Reg-ulations 2021 (SI 2021/674) amended reg.12 in the following ways:
(a) in para.(1)(b) by substituting "a prescribed state who is not a person subject to immigration control and" for "another EEA state";

(b) in para.(2)(a)(ii) by substituting "a prescribed" for "another EEA";

(c) by inserting at the end of para.(2)(b) the following new sub-paragraphs:

"; or

(c) a person who has applied within the applicable time limits for leave to enter or remain under the EU Settlement Scheme and the application has not been determined or there is an outstanding appeal."; and

(d) by inserting in para.(3) after the definition of "double taxation arrangements" the following new definition:

"EU Settlement Scheme" means—

(i) the residence scheme immigration rules in Appendix EU to the immigration rules except those rules or changes to that appendix which are identified in the immigration rules as not having effect in the residence scheme that operates in connection with the withdrawal of the United Kingdom from the EU; and

(ii) any other rules which are identified in the immigration rules as having effect in connection with the withdrawal of the United Kingdom from the EU;".

With effect from November 12, 2021, reg.5 of the Childcare (Early Years Provision Free of Charge) (Extended Entitlement) (Amendment) (No. 2) Regulations 2021 (SI 2021/1168) further amended reg.12 by making the following four amendments: (1) inserting "or" at the end of para.(2)(a)(ii); (2) substituting "." for "; or" at the end of para.(2)(b); (3) omitting para.(2)(c); and (4) omitting the definition of "EU Settlement Scheme" in para.(3).

pp.1383-1834, *annotation to the Childcare (Early Years Provision Free of Charge) (Extended Entitlement) Regulations 2016 (SI 2016/1257) reg.15 (Period of time for which the first declaration has effect)*

5.063   In *HMRC v JS, EL and LG* [2021] UKUT 264 (AAC) Upper Tribunal Judge Gray expressed the view (obiter) that by virtue of reg.15 a FTT decision has prospective effect only: "it provides that where a tribunal decides a case under regulation 24 the date of the tribunal decision is the first day of the first period in which the declaration has effect. Somebody appealing to the FTT can therefore only obtain 30 hours free childcare from a date significantly in advance of their initial declaration."

p.1436, *annotation to the Social Security (Scotland) Act 2018 s.41 (Right to request re-determination)*

5.064   The period prescribed for requesting a re-determination of entitlement to child disability payment is 42 days (reg.37(1) of the Disability Assistance for Children and Young People (Scotland) Regulations 2021–see Part I of this Supplement).

Contrary to what is stated in the last sentence of the annotation in the main work, the amendments made to s.41 by the Coronavirus (Scotland) Act 2020 are not temporary. See the supplemental annotation to s.52A, below.

pp.1437–1438, *annotation to the Social Security (Scotland) Act 2018 s.43 (Duty to re-determine)*

The prescribed period allowed for a re-determination of entitlement to   5.065
child disability payment is 56 days from the date that the request is received by Scottish Minsters or, if it was late, the date that they decided that the person making the request had a good reason for not making it sooner (reg.37(2) of the Disability Assistance for Children and Young People (Scotland) Regulations 2021–see Part I of this Supplement).

The modifications to s.43 made by the Coronavirus (Scotland) Act 2020 expired at the end of September 30, 2021 (see s.2(1) and (7)(a) of the Coronavirus (Extension and Expiry) (Scotland) Act 2021).

p.1440, *annotation to the Social Security (Scotland) Act 2018 s.48 (Deadline for appealing)*

Contrary to what is stated in the last sentence of the annotation in the   5.066
main work, the amendment made to s.48 by the Coronavirus (Scotland) Act 2020 is not temporary. See the supplemental annotation to s.52A, below.

p.1441, *amendment to the Social Security (Scotland) Act 2018 s.51 (Determination on basis of ongoing entitlement)*

With effect from July 26, 2021, the Social Security Administration and   5.067
Tribunal Membership (Scotland) Act 2020 (Commencement No. 2) Regulations 2021 (SSI 2021/232) brought into force s.12 of the 2020 Act, subs.(1) and (2) of which modify s.51 of the 2018 Act.

In subs.(2), the "and" at the end of para.(a) is repealed and, after para.(a) there is inserted—

"(aa) make provision, in accordance with Schedule 11, about—
   (i) the circumstances in which an individual who has an entitlement to assistance in respect of a period under such a determination is not to become entitled to be given some or all of that assistance at the time at which the individual otherwise would in accordance with provision under paragraph (a), and
   (ii) in that event, how and when the individual is to become entitled to be given that assistance, and".

After subs.(3), there is inserted—

"(3A) Schedule 11 makes provision about the exercise of the power conferred by subsection (2)(aa).".

p.1442, *annotation to the Social Security (Scotland) Act 2018 s.52A (Re-determination and appeal deadlines)*

5.068 Contrary to what is stated in the main work, ss.52A and 52B are not temporary. They were introduced by way of amendment rather than modification and so, although the provision introducing them expired on September 29, 2020, they remain effective. However, of course, they have effect only insofar as delay "is related to coronavirus". Section 1 of the Coronavirus (Scotland) Act 2020, which defines "coronavirus" as "severe acute respiratory syndrome coronavirus 2 (SARS-CoV-2)" and is applied for these purposes by ss.52A(4) and 52B(4), remains in force.

p.1443, *movement and renumbering of the Social Security (Scotland) Act 2018 s.53 (Duty to inform about possible eligibility)*

5.069 With effect from July 26, 2021, the Social Security Administration and Tribunal Membership (Scotland) Act 2020 (Commencement No.2) Regulations 2021 (SSI 2021/232) brought into force ss.9 and 10 of the 2020 Act. Section 9 of the 2020 Act modified the 2018 Act by moving s.53 to after s.84B, renumbering it as s.84C and amending it (see below). Section 10 of the 2020 Act provides that anything done under s.53 of the 2018 Act is to be treated as having been done under section 84C of that Act, and that any reference to s.53 in any enactment or other document is to be read accordingly.

pp.1443-1444, *amendment to the Social Security (Scotland) Act 2018 s.54 (Obligation to provide information on request)*

5.070 With effect from July 26, 2021, the Social Security Administration and Tribunal Membership (Scotland) Act 2020 (Commencement No.2) Regulations 2021 (SSI 2021/232) brought into force s.12 of the 2020 Act, subss.(1) and (3) of which modify s.54 of the 2018 Act.
In subs.(1), for paras. (a) and (b) there are substituted—

"(a) the Scottish Ministers are either—
    (i) determining an individual's entitlement to assistance (whether under section 37 or 43), or
    (ii) considering whether regulations under section 52 require them to make a determination of an individual's entitlement to assistance without receiving an application, and
(b) they require further information in order to satisfy themselves about any matter material to the making of the determination of entitlement or (as the case may be) to their consideration of whether they are required to make a determination without receiving an application,",

After subs.(1), there is inserted—

"(1A) If—
    (a) the Scottish Ministers are either—
        (i) determining the individual's entitlement to a type of assistance that the individual has ongoing entitlement to, or

(ii) considering whether regulations under section 52 require them to make a determination of the individual's entitlement to assistance without receiving an application,

(b) the individual fails to provide the requested information by the end of the period specified under subsection (1), and

(c) it is the first time that the individual has failed to provide the Scottish Ministers with the requested information within a specified period since they began making the determination or considering the matter mentioned in paragraph (a)(ii),

the Scottish Ministers may issue a decision to suspend the assistance to the individual in accordance with regulations under section 51(2)(aa).

(1B) Where the Scottish Ministers issue such a decision, they must, at the same time, request that the individual provide them with the information within such further period as they specify.",

In subs.(2), for "specified period" there is substituted "the period specified under subsection (1) or (1B)".

After subs.(3), there is inserted—

"(4) The reference in subsection (1A)(a) to an individual having ongoing entitlement to a type of assistance is to an individual being entitled to be given the type of assistance in question under section 24 under a determination made on the basis that the individual has ongoing entitlement to that type of assistance.".

p.1447, *insertion of the Social Security (Scotland) Act 2018 s.62A (Non-disclosure of health information)*

With effect from July 26, 2021, the Social Security Administration and Tribunal Membership (Scotland) Act 2020 (Commencement No. 2) Regulations 2021 (SSI 2021/232) brought into force s.3 of the 2020 Act, which inserts s.62A into the 2018 Act—   5.071

"Non-disclosure of health information

Non-disclosure of information about individual's health

62A.—(1) This section applies in relation to a duty of the Scottish Ministers arising from section 38(5), 40(1), 41(6), 42(2), 44(1) or 53(2) to inform a person ("the recipient") of certain things in connection with the determination of an individual's entitlement to assistance.

(2) Nothing in the duty is to be regarded as requiring the Scottish Ministers to disclose information if subsection (3) applies to it.

(3) This subsection applies to information if—

(a) it relates to the physical or mental health of the individual, and

(b) a registered medical practitioner or a registered nurse has informed the Scottish Ministers that disclosure of the information would be likely to cause serious harm to the physical or mental health of the recipient.".

p.1449, *repeal of the Social Security (Scotland) Act 2018 s.68 (First-tier Tribunal's jurisdiction)*

5.072   With effect from November 11, 2020, s.14 of the Social Security Administration and Tribunal Membership (Scotland) Act 2020 repealed this section and replaced it with by s.87A, which is omitted from the main work but provides for more extensive powers to transfer to the First-tier Tribunal the sheriff's jurisdiction in relation to the recovery of overpayments of benefits payable under this Act. On September 30, 2021, the Scottish Government launched a consultation on proposals to exercise those powers.

p.1450, *movement and renumbering of the Social Security (Scotland) Act 2018 ss.77 and 78 (Uprating for inflation)*

5.073   With effect from October 11, 2021, the Social Security Administration and Tribunal Membership (Scotland) Act 2020 (Commencement No. 3) Regulations 2021 (SSI 2021/338) brought into force s.7 of the 2020 Act which modified the 2018 Act by deleting Chapter 7 of Part 2 and moving ss. 77 and 78 to after s.86, renumbering them as ss. 86A and 86B and amending them. Section 8 of the 2020 Act (brought into force with effect from 20 November 2021 by the Social Security Administration and Tribunal Membership (Scotland) Act 2020 (Commencement No. 4) Regulations 2021 (SSI 2021/352)) provides that anything done under s.77 or s.78 of the 2018 Act is to be treated as having been done under s.86A or s.86B of that Act, respectively, and that any reference to s.77 or s.78 in any enactment or other document is to be read accordingly.

p.1452, *amendment to the Social Security (Scotland) Act 2018 s.81 (Carer's Allowance Supplement)*

5.074   With effect from November 16, 2021, s.1 of the Carer's Allowance Supplement (Scotland) Act 2021 amends s.81 of the 2018 Act by inserting "(but see also subsection (4B))" after "formula" in subs.(4) and inserting after that subsection (in place of subs.(4A) which has expired)—

   "(4B) The amount of a carer's allowance supplement in respect of the period of 1 October 2021 to 31 March 2022 is £231.40 greater than that calculated according to the formula in subsection (4).".

See the annotation below.

p.1454, *annotation to the Social Security (Scotland) Act 2018 s.81 (Carer's Allowance Supplement)*

5.075   The modifications to s.81 made by the Coronavirus (Scotland) (No.2) Act 2020 expired at the end of September 30, 2021 (see s.2(8)(b) of the Coronavirus (Extension and Expiry) (Scotland) Act 2021). In any event, the period covered by subs.(4A) had ended on September 30, 2020. The amount of a carer's allowance supplement for the period 1 April to 30

September 2021 was therefore only the £231.40 calculated under the formula in subs.(4), but the effect of the new subs.(4B), inserted by s.1 of the Carer's Allowance Supplement (Scotland) Act 2021, is to double that amount in respect of the period from 1 October 2021 to 30 March 2022, "in recognition of the pressures unpaid carers face because of the pandemic" (*https://www.mygov.scot/carers-allowance-supplement*). Section 2 of that Act will insert a subs.(4C) giving Scottish Ministers a permanent power, subject to the affirmative procedure in the Scottish Parliament, to make regulations modifying this section "so as to provide that the amount of a carer's allowance supplement in respect of such period as may be specified in the regulations is an amount greater than the amount calculated according to the formula in subsection (4)", but it has not yet been brought into force.

p.1454, *insertion of the Social Security (Scotland) Act 2018 s.84C (Duty to inform about possible eligibility)*

With effect from July 26, 2021, the Social Security Administration and Tribunal Membership (Scotland) Act 2020 (Commencement No. 2) Regulations 2021 (SSI 2021/232) brought into force ss.9 and 10 of the 2020 Act. Section 9 of the 2020 Act modified the 2018 Act by moving s.53 to after s.84B, renumbering it as s.84C and amending it as follows (amendments in square brackets)— 5.076

"Identifying possible eligibility

Duty to inform about possible eligibility

84C.—(1) Subsection (2) applies if, in the course of their making a determination of an individual's entitlement to assistance [under Part 2 or (as the case may be) regulations under section 79,], it appears to the Scottish Ministers that the individual may be eligible for other assistance.

(2) The Scottish Ministers must—

(a) inform the individual that the individual may be eligible for the other assistance, and

(b) either—

(i) provide the individual with information about how to apply for it, or

(ii) if regulations under section 52 [, or (as the case may be) section 79] so allow, ask the individual whether they should proceed with making a determination of the individual's entitlement to the other assistance without receiving an application.

(3) Subsection (2)(b)(ii) does not preclude the Scottish Ministers from requesting further information under section 54(1) [, or (as the case may be) regulations under section 79] for the purpose of determining the individual's entitlement to the other assistance.

(4) In this section, "other assistance" means—

[(a) where the determination mentioned in subsection (1) relates to an individual's entitlement to assistance under Part 2—

>> (i) a different type of assistance described in Chapter 2 of that Part from the type of assistance that the determination mentioned in subsection (1) relates to,
>> (ii) the same type of assistance as that determination relates to, but in respect of a different period or (as the case may be) event, or
>> (iii) assistance under regulations under section 79,
>
> (b) where the determination mentioned in subsection (1) relates to an individual's entitlement to assistance under regulations under section 79—
>> (i) a different type of assistance described in regulations under section 79 from the type of assistance that the determination mentioned in subsection (1) relates to,
>> (ii) the same type of assistance as that determination relates to, but in respect of a different period or (as the case may be) event, or
>> (iii) a type of assistance described in Chapter 2 of Part 2.]".

By virtue of s.10 of the Social Security Administration and Tribunal Membership (Scotland) Act 2020, anything done under s.53 of the 2018 Act is to be treated as having been done under section 84C of that Act, and any reference to s.53 in any enactment or other document is to be read accordingly.

p.1458, *annotation to the Social Security (Scotland) Act 2018 s.85B (Appointment of person to act in other circumstances)*

5.077   Section 85B is not yet fully in force. Only subss.(1) to (11) came into force on December 23, 2020 and then only in connection with child payment and only where the condition in s.85B(3)(b) is met (see the Social Security Administration and Tribunal Membership (Scotland) Act 2020 (Commencement No.1) Regulations 2020 (SSI 2020/422) reg.3). It will come more fully into force on January 24, 2022, when s.58 will be repealed, but it will still not come into force for the purpose of enabling appointments to be made under subss.(3)(a) and (4) (see the Social Security Administration and Tribunal Membership (Scotland) Act 2020 (Commencement No. 5 and Transitional Provisions) Regulations 2021 (SSI 2021/442) reg.2(b)).

p.1458, *insertion of the Social Security (Scotland) Act 2018 s.85C (Guidelines for decisions about appointees) and ss.86A and 86B (Uprating for inflation)*

5.078   With effect from July 26, 2021, the Social Security Administration and Tribunal Membership (Scotland) Act 2020 (Commencement No. 2) Regulations 2021 (SSI 2021/232) brought into force s.2(5) of the 2020 Act, which inserts s.85C into the 2018 Act—

"Guidelines for decisions about appointees

85C.—(1) The Scottish Ministers—

(a) must prepare guidelines governing their decisions in connection with appointments under sections 85A and 85B,

(b) may revise the guidelines,

(c) must make the latest version of the guidelines publicly available by such means as they consider appropriate.

(2) The guidelines must, in particular, set out—

(a) the steps that the Scottish Ministers will take to determine that a person is suitable for appointment,

(b) how a request that an appointment be made or terminated may be made and how it will be handled,

(c) the process by which persons with an interest in the making or termination of an appointment will be involved in those decisions,

(d) the steps that the Scottish Ministers will take to review appointments periodically (being in any case no more than 5 years) and the process by which that will occur,

(e) how concerns about the acts, or omissions, of an appointee may be raised and how any concerns raised will be handled.

(3) In preparing or revising the guidelines, the Scottish Ministers must have regard (among other things) to the following considerations—

(a) that an appointment in the case of a living individual should be made only if it appears to secure a benefit in respect of the individual that cannot reasonably be achieved without the appointment,

(b) that such an appointment should last for only so long as it continues to secure that benefit,

(c) that, so far as reasonably practicable, before decisions are made—

(i) persons who may be affected are consulted, and

(ii) due account is taken of their views (or, if they are incapable within the meaning of the Adults with Incapacity (Scotland) Act 2000, their wishes and feelings),

(d) that decisions should be made on the basis of good information,

(e) that decision-making processes should, so far as reasonably practicable, take account of the circumstances of individual cases,

(f) that persons who may be affected by decisions are given adequate information and support in relation to their involvement in the decision-making process.

(4) In preparing or revising the guidelines, the Scottish Ministers must consult—

(a) the Commissioner for Children and Young People in Scotland,

(b) the Mental Welfare Commission for Scotland,

    (c) the Public Guardian (established by section 6 of the Adults with Incapacity (Scotland) Act 2000), and

    (d) local authorities.".

Section 86 of the 2018 Act is not yet in force.

With effect from October 11, 2021, the Social Security Administration and Tribunal Membership (Scotland) Act 2020 (Commencement No. 3) Regulations 2021 (SSI 2021/338) brought into force s.7 of the 2020 Act which modified the 2018 Act by deleting Chapter 7 of Part 2 and moving ss. 77 and 78 to after s.86, renumbering them as ss. 86A and 86B and amending them. Section 8 of the 2020 Act (brought into force with effect from 20 November 2021 by the Social Security Administration and Tribunal Membership (Scotland) Act 2020 (Commencement No. 4) Regulations 2021 (SSI 2021/352)) provides that anything done under s.77 or s.78 of the 2018 Act is to be treated as having been done under s.86A or s.86B of that Act, respectively and that any reference to s.77 or s.78 in any enactment or other document is to be read accordingly. Sections 86A and 86B are omitted from this work.

pp.1460–1462, *amendment to the Social Security (Scotland) Act 2018 Sch.2 (Carer's assistance regulations)*

5.079   With effect from July 26, 2021, the Social Security Administration and Tribunal Membership (Scotland) Act 2020 (Commencement No.2) Regulations 2021 (SSI 2021/232) brought into force s.13 of the 2020 Act, subs.(1) and (2) of which modify Sch.2 of the 2018 Act.

After para.11, there is inserted—

"Power to set value of assistance as nil

11A.—(1) Provision may be made in the regulations for the value of the carer's assistance that is to be given to an individual in respect of a period to be £0, but—

    (a) such provision must be framed so as to apply by reference to at least one of the following matters—

        (i) the individual being resident and present in a particular place during the period,

        (ii) the individual being in receipt of another type of assistance (whether under this Act or another enactment) during the period, and

    (b) the Scottish Ministers may only make such provision where they consider that it would be in the interests of the individuals to whom it applies to be entitled to carer's assistance with a value of £0 in respect of a period rather than not being entitled to carer's assistance at all.

(2) Nothing in sub-paragraph (1)(a) is to be taken to preclude provision being framed so as to apply by reference to further matters in addition to those mentioned there.".

In para.12(b), for "paragraph 11" there is substituted "paragraphs 11 and 11A".

pp.1464-1467, *amendment to the Social Security (Scotland) Act 2018 Sch.5 (Disability assistance regulations)*

With effect from July 26, 2021, the Social Security Administration and Tribunal Membership (Scotland) Act 2020 (Commencement No.2) Regulations 2021 (SSI 2021/232) brought into force ss.11 and 13 of the 2020 Act which modify Sch.5 of the 2018 Act.   **5.080**

Part 1 of the Schedule is modified by s.11 of the 2020 Act.

In para.1(2), for "a registered medical practitioner" there is substituted "an appropriate healthcare professional".

After para.1(2), there is inserted—

"(2A) The regulations may provide that, in the situation mentioned in sub-paragraph (2B), an individual who is not resident in the United Kingdom is to be regarded as having a terminal illness despite the clinical judgement described in sub-paragraph (2) not having been formed with regard to the guidance mentioned in sub-paragraph (3).

(2B) The situation referred to in sub-paragraph (2A) is that it would not be reasonable in the circumstances to insist on a clinical judgement being provided that has been formed with regard to the guidance.

(2C) The regulations are to define "appropriate healthcare professional" for the purpose of determining entitlement to disability assistance on the basis of an individual having a terminal illness.

(2D) In defining "appropriate healthcare professional" the regulations—

(a) must provide that being a registered medical practitioner or registered nurse is a requirement for being an appropriate healthcare professional,

(b) may provide that being a registered member of a healthcare profession otherwise than as mentioned in paragraph (a) is a requirement for being an appropriate healthcare professional,

(c) may include additional requirements that a person must satisfy in order to be an appropriate healthcare professional, including by reference to a person's—

    (i) skills, training, qualifications and experience,

    (ii) professional relationship to the individual in question,

    (iii) being authorised to act as an appropriate healthcare professional in relation to the individual in question by—

        (A) a Health Board constituted under section 2(1)(a) of the National Health Service (Scotland) Act 1978,

        (B) a Special Health Board constituted under section 2(1)(b) of that Act,

        (C) the Scottish Ministers.

(d) may make different provision about the requirements for being an appropriate healthcare professional for the purposes of determining the entitlement to disability assistance of individuals who are resident in the United Kingdom and those who are not.",

For para.1(3), there is substituted—

"(3) The Chief Medical Officer of the Scottish Administration is—
  (a) to prepare and from time to time revise, and
  (b) to make publicly available by such means as the Chief Medical Officer considers appropriate,
guidance that sets out when a progressive disease can reasonably be expected to cause an individual's death for the purpose of determining entitlement to disability assistance.

(4) Before preparing or revising guidance under sub-paragraph (3), the Chief Medical Officer must consult appropriate healthcare professionals (as defined in sub-paragraph (2C)) who are registered in the United Kingdom as members of a healthcare profession.".

In para.10, for "a registered medical practitioner" there is substituted "an appropriate healthcare professional (see paragraph 1(2C))".

Part 2 of the schedule is modified by s.13(1) and (3) of the 2020 Act.

After para.14, there is inserted—

"Power to set value of assistance as nil

14A.—(1) Provision may be made in the regulations for the value of the disability assistance that is to be given to an individual in respect of a period to be £0, but—
  (a) such provision must be framed so as to apply by reference to at least one of the following matters—
    (i) the individual being resident and present in a particular place during the period,
    (ii) the individual being in receipt of another type of assistance (whether under this Act or another enactment) during the period, and
  (b) the Scottish Ministers may only make such provision where they consider that it would be in the interests of the individuals to whom it applies to be entitled to disability assistance with a value of £0 in respect of a period rather than not being entitled to disability assistance at all.

(2) Nothing in sub-paragraph (1)(a) is to be taken to preclude provision being framed so as to apply by reference to further matters in addition to those mentioned there.".

In para.19, after sub-para.(c) there is inserted—

"(ca) paragraph 14A in Chapter 1 of Part 2,".

p.1467, *annotation to the Social Security (Scotland) Act 2018 Sch.5 (Disability assistance regulations)*

The Disability Assistance Regulations 2021 (see Part I of this Supple-   **5.081** ment) are made under this schedule and came into force on July 26, 2021.

p.1471, *insertion of the Social Security (Scotland) Act 2018 Sch.11 (Suspension of assistance)*

With effect from July 26, 2021, the Social Security Administration and   **5.082** Tribunal Membership (Scotland) Act 2020 (Commencement No.2) Regulations 2021 (SSI 2021/232) brought into force s.12 of the 2020 Act, subss.(1) and (4) of which insert Sch.11 into the 2018 Act.

"SCHEDULE 1

(introduced by section 51)

SUSPENSION OF ASSISTANCE

Circumstances in which assistance may be suspended

1.—(1) The regulations may provide for an individual's assistance to be suspended in the following circumstances only—
  (a) under section 54(1A) the Scottish Ministers have issued a decision to suspend assistance to the individual due to a failure to provide information which the individual is yet to provide,
  (b) where the Scottish Ministers have made arrangements (whether under section 85A, 85B or otherwise) for a person to receive the assistance on the individual's behalf, and the Ministers consider that it is necessary to suspend the assistance—
    (i) in order to protect the individual from the risk of financial abuse,
    (ii) because the person with whom the Ministers have made arrangements is unable to continue to receive the assistance, or
    (iii) for any other reason specified in the regulations, or
  (c) the individual has requested that the Scottish Ministers temporarily stop giving the assistance in question and is yet to request that they resume doing so.

(2) For the purpose of sub-sub-paragraph (1)(b), "financial abuse" includes—
  (a) having money or other property stolen,
  (b) being defrauded,
  (c) being put under pressure in relation to money or other property,
  (d) having money or other property misused.

Safeguards: requirement to consider financial circumstances before suspension

2. The regulations must require the Scottish Ministers, before suspending the assistance given to an individual, to have regard to the financial circumstances of the individual.

Safeguards: right to review suspension

3. The regulations must confer a right on an individual whose assistance has been suspended to require the Scottish Ministers to review their decision to suspend the individual's assistance.

Safeguards: information to be given following suspension

4.—(1) The regulations must require the Scottish Ministers to inform an individual whose assistance they have suspended—
  (a) of their decision to suspend the individual's assistance,
  (b) of the reasons for their decision,
  (c) of any steps which might be taken by the individual in order for the Scottish Ministers to consider ending the suspension, and
  (d) of the individual's right in accordance with the regulations to require the Scottish Ministers to review their decision to suspend the individual's assistance.

(2) The regulations must provide that the Scottish Ministers are to fulfil the duty described by sub-paragraph (1) in a way that leaves the individual with a record of the information which the individual can show to, or otherwise share with, others.

Safeguards: effect of suspension ending

5. The regulations must provide that when—
  (a) the suspension of an individual's assistance ends, and
  (b) under the latest determination of the individual's entitlement to the type of assistance in question, the individual would have become entitled to be given assistance during the period of the suspension,
the individual is immediately to be given under section 24 the assistance that the individual would have become entitled to be given under the determination during that period.

Generality of enabling power unaffected

6. Nothing in this schedule is to be taken to limit the provision that may be included in the regulations except to the extent stated.

Interpretation

7. In this schedule—
  (a) references to an individual's assistance being suspended are to an individual, by virtue of the regulations, not becoming entitled to be given some or all of the assistance in respect of a period that the individual otherwise would at the time, or times, prescribed by regulations under section 51(2)(a),

(b) "the regulations" means regulations under section 51(1).".

pp.1481–1482, *amendment to the Early Years Assistance (Best Start Grants) (Scotland) Regulations 2018 (SSI 2018/370) Sch.2 para.4 (Pregnancy and Baby Grant–Residence requirement)*

With effect from December 31, 2020, reg.3(1) and (2) of the Social Security Co-ordination (EU Exit) (Scotland) (Amendment etc.) Regulations 2020 (SSI 2020/399) substituted "or the Isle of Man" for ", the Isle of Man, the European Economic Area or Switzerland" in head (a) of para.4(2) of Sch.2 and inserted after that head—   5.083

"(aa)   a person who, or has a partner who, is habitually resident in the European Economic Area or Switzerland and—
   (i) is a qualified person within the meaning of regulation 6(1)(a) (jobseeker), (b) (worker), (c) (self-employed person), (d) (self-sufficient person) or (e) (student) of the Immigration (European Economic Area) Regulations 2016 (the EEA Regulations);
   (ii) retains the status referred to in sub-head (i) pursuant to regulation 6(2) or (4) of the EEA Regulations;
   (iii) is a family member of a person referred to in sub-head (i) or (ii) within the meaning of regulation 7(1) of the EEA Regulations;
   (iv) has a right to reside permanently in the United Kingdom by virtue of regulation 15(1) of the EEA Regulations; or
   (v) has been granted indefinite or limited leave to enter, or remain in, the United Kingdom under the Immigration Act 1971 by virtue of Appendix EU to the immigration rules made under section 3(2) of that Act.".

With effect from September 15, 2021, reg.3(1) and (2) of the Social Security (Residence Requirements) (Afghanistan) (Scotland) Regulations 2021 (SSI 2021/320) inserts, after head (aa) of para.4(2), a new head (ab)—

"(ab)   a person who—
   (i) leave to enter or remain in the United Kingdom granted under the immigration rules made under section 3(2) of the Immigration Act 1971, by virtue of—
      (ia) the Afghan Relocations and Assistance Policy, or
      (ib) the previous scheme for locally-employed staff in Afghanistan (sometimes referred to as the ex-gratia scheme),
   (ii) has been granted discretionary leave outside the immigration rules as a dependant of a person referred to in sub-head (i), or
   (iii) has leave granted under the Afghan Citizens Resettlement Scheme."

and also, after para. 4(2), inserts—

"(3) In this paragraph, "the Afghan Citizens Resettlement Scheme" means the scheme announced by the United Kingdom Government on 18 August 2021.".

The word "has" is obviously missing from the beginning of head (ab)(i).

pp.1484–1485, *amendment to the Early Years Assistance (Best Start Grants) (Scotland) Regulations 2018 (SSI 2018/370) I 2018/370) Sch.3 para.3 (Early Learning Grant–Residence requirement)*

5.084   With effect from December 31, 2020, reg.3(1) and (3) of the Social Security Co-ordination (EU Exit) (Scotland) (Amendment etc.) Regulations 2020 (SSI 2020/399) substituted "or the Isle of Man" for ", the Isle of Man, the European Economic Area or Switzerland" in head (a) of para.3(2) of Sch.3 and inserted after that head—

"(aa) a person who, or has a partner who, is habitually resident in the European Economic Area or Switzerland and—
  (i) is a qualified person within the meaning of regulation 6(1)(a) (jobseeker), (b) (worker), (c) (self-employed person), (d) (self-sufficient person) or (e) (student) of the Immigration (European Economic Area) Regulations 2016 (the EEA Regulations);
  (ii) retains the status referred to in sub-head (i) pursuant to regulation 6(2) or (4) of the EEA Regulations;
  (iii) is a family member of a person referred to in sub-head (i) or (ii) within the meaning of regulation 7(1) of the EEA Regulations;
  (iv) has a right to reside permanently in the United Kingdom by virtue of regulation 15(1) of the EEA Regulations; or
  (v) has been granted indefinite or limited leave to enter, or remain in, the United Kingdom under the Immigration Act 1971 by virtue of Appendix EU to the immigration rules made under section 3(2) of that Act.".

With effect from September 15, 2021, reg.3(1) and (3) of the Social Security (Residence Requirements) (Afghanistan) (Scotland) Regulations 2021 (SSI 2021/320) inserts, after head (aa) of para.3(3), a new head (ab)—

"(ab) a person who—
  (i) leave to enter or remain in the United Kingdom granted under the immigration rules made under section 3(2) of the Immigration Act 1971, by virtue of—
    (ia) the Afghan Relocations and Assistance Policy, or
    (ib) the previous scheme for locally-employed staff in Afghanistan (sometimes referred to as the ex-gratia scheme),

(ii) has been granted discretionary leave outside the immigration rules as a dependant of a person referred to in sub-head (i), or

(iii) has leave granted under the Afghan Citizens Resettlement Scheme."

and also, after para.3(2), inserts—

"(3) In this paragraph, "the Afghan Citizens Resettlement Scheme" means the scheme announced by the United Kingdom Government on 18 August 2021.".

pp.1486-1487, *amendment to the Early Years Assistance (Best Start Grants) (Scotland) Regulations 2018 (SSI 2018/370) Sch.4 para.4 (School-age Grant– Residence requirement)*

With effect from December 31, 2020, reg.3(1) and (4) of the Social Security Co-ordination (EU Exit) (Scotland) (Amendment etc.) Regulations 2020 (SSI 2020/399) substituted "or the Isle of Man" for ", the Isle of Man, the European Economic Area or Switzerland" in head (a) of para.4(2) of Sch.4 and inserted after that head— 5.085

"(aa) a person who, or has a partner who, is habitually resident in the European Economic Area or Switzerland and—
(i) is a qualified person within the meaning of regulation 6(1)(a) (jobseeker), (b) (worker), (c) (self-employed person), (d) (self-sufficient person) or (e) (student) of the Immigration (European Economic Area) Regulations 2016 (the EEA Regulations);
(ii) retains the status referred to in sub-head (i) pursuant to regulation 6(2) or (4) of the EEA Regulations;
(iii) is a family member of a person referred to in sub-head (i) or (ii) within the meaning of regulation 7(1) of the EEA Regulations;
(iv) has a right to reside permanently in the United Kingdom by virtue of regulation 15(1) of the EEA Regulations; or
(v) has been granted indefinite or limited leave to enter, or remain in, the United Kingdom under the Immigration Act 1971 by virtue of Appendix EU to the immigration rules made under section 3(2) of that Act.".

With effect from September 15, 2021, reg.3(1) and (4) of the Social Security (Residence Requirements) (Afghanistan) (Scotland) Regulations 2021 (SSI 2021/320) inserts, after head (aa) of para.4(2), a new head (ab)–

"(ab) a person who—
(i) leave to enter or remain in the United Kingdom granted under the immigration rules made under section 3(2) of the Immigration Act 1971, by virtue of—
(ia) the Afghan Relocations and Assistance Policy, or

(ib) the previous scheme for locally-employed staff in Afghanistan (sometimes referred to as the ex-gratia scheme),

(ii) has been granted discretionary leave outside the immigration rules as a dependant of a person referred to in sub-head (i), or

(iii) has leave granted under the Afghan Citizens Resettlement Scheme."

and also, after para.4(2), inserts—

"(3) In this paragraph, "the Afghan Citizens Resettlement Scheme" means the scheme announced by the United Kingdom Government on 18 August 2021.".

p.1493, *amendment to the Funeral Expense Assistance (Scotland) Regulations 2019 (SSI 2019/292) reg.9 (Residence conditions, place of funeral and status)*

5.086 The number of the Social Security Co-ordination (EU Exit) (Scotland) (Amendment etc.) Regulations 2020, which substituted reg.9(3), is SSI 2020/399 and the amendment came into effect on December 31, 2020.

pp.1501-1503, *amendment to Carer's Assistance (Young Carer Grants) (Scotland) Regulations 2019 (SSI 2019/324) reg.8 (Conditions relating to residence)*

5.087 With effect from September 15, 2021, reg.5 of the Social Security (Residence Requirements) (Afghanistan) (Scotland) Regulations 2021 (SSI 2021/320) inserts—

"(aa) a person who—
(i) has leave to enter or remain in the United Kingdom granted under the immigration rules made under section 3(2) of the Immigration Act 1971, by virtue of—
(ia) the Afghan Relocations and Assistance Policy, or
(ib) the previous scheme for locally-employed staff in Afghanistan (sometimes referred to as the ex-gratia scheme),
(ii) has been granted discretionary leave outside the immigration rules as a dependant of a person referred to in sub-head (i), or
(iii) has leave granted under the Afghan Citizens Resettlement Scheme."

It also inserts, as the first definition in para.(10)—
""the Afghan Citizens Resettlement Scheme" means the scheme announced by the United Kingdom Government on 18 August 2021.".

p.1527, *amendment to the Winter Heating Assistance for Children and Young People (Scotland) Regulations 2020 (SSI 2020/352) reg.2 (Interpretation)*

With effect from July 26, 2021, reg.18(1) and (2) of the Disability Assistance for Children and Young People (Consequential Amendment and Transitional Provision) (Scotland) Regulations 2021 (SSI 2021/73) inserts new definitions into reg.2 of the 2020 Regulations— 5.088

"the 2021 Regulations" means the Disability Assistance for Children and Young People (Scotland) Regulations 2021,

"Child Disability Payment" means disability assistance for children and young people given in accordance with the 2021 Regulations.

With effect from November 16, 2021, reg.2(1) and (2) of the Winter Heating Assistance for Children and Young People (Scotland) Amendment Regulations 2021 (SSI 2021/415) inserts further definitions into reg.2 of the 2020 Regulations—

"the 2013 Regulations" means the Social Security (Personal Independence Payment) Regulations 2013,

"the 2016 Regulations" means the Personal Independence Payment Regulations (Northern Ireland) 2016,

"first qualifying week" means the qualifying week in the same calendar year these Regulations came into force,

"Personal Independence Payment" means personal independence payment under—

(a) Part 4 of the Welfare Reform Act 2012, or

(b) article 82 of the Welfare Reform (Northern Ireland) Order 2015.

p.1528, *amendment to the Winter Heating Assistance for Children and Young People (Scotland) Regulations 2020 (SSI 2020/352) reg.4 (Eligibility rules for child winter heating assistance)*

With effect from July 26, 2021, reg.18(1) and (3) of the Disability Assistance for Children and Young People (Consequential Amendment and Transitional Provision) (Scotland) Regulations 2021 (SSI 2021/73) amends reg.4 of the 2020 Regulations. Amendments made to paras. (1)(b) and (2) have been overtaken by later amendments (see below) but, in addition, there were inserted after para.(2)— 5.089

"(3) For the purposes of the rule in paragraph (1)(b)(ii), an individual is to be treated as being entitled to receive payment even if, throughout the qualifying week—

(a) regulation 17(2) (effect of admission to a care home on ongoing entitlement to care component) of the 2021 Regulations applies to the individual, or

(b) regulation 20 (entitlement beginning while in alternative accommodation) of the 2021 Regulations applies to the individual due to the individual being resident in a care home.

(4) In paragraph (3), "care home" has the meaning given in regulation 2 of the 2021 Regulations.".

With effect from November 16, 2021, reg.2(1) and (3) of the Winter Heating Assistance for Children and Young People (Scotland) Amendment Regulations 2021 (SSI 2021/415) substitutes for para.(1)(b)—

"(b) entitled to receive payment of—
    (i) the highest rate of the care component of—
        (aa) Disability Living Allowance, or
        (bb) Child Disability Payment, or
    (ii) the enhanced rate of the daily living component of Personal Independence Payment, and".

In para.(2), for what was originally "paragraph (1)(b)" and had become from July 26, 2021 "paragraph (1)(b)(i)", there is substituted "paragraph (1)(b)(i)(aa)" and, after "week," there is inserted "regulation 8 (Hospitalisation of persons aged 18 or over), or". In para.(3) (see above), for "paragraph (1)(b)(ii)" there is substituted "paragraph (1)(b)(i)(bb)". After para.(4) (see above), there is inserted—

"(5) For the purposes of the rule in paragraph (1)(b)(ii), an individual is to be treated as being entitled to receive payment even if, throughout the qualifying week—
    (a) regulation 28 (care home residents) of either the 2013 Regulations or the 2016 Regulations applies to the individual due to the individual being resident in a care home, or
    (b) regulation 29 (hospital in-patients aged 18 or over) of either the 2013 Regulations or the 2016 Regulations applies to the individual due to the individual being an in-patient in hospital.
(6) In paragraph (5)—
    (a) "care home" has the meaning given in section 85(3) of the Welfare Reform Act 2012 or article 90(3) of the Welfare Reform Act (Northern Ireland) Order 2015, and
    (b) "hospital" has the meaning given in regulation 29 of the 2013 Regulations or regulation 29 of the 2016 Regulations.
(7) An individual is entitled to be paid child winter heating assistance in respect of the first qualifying week if it appears to the Scottish Ministers from information available to them that the individual would have been entitled to be paid child winter heating assistance had the requirement in regulation 4(1)(b)(ii) had effect beginning with the day upon which these Regulations came into force.".

p.1528, *amendment to the Winter Heating Assistance for Children and Young People (Scotland) Regulations 2020 (SSI 2020/352) reg.5 (Determination of entitlement to child winter heating assistance without application)*

5.090   With effect from November 16, 2021, reg.2(1) and (4) of the Winter Heating Assistance for Children and Young People (Scotland) Amendment Regulations 2021 (SSI 2021/415) amends reg.5 by omitting "by the end of December in any year".

p.1529, *amendment to the Winter Heating Assistance for Children and Young People (Scotland) Regulations 2020 (SSI 2020/352) reg.8 (Determination following backdated award of assistance)*

With effect from July 26, 2021, reg.18(1) and (4) of the Disability   5.091
Assistance for Children and Young People (Consequential Amendment and Transitional Provision) (Scotland) Regulations 2021 (SSI 2021/73) amended reg.8(b) of the 2020 Regulations by substituting a new version of sub-para.(b)(i) but that has now itself been substituted, with effect from November 16, 2021, by reg.2(1) and (5) of the Winter Heating Assistance for Children and Young People (Scotland) Amendment Regulations 2021 (SSI 2021/415). It now reads—

> "(i) following an appeal, an award of—
>> (aa) the highest rate of the care component of Disability Living Allowance,
>> (bb) the highest rate of the care component of Child Disability Payment, or
>> (cc) the enhanced rate of the daily living component of Personal Independence Payment,
> is made that is a backdated award, and".

pp.1529-1530, *amendment to the Winter Heating Assistance for Children and Young People (Scotland) Regulations 2020 (SSI 2020/352) reg.10 (value and form of child winter heating assistance)*

With effect from November 16, 2021, reg.2(1) and (6) of the Winter   5.092
Heating Assistance for Children and Young People (Scotland) Amendment Regulations 2021 (SSI 2021/415) amends reg.10(1) by substituting for "The value", the words "Subject to paragraph (1A), the value". After para.(1), there is inserted—

> "(1A) Where an individual is entitled to be paid child winter heating assistance by virtue of regulation 4(7), the value of child winter heating assistance payable is the value specified in paragraph (1) as it had effect on the day these Regulations came into force.".

p.1530, *amendment to the Winter Heating Assistance for Children and Young People (Scotland) Regulations 2020 (SSI 2020/352) reg.11 (value and form of child winter heating assistance)*

With effect from November 16, 2021, reg.2(1) and (7) of the Winter   5.093
Heating Assistance for Children and Young People (Scotland) Amendment Regulations 2021 (SSI 2021/415) amends reg.11(1) by substituting for "young person" in each place where it occurs the words "child or young person".

p.1535, *The Carer's Allowance Supplement and Young Carer Grants (Residence Requirements and Procedural Provisions) (EU Exit) (Scotland) Regulations 2020 (SSI 2020/475) Pt 3 and Sch.1*

5.094   The reference to SSI 2020/324 in the entry for reg.11 should be to SSI 2019/324.

The words "Regulation 10" immediately below the entry for Sch.1 are a typographical error and should be ignored.

pp.1548–1549, *annotation to the Tribunals (Scotland) Act 2014 s.1 (Establishment of the Tribunals)*

5.094.1   Since 7 December 2021, provision has been made for a seventh chamber of the First-tier Tribunal. However, it remains the case that only five of the chambers have so far had functions allocated to them. These are the Housing and Property Chamber, the Health and Education Chamber, the General Regulatory Chamber, the Tax Chamber and the Social Security Chamber.

The Mental Health Chamber is expected to take over the functions of the Mental Health Tribunal for Scotland during 2022 and the new Local Taxation Chamber is expected to start receiving cases in January 2023.

pp.1549–1550, *annotation to the Tribunals (Scotland) Act 2014 s.43 (Review of Decisions)*

5.094.2   In *South Lanarkshire Council v Boyd* [2021] UT 31, the Upper Tribunal was content to assume, but not decide, that it should take the same approach when it was reviewing one of its decisions as the First-tier Tribunal should take when exercising its power of review and it referred to *Point West GR Ltd v Bassi* [2020] EWCA Civ 765, where the approach of the United Kingdom Upper Tribunal in *R. (RB) v First-tier Tribunal (Reviews)* [2010] UKUT 160 (AAC); [2010] AACR 41 (mentioned in the annotation in the main work) had been approved.

pp.1551-1553, *annotation to the Tribunals (Scotland) Act 2014 s.46 (Appeal from the Tribunal)*

5.095   In *Cowan v Somasundaram* [2021] UT 4, the Upper Tribunal applied the approach taken in *Advocate General for Scotland v Murray Group Holdings Limited* [2015] CSIH 77; 2016 SC 201 at [39] and held that it is competent for permission to appeal to be granted by the Upper Tribunal on grounds not argued before the First-tier Tribunal, although the Upper Tribunal should be slow to allow such an appeal, particularly where additional findings in fact are required, and should not do so if unfairness results. However, as the grounds advanced on behalf of Mr Cowan were not arguable, he was refused permission to appeal.

By way of contrast, in *Hughes v Glasgow City Council Private Sector* [2021] UT 12, the Appellant had raised a new argument when applying to the First-tier Tribunal for permission to appeal and the First-tier

Tribunal had granted unlimited permission to appeal without giving reasons for considering the point to be arguable. The Upper Tribunal commented that that made it difficult for the Upper Tribunal to rule on the issue and it raised the question whether the First-tier Tribunal could err on an issue that it had not considered or ruled upon, and it also was concerned as to whether the First-tier Tribunal had made sufficient findings to enable the Upper Tribunal to deal with the issue, but in the end it grasped the nettle and did in fact rule on the point of law, deciding it against the appellant.

In *Ostendorf v Rollos Solicitors & Estate Agents* [2021] UT 11, in which the appeal raised a not entirely straightforward point of law and both parties had legal representation, the Upper Tribunal commented—

"Both parties supplied little by way of submission to this Tribunal. The failure of both parties to provide any serious analysis in support of their respective positions in this appeal is disappointing. . . . . It is important that professional representatives make substantive submissions to the Tribunal in appeals of this kind."

Breaches of procedural provisions, such as the duty to provide proper and adequate reasons can amount to errors of law. For the standard of reasoning required from the First-tier Tribunal, see the supplemental annotation to r.29 of the procedural rules in the schedule of the First-tier Tribunal for Scotland Social Security Chamber (Procedure) Regulations 2018, below.

p.1553, *annotation to the Tribunals (Scotland) Act 2014 s.47 (Disposal of an appeal)*

In *New Lanark Hotels Limited v Office of the Scottish Charity Regulator* **5.096** [2020] UT 9 *and New Lanark Trading Limited v Office of the Scottish Charity Regulator* [2020] UT 10, the Upper Tribunal held that when making its own decisions, having found the First-tier Tribunal to have erred in law, it must proceed on the basis of the findings in fact specifically made by the First-tier Tribunal, or obviously arising from its decision (the First-tier Tribunal decision not always clearly discriminating between what was properly stated as a finding in fact and what was a reason) insofar as they were not vitiated by the error of law, but that it was also appropriate, in the exercise of its power under s.47(3)(b) of the 2014 Act, to make additional findings based upon evidence led before the First-tier Tribunal, where such findings were not in any way inconsistent with other findings made, or to be attributed to, the First-tier Tribunal. It was not suggested by the parties that it should hear any additional evidence as the primary facts were not really in dispute. Appeals by the Regulator were subsequently dismissed by the Court of Session (*Office of the Scottish Charity Regulator v New Lanark Hotels Limited and New Lanark Trading Limited* [2021] CSIH 7), the Court emphasising that the Upper Tribunal was required to make a decision "of new" and was not merely exercising a supervisory jurisdiction.

p.1555, *annotation to the Tribunals (Scotland) Act 2014 s.50 (Procedure on second appeal)*

5.096.1   The criteria for giving permission for a second appeal were considered in *South Lanarkshire Council v Boyd* [2021] UT 31, where the Upper Tribunal decided that permission to appeal should be refused even though the would-be appellant had an arguable point of law.

p.1584, *annotation to the First-tier Tribunal for Scotland Social Security Chamber (Procedure) Regulations 2018 (SSI 2018/273) Sch.—r.21 (Response of the decision maker to notice of appeal against a determination of entitlement)*

5.097   The list of amendments should show that paras. (1) and (2) were substituted by the First-tier Tribunal for Scotland Social Security Chamber and Upper Tribunal for Scotland (Allocation of Functions, Procedure and Composition) (Miscellaneous Amendments) Regulations 2020 (SSI 2020/476) reg.5(1) and (3)(d) (December 24, 2020).

p.1586, *annotation to the First-tier Tribunal for Scotland Social Security Chamber (Procedure) Regulations 2018 (SSI 2018/273) Sch.—r.25 (Notice of hearings)*

5.097.1   In *Arshad v Khawaja* [2021] UT 33, a landlord applied for the post-ponement of a hearing scheduled to be heard on 20 February 2021. Both the landlord and the tenant were sent by the First-tier Tribunal a letter saying that the application had been refused for specified reasons but also that the hearing "will therefore go ahead as scheduled on Wednesday, 10 December 2021". The landlord did not attend the hearing, although the tenant did. The landlord subsequently appealed on the ground that he had not attended because he had been misled by the letter. The appeal was allowed, notwithstanding the internal incon-sistency of the letter and the view of the First-tier Tribunal, when refusing permission to appeal, that the landlord should have realised that there had been an error. The Upper Tribunal held that the rule in the procedure regulations for the Housing and Property Chamber that is equivalent to this rule had not been complied with and that "[t]he appellant did not have proper intimation of the date of the hearing following his request to postpone".

p.1588, *annotation to the First-tier Tribunal for Scotland Social Security Chamber (Procedure) Regulations 2018 (SSI 2018/273) Sch.—r.29 (Reasons for decision)*

5.098   In *Wordie Property Co Ltd v Secretary of State for Scotland* 1984 SLT 345 at page 348, it was said that a decision maker was required to—

" . . . give proper and adequate reasons . . . which deal with the sub-stantial questions in issue in an intelligible way. The decision must, in short, leave the informed reader and the court in no real and sub-stantial doubt as to what the reasons for it were and what were the material considerations which were taken into account in reaching it."

A failure by the First-tier Tribunal to give proper and adequate reasons is a breach of r.29 and therefore, if the breach is material, is an error of law. When considering whether the First-tier Tribunal had erred in law in *Midlothian Council v Barr* [2021] UT 17 at [25], the Upper Tribunal adopted the submissions of the appellant's representative, which it had summarised at [15]—

"[15] A decision must leave the informed reader in no real and substantial doubt as to what the reasons for it were and what were the material considerations which were taken into account in reaching it: *Wordie Property Co Ltd v Secretary of State for Scotland* 1984 SLT 345, at pages 347-348. A statement of reasons must identify what the decision maker decided to be the material considerations; must clearly and concisely set out his evaluation of them; and must set out the essence of the reasoning that has led him to his decision: *Ritchie v Aberdeen City Council* 2011 SC 579, Lord President (Gill) at paragraph 12; *JC v Midlothian Council* [2012] CSIH 77, Lord Menzies, paragraph 30, citing *Uprichard v Scottish Ministers* 2012 SC 172, Lord President (Gill) at paragraph 26. It was necessary to read the reasons as a whole: *City of Edinburgh Council v MDN* 2011 SC 513, paragraph 28."

Having found that the First-tier Tribunal's reasons were not adequate in that case, the Upper Tribunal made the following further observations—

"[57] I am conscious that tribunals need to provide reasonably concise and understandable decisions, and with that in mind, make the following additional observations in the context of this case.
[58] The FTT in this case wrote:

"It is not practical, appropriate or necessary to narrate every aspect of the evidence in this written decision. We note that many of the witnesses lodged written mini-CVs to assist the Tribunal. We also were provided with written statements which were entered into evidence."

and

"We do not seek to rehearse all the evidence before us. The Findings of Fact record the evidence we accepted."

[59] Fact-finding tribunals, such as the FTT is in a case of this sort, are under no obligation to narrate all of the evidence led before them, or to narrate in detail all of the evidence they rejected. There is no merit in a mechanistic recital of all of the evidence, and that sort of exercise should be avoided. The FTT does require to bear in mind, however, that the audience for a decision includes not only parties who were present at the hearing, but also, potentially, an appellate tribunal. The FTT's decision is the primary source of information for the appellate tribunal as to what the oral evidence was. It is also important more generally that a reader unconnected with the case should be able

to understand why the decision was made. Anonymised decisions in cases of this type may be published. It is an aspect of open justice that members of the public should be able to see and understand the decisions of tribunals. The provision of comprehensible written reasons contributes to the maintenance of public confidence in the decision making process: *Chief Constable, Lothian and Borders Police v Lothian and Borders Police Board* 2005 SLT 315, paragraph 63.

[60] As I observed in the decision relating to permission to appeal in this case, findings in fact are expressions of a conclusion as to a matter of fact, formed on the basis of evidence. Some of the findings in fact in this case conform to that model. Some, however, include narrations of evidence. A number read "[name of witness] stated . . . ". Some include discussions of the law. Finding in fact 25, for example, is in these terms:

"The burden of proof in this placing request rests with the Authority. The appeal hearing is a full reconsideration of the evidence and it is the current circumstances that apply at the date of the hearing that are relevant."

Others record findings in fact and law, rather than matters of fact, for example:

"The child has additional support needs in terms of section 1 of [the 2004 Act]"

The way in which the findings in fact in this case have been written means that they are less useful than the FTT must have intended in providing an indication as to the evidence that was accepted. In relation to an issue essential to the decision-making process of the tribunal, a decision should set out intelligibly the findings of fact relevant to that matter. Elsewhere in the decision a tribunal should make clear what evidence those findings were based on. Where there has been evidence to contrary effect, the decision should set out also what that evidence was, and why the competing bodies of evidence have, respectively, been accepted and rejected. The FTT should do so as concisely as is consistent with the nature and extent of the evidence in question.

[61] I have already referred to a finding in fact which expressed conclusions about mixed questions of fact and law. Another example is this:

"School A is suited to the ability and aptitude of the child".

I observe that the FTT should have been considering whether it was satisfied that the education normally provided at School A was not suited to the child's age, ability or aptitude. Ideally, findings in fact relevant to an issue of this sort would be factual findings as to the education normally provided at School A, and about the child's ability and his aptitude (and age, if that were a live issue). The reasons for the decision would then go on to explain what those factual findings demonstrated about the suitability or otherwise of that education for the child's age, ability and aptitude.

[62] The reader ought to be able to discern how the evidence related to the facts found, and how the facts found have been employed in considering whether the legal tests have been satisfied. A rigorous focus on the matters of fact relevant to each of the legal tests individually will be helpful in this regard."

In *South Lanarkshire Council v Boyd* [2021] UT 24, the Upper Tribunal followed the approach taken by Lord Hope of Craighead in *AH (Sudan) v Secretary of State for the Home Department* [2007] UKHL 49; [2008] AC 678 at [19], where he said—

"I agree also with what my noble and learned friend Baroness Hale of Richmond says about the caution with which the ordinary courts should approach the decision of an expert tribunal. A decision that is clearly based on a mistake of law must, of course, be corrected. Its reasoning must be explained, but it ought not to be subjected to an unduly critical analysis. As your Lordships have indicated, there are passages in the decision that is before us which might, when read in isolation, suggest that the tribunal misdirected itself. But I am quite satisfied that the decision as a whole was soundly based, and that a more accurate wording of the passages that have attracted criticism would have made no difference to the tribunal's conclusion on the facts that the Secretary of State's refusal of asylum in these cases should be upheld."

At [55] of its decision, the Upper Tribunal said—

"Where, as here, a challenge is based on a failure to give reasons, in some cases quite minimal explanation might suffice; reasons could be stated briefly, and the level of detail required would be dictated by the issues requiring determination. The informed reader should be left in no real or substantial doubt as to why the decision was taken: *Stefan v General Medical Council* [1999] UKPC 10 at [24]; [1999] 1 W.L.R. 1293 at p.1301F; *South Bucks District Council v Porter (No 2)* [2004] UKHL 33; [2004] 1 W.L.R. 1953, paragraph 36. In my view there is no doubt as to why the decision was taken. It also needs to be remembered that the tribunal decision is governed by the evidence and submissions which parties elect to place before it. The tribunal did not have the benefit of the comprehensive submissions made by Mr Upton. The tribunal is obliged to make its decision on the basis of the evidence and submissions which it has before it at the time of the hearing."

It is important to note that the Upper Tribunal referred to evidence as well as submissions. It therefore needs to be borne in mind that issues may arise on the evidence even if no party has explicitly raised them, so that, particularly when litigants are acting in person, a tribunal ought not to confine itself to issues raised in the parties' submissions but ought to address any other questions that are obviously raised by the evidence.

p.1589, *annotation to the First-tier Tribunal for Scotland Social Security Chamber (Procedure) Regulations 2018 (SSI 2018/273) Sch.—r.33 (Application for permission to appeal against a decision of the First-tier Tribunal)*

5.099   In the course of a 45-paragraph refusal of permission to appeal from a decision of the General Regulatory Chamber of the First-tier Tribunal, the Upper Tribunal held in *Doherty v City of Edinburgh Council* [2021] UT 10 that the First-tier Tribunal had been right to refuse permission to appeal on the ground that the applicant had failed to comply with the provision in the relevant procedure rules that was equivalent to r.33(2)(c) of these Rules, because he had not stated the result that he was seeking. The applicant argued that it was obvious what result he was seeking, but the Upper Tribunal held that it was not for the First-tier Tribunal to infer that from the surrounding circumstances.

However, even if that is the correct approach in the General Regulatory Chamber under the procedure rules applicable in that case, it is difficult to see how it could be the correct approach in the Social Security Chamber, where there is an express power under r.6(2) to waive a requirement in these Rules.

Allegations of bias must be properly particularised and appropriately evidenced if permission to appeal is to be given on that ground (*Wilson v Fife Properties Ltd* [2021] UT 27, applying the approach taken in *Singh v Secretary of State for the Home Department* [2016] EWCA Civ 492).

In *Mahmood v Glasgow West Enterprises Ltd* [2021] UT 29, an important document was not sent to the applicant in advance of the hearing before the First-tier Tribunal but, when the applicant was offered an opportunity to apply for an adjournment so that he could consider the document, he declined to do so. The applicant accepted that the First-tier Tribunalís decision was not wrong in law on the evidence that was before it and the Upper Tribunal refused to give permission to appeal in order to allow the applicant to introduce new evidence to challenge the accuracy of the important document.

p.1596, *annotation to Upper Tribunal for Scotland (Social Security Rules of Procedure) Regulations 2018 (SSI 2018/274) Sch.—r.3 (Application for permission to appeal against a decision of the First-tier Tribunal)*

5.100   As the Upper Tribunal made clear in *PD v Midlothian Council* [2021] UT 19 at [10], when a judge is reconsidering under r.3(6) and (7) a refusal of permission to appeal, he or she is not reviewing the earlier decisions of the First-tier Tribunal and the Upper Tribunal to refuse permission; his or her task is simply to decide afresh whether the grounds of appeal disclose an arguable material error of law on the part of the First-tier Tribunal in its substantive decision. The Upper Tribunal was content in *Balloch v Bernisdale Homes Ltd* [2021] UT 34 to consider a ground of appeal that had not been considered by the First-tier Tribunal. Reference was made to *Advocate General for Scotland v Murray Group Holdings Ltd* [2015] CSIH 77; 2016 S.C. 201, but the Upper Tribunal found the relevant ground of appeal to be unarguable and so permission was refused anyway.

PART VI

UPDATING MATERIAL
VOLUME V

INCOME SUPPORT
AND THE LEGACY BENEFITS

Commentary by

John Mesher

Tom Royston

Nick Wikeley

pp.329-330, *amendment to the Income Support (General) Regulations 1987 (SI 1987/1967) reg.21AA (Special cases: supplemental—persons from abroad)*

With effect from September 15, 2021, reg.2 of the Social Security 6.001
(Habitual Residence and Past Presence) (Amendment) Regulations 2021 amended regulation 21AA(4) (which prescribes persons who are not a 'person from abroad'). The amendment inserts before sub-paragraph (za):

"(zza) a person granted leave in accordance with the immigration rules made under section 3(2) of the Immigration Act 1971(10), where such leave is granted by virtue of—
  (i) the Afghan Relocations and Assistance Policy; or
  (ii) the previous scheme for locally-employed staff in Afghanistan (sometimes referred to as the ex-gratia scheme);
  (zzb) a person in Great Britain not coming within sub-paragraph (zza) or (h)(iv) who left Afghanistan in connection with the collapse of the Afghan government that took place on 15th August 2021;".

From the same date the amendment also adds a new Reg 21AA(4) (h)(iv), so sub-paragraph (h) now reads:

"(h) a person who has been granted leave or who is deemed to have been granted leave outside the rules made under section 3(2) of the Immigration Act 1971 where that leave is—
  (i) discretionary leave to enter or remain in the United Kingdom,
  (ii) leave to remain under the Destitution Domestic Violence concession, [. . .]
  (iii) leave deemed to have been granted by virtue of regulation 3 of the Displaced Persons (Temporary Protection) Regulations 2005; [or
  [(iv) granted under the Afghan Citizens Resettlement Scheme;]"

p.385, *annotation to the Income Support (General) Regulations 1987 (SI 1987/1967) reg.35(1)(d) (Earnings of employed earners—holiday pay)*

Replace the second paragraph of 2.265 (starting "Holiday pay") with 6.001.1
the following:

Holiday pay outside this sub-paragraph is to be treated as capital (reg.48(3)), with no disregard. It then appears that it cannot be taken into account as actual income, whether it would in the absence of reg.48(3) be regarded as earnings under the general meaning in reg.35(1) or as income other than earnings. In either case there is also a disregard (Sch.8, paras 1–2, and Sch.9, para.32).

p.396, *annotation to the Income Support (General) Regulations 1987 (SI 1987/1967) reg.37 (Earnings of self-employed earners)*

6.002   The two Business Interruption Loan Schemes and the Bounce Back Loan Scheme ceased to operate on March 31, 2021, to be replaced by the Recovery Loan Scheme.

p.482, *annotation to the Income Support (General) Regulations 1987 (SI 1987/1967) reg.51(1) (Notional capital—deprivation)*

6.003   See the entry for pp.1029-30 for the acceptance of the position under reg.113(1) of the JSA Regulations 1996 in *DB v DfC (JSA)* [2021] NICom 43. There, it was found that the claimant had deprived herself of capital while in receipt of income-related ESA. It was inherently improbable that when doing so, more than a year before she claimed JSA, she had possible entitlement to JSA or income support in mind. The tribunal had failed to make necessary findings of fact in concluding that her purpose had been the securing of entitlement to JSA. The principle would apply even more so to reg.51(1), where the test of purpose is still restricted to income support (but contrast the position under reg.115(1) of the ESA Regulations 2008).

The decision also illustrates that on a new claim neither the decision-maker nor a tribunal on appeal is bound by the findings of fact on capital that have underpinned a decision of non-entitlement on capital grounds. The basis of the ESA decision, that the claimant as at that date still had actual capital of more than £40,000, did not have to be adopted on the JSA claim.

p.651, *amendment to the Income Support (General) Regulations 1987 (SI 1987/1967) Sch.9 (Sums to be disregarded in the calculation of income other than earnings)*

6.004   With effect from July 26, 2021, art.11(2) of the Social Security (Scotland) Act 2018 (Disability Assistance, Young Carer Grants, Short-term Assistance and Winter Heating Assistance) (Consequential Provision and Modifications) Order 2021 (SI 2021/886) inserted the following after para.85:

"**86.** Any disability assistance given in accordance with regulations made under section 31 of the Social Security (Scotland) Act 2018."

The relevant regulations under s.31 of the 2018 Act so far are the Disability Assistance for Children and Young People (Scotland) Regulations 2021 (SSI 2021/174), also in effect from July 26, 2021, providing for the benefit known as a child disability payment. The regulations also authorise the payment of short-term assistance, to be disregarded under para.85.

p.676, *annotation to the Income Support (General) Regulations 1987 (SI 1987/1967) Sch.9, para.31A (Sums to be disregarded in the calculation of income other than earnings—local welfare provision)*

No doubt, payments under the Household Support Fund, in opera-   **6.005**
tion from October 2021 to March 2022, constitute "local welfare provision", as with the schemes mentioned in the main volume. See para.18A of Sch.10 for the capital disregard.

p.681, *amendment to the Income Support (General) Regulations 1987 (SI 1987/1967) Sch.10, para.7(1)(a) (Capital to be disregarded)*

With effect from July 26, 2021, art.11(3) of the Social Security (Scot-   **6.006**
land) Act 2018 (Disability Assistance, Young Carer Grants, Short-term Assistance and Winter Heating Assistance) (Consequential Provision and Modifications) Order 2021 (SI 2021/886) substituted "84, 85 or 86" for "84 or 85". See the entry for p.651 for the new para.86 of Sch.9.

p.707, *annotation to the Income Support (General) Regulations 1987 (SI 1987/1967) Sch.10 para.7 (Capital to be disregarded—arrears of certain benefits)*

With effect from October 18, 2021, the Social Security Benefits   **6.007**
(Claims and Payments) (Amendment) Regulations 2021 (SI 2021/1065) have permitted the payment of arrears of many benefits to be made in instalments, where necessary to protect the interests of the beneficiary and the latter agrees. Once such payments become capital (see the main volume), presumably the 52-week limit on the para.7(1) disregard runs separately from the date of receipt of each instalment. The application of the conditions in para.7(2) for a longer disregard might be more problematic.

p.742, *amendment to the Fines (Deductions from Income Support) Regulations 1992 (SI 1992/2182) reg.4 (Deductions from offender's income support, universal credit, state pension credit or jobseeker's allowance)*

With effect from October 29, 2021, the Fines (Deductions from   **6.008**
Income Support) (Miscellaneous Amendments) Regulations 2021 (SI 1077/2021) substituted a new Reg 4(1B):

"(1B) The amount that may be deducted under paragraph (1A) is 5 per cent. of the appropriate universal credit standard allowance for the offender for the assessment period in question, as specified under regulation 36 of the UC Regulations.".

This amendment follows the decision of Kerr J in *R (Blundell) v Secretary of State for Work and Pensions* [2021] EWHC 608 (Admin), [2021] PTSR 1342, where the Secretary of State's policy on deductions was found to be unlawfully fettering her discretion about the amount to deduct under reg.4(1B). The new regulation removes that discretion, by limiting deductions to the smallest amount which could previously have been deducted.

pp.975-976, *amendment to the Jobseeker's Allowance Regulations 1996 (SI 1996/207) reg.85A (Special cases: supplemental—persons from abroad)*

6.009   With effect from September 15, 2021, reg.2 of the Social Security (Habitual Residence and Past Presence) (Amendment) Regulations 2021 amended regulation 85A(4) (which prescribes persons who are not a 'person from abroad'). The amendment inserts before sub-paragraph (za):

"(zza) a person granted leave in accordance with the immigration rules made under section 3(2) of the Immigration Act 1971(10), where such leave is granted by virtue of—
   (i) the Afghan Relocations and Assistance Policy; or
   (ii) the previous scheme for locally-employed staff in Afghanistan (sometimes referred to as the ex-gratia scheme);
(zzb) a person in Great Britain not coming within sub-paragraph (zza) or (h)(iv) who left Afghanistan in connection with the collapse of the Afghan government that took place on 15th August 2021;".

From the same date the amendment also adds a new reg.85A(4)(h)(iv), so sub-paragraph (h) now reads:

"(h) a person who has been granted leave or who is deemed to have been granted leave outside the rules made under section 3(2) of the Immigration Act 1971 where that leave is—
   (i)   discretionary leave to enter or remain in the United Kingdom,
   (ii) leave to remain under the Destitution Domestic Violence concession, [. . .]
   (iii) leave deemed to have been granted by virtue of regulation 3 of the Displaced Persons (Temporary Protection) Regulations 2005; [or
   [(iv) granted under the Afghan Citizens Resettlement Scheme;]"

pp.1029-1030, *annotation to the Jobseeker's Allowance Regulations 1996 (SI 1996/207) reg.113(1) (Notional capital—deprivation)*

6.010   *DB v DfC (JSA)* [2021] NICom 43 takes the same approach as set out in the main volume to the scope of the Northern Ireland equivalent (in identical terms) of reg.113(1). The claimant had been entitled to old style ESA. On November 25, 2016 the decision was given that she was not entitled from August 2015, apparently on the basis that, although she asserted that she had disposed of some £40,000 of capital that she said did not belong to her, it was her capital and she had not shown that she had disposed of it. She claimed old style JSA on September 14, 2017. On October 16, 2017 it was decided that she was not entitled, on the basis that her actual capital exceeded £16,000, despite her further assertions of having depleted bank accounts. A revision of that decision and submissions made on appeal were hopelessly confused as between actual and notional capital, but the decision of October 16, 2017 was never formally changed. The appeal tribunal found that the claimant had deprived herself of more than £40,000 in 2016 for the principal purpose of bringing her capital below the limits to obtain benefits including JSA, so that she was treated as having notional income over £16,000 after the application of the diminishing notional capital rule (reg.114). The Chief Commissioner held, as had been submitted by the DfC, that because reg.113(1) could only bite when the claimant's purpose was securing entitlement to or increasing the amount of old style JSA or income support, the appeal tribunal had failed to make the necessary findings of fact or show that it had applied the legally correct approach. It was inherently improbable that when depriving herself of capital while in receipt of ESA, more than a year before she claimed JSA, the claimant had possible entitlement to JSA in mind.

The decision also illustrates that on a new claim neither the decision-maker nor a tribunal on appeal is bound by the findings of fact on capital that have underpinned a decision of non-entitlement on capital grounds. The basis of the ESA decision, that the claimant as at that date still had actual capital of more than £40,000, did not have to be adopted on the JSA claim.

p.1156, *amendment to the Jobseeker's Allowance Regulations 1996 (SI 1996/207) Sch.7 (Sums to be disregarded in the calculation of income other than earnings)*

With effect from July 26, 2021, art.12(2) of the Social Security (Scotland) Act 2018 (Disability Assistance, Young Carer Grants, Short-term Assistance and Winter Heating Assistance) (Consequential Provision and Modifications) Order 2021 (SI 2021/886) inserted the following after para.81: 6.011

"**82.** Any disability assistance given in accordance with regulations made under section 31 of the Social Security (Scotland) Act 2018."

The relevant regulations under s.31 of the 2018 Act so far are the Disability Assistance for Children and Young People (Scotland) Regulations 2021 (SSI 2021/174), also in effect from July 26, 2021, providing for the benefit known as a child disability payment. The regulations also authorise the payment of short-term assistance, to be disregarded under para.81.

p.1165, *amendment to the Jobseeker's Allowance Regulations 1996 (SI 1996/207) Sch.8, para.12(1)(a) (Capital to be disregarded)*

With effect from July 26, 2021, art.12(3) of the Social Security (Scotland) Act 2018 (Disability Assistance, Young Carer Grants, Short-term Assistance and Winter Heating Assistance) (Consequential Provision and Modifications) Order 2021 (SI 2021/886) substituted "80, 81 or 82" for "80 or 81". See the entry for p.1156 for the new para.82 of Sch.7. 6.012

p.1238, *amendment to the Employment and Support Allowance Regulations 2008 (SI 2008/794) reg.18 (Circumstances in which the condition that the claimant is not receiving education does not apply)*

6.013   With effect from July 26, 2021, art.16 and Sch. 9, para.3 of the Social Security (Scotland) Act 2018 (Disability Assistance for Children and Young People) (Consequential Modifications) Order 2021 (SI 2021/786) amended reg.18 by inserting ", child disability payment" after "disability living allowance",

p.1260, *annotation to the Employment and Support Allowance Regulations 2008 (SI 2008/794) reg.24 (Matters to be taken into account in determining good cause in relation to regulations 22 or 23)*

6.014   See also the unsuccessful application for a new inquest in *Dove v HM Assistant Coroner for Teesside and Hartlepool, Rahman and SSWP* [2021] EWHC 2511 (Admin), Mrs Dove's daughter, Ms W, had died of an overdose shortly after her ESA award had been stopped. Mrs Dove applied to the High Court under the Coroners Act 1988 s.13, (a) to quash the coroner's suicide verdict; and (b) to order a new inquest covering the circumstances surrounding her daughter's death. Ms W had a history of mental health problems, suicidal ideation and overdoses, as well as physical ill-health. She had been in receipt of ESA for several years. In 2016, on a periodic review, she asked for a home visit. The DWP neglected to deal with that request and required her to attend an HCP assessment, which she failed to attend. The DWP decided that Ms W had shown neither good cause for the failure to attend nor that she had limited capability for work. Ms W's ESA was duly stopped on February 7, 2017, and she died a fortnight later. Mrs Dove believed that the withdrawal of benefit had created extra stress and contributed to her daughter's death. The coroner ruled that questioning the DWP's decisions was beyond her remit under the Coroners and Justice Act 2009.

Mrs Dove submitted that (1) the coroner's inquiry was insufficient in scope and should have covered the DWP's failings; (2) those failings meant that the state was in breach of ECHR art.2, so requiring a wider inquiry; (3) fresh evidence (in the form of an ICE report on a complaint about the DWP's handling of Ms W's claim and a psychiatrist's report) showed that a new inquest was necessary. A strong Administrative Court (Warbey LJ, Farbey J and HH Judge Teague QC) dismissed the application on the following grounds:

(1) Scope of inquiry—coroner's inquiry was sufficient. Her function was to conduct an inquest in accordance with the Coroners and Justice Act 2009, and her rulings involved no *Wednesbury* or other public law error. She was not required by the public interest to undertake a wider inquiry about the DWP's handling of Ms W's case. Coroners had no specialism in social security issues and were not well-equipped to undertake such an inquiry. Other forms of scrutiny existed (e.g. via the DWP's complaints procedure, which was subject to judicial review, and via the statutory appeals process to a tribunal against substantive ESA decisions).

It would be contrary to the administration of justice for coroners to stand in the shoes of specialist tribunal judges, who were best placed to balance the rights of vulnerable social security claimants with the fair and proportionate allocation of public resources (see paras 71-75 of the judgment).

(2) ECHR art.2—In protecting a person's right to life, art.2 imposed an operational duty on the state to take reasonable steps to prevent real and immediate risk to life (including the risk of suicide), and a systems duty to establish a framework of laws, procedures and means of enforcement to protect life. Where art.2 was engaged, the scope of an inquest could expand to include the wider circumstances of death. However, it was not engaged in the present case. So far as any operational duty was concerned the DWP, in providing funds by way of welfare benefits, had not assumed responsibility for preventing the suicide of those who received such funds. Further, although Ms W undoubtedly had both mental and physical and health problems that made her particularly vulnerable, she was not under the control or care of the state. There was no general obligation on the state to prevent suicide in the absence of the assumption of responsibility. So far as any systems duty was concerned, the DWP's undoubted errors constituted individual failings attributable to errors or poor judgement and were not systemic in nature.

(3) *Fresh evidence*—It was not in the interests of justice to order a new inquest in light of the fresh evidence. The ICE report certainly concluded that there had been significant failings on the part of DWP staff in dealing with Ms W's case, in breach of departmental guidance on safeguarding vulnerable claimants. But this did not mean that an inquest needed to hear further evidence about such matters. The psychiatrist's report drew a causal link between the DWP's failings and Ms W's state of mind, rather than her death. It did not say in terms that the DWP's decision to stop her ESA had caused Ms W to take her own life, and did not rule out other causative stress factors. It would be very difficult for a new inquest to conclude that the DWP caused her death (paras 91-94).

pp.1341-1342, *amendment to the Employment and Support Allowance Regulations 2008 (SI 2008/794) reg.70 (Special cases: supplemental—persons from abroad)*

With effect from September 15, 2021, reg.2 of the Social Security (Habitual Residence and Past Presence) (Amendment) Regulations 2021 amended regulation 70(4) (which prescribes persons who are not a 'person from abroad'). The amendment inserts before sub-paragraph (za): **6.015**

"(zza) a person granted leave in accordance with the immigration rules made under section 3(2) of the Immigration Act 1971(10), where such leave is granted by virtue of—
(i) the Afghan Relocations and Assistance Policy; or

(ii) the previous scheme for locally-employed staff in Afghanistan (sometimes referred to as the ex-gratia scheme);

(zzb) a person in Great Britain not coming within sub-paragraph (zza) or (h)(iv) who left Afghanistan in connection with the collapse of the Afghan government that took place on 15th August 2021;".

From the same date the amendment also adds a new reg.70(4)(h)(iv), so sub-paragraph (h) now reads:

"(h) a person who has been granted leave or who is deemed to have been granted leave outside the rules made under section 3(2) of the Immigration Act 1971 where that leave is—

(i) discretionary leave to enter or remain in the United Kingdom,

(ii) eave to remain under the Destitution Domestic Violence concession, [. . .]

(iii) leave deemed to have been granted by virtue of regulation 3 of the Displaced Persons (Temporary Protection) Regulations 2005; [or

[(iv) granted under the Afghan Citizens Resettlement Scheme;]".

p.1548, *amendment to the Employment and Support Allowance Regulations 2008 (SI 2008/794) Sch.8 (Sums to be disregarded in the calculation of income other than earnings)*

6.016   With effect from July 26, 2021, art.16(2) of the Social Security (Scotland) Act 2018 (Disability Assistance, Young Carer Grants, Short-term Assistance and Winter Heating Assistance) (Consequential Provision and Modifications) Order 2021 (SI 2021/886) inserted the following after para.73:

"**74.** Any disability assistance given in accordance with regulations made under section 31 of the Social Security (Scotland) Act 2018.".

The relevant regulations under s.31 of the 2018 Act so far are the Disability Assistance for Children and Young People (Scotland) Regulations 2021 (SSI 2021/174), also in effect from July 26, 2021, providing for the benefit known as a child disability payment. The regulations also authorise the payment of short-term assistance, to be disregarded under para.73.

p.1556, *amendment to the Employment and Support Allowance Regulations 2008 (SI 2008/794) Sch.9 para.11(1)(a) (Capital to be disregarded)*

6.017   With effect from July 26, 2021, art.16(3) of the Social Security (Scotland) Act 2018 (Disability Assistance, Young Carer Grants, Short-term Assistance and Winter Heating Assistance) (Consequential Provision and Modifications) Order 2021 (SI 2021/886) substituted "72, 73 or 74" for "72 or 73". See the entry for p.1549 for the new para.74 of Sch.8.

190

pp.1826-1829, *annotation to the Immigration (European Economic Area) Regulations 2016 reg.4 ("Worker", "self-employed person", "self-sufficient person" and "student") Self-sufficient persons*

In *VI v Commissioners for Her Majesty's Revenue & Customs* (C-247/20   **6.018** O, September 30, 2021), §§56-64 AG Hogan's opinion describes a "fundamental question" in that case as "probably" being whether free access to the NHS satisfies the requirement to have CSI, and laments that the UK Government had not made any submissions about that issue. However, he does not give his own answer to the question, and cautions the Court against doing so; therefore when the Court gives judgment it seems unlikely that any further light will be thrown.

PART VII

FORTHCOMING CHANGES AND UP-RATING OF BENEFITS

FORTHCOMING CHANGES

Statutory sick pay

7.001 The Statutory Sick Pay (Medical Evidence) Regulations 2021(SI 2021/1453), in force from December 17, 2021, deal with the length of the period for which employees are *not* required to provide medical evidence of sickness absences for statutory sick pay (SSP) purposes. The new Regulations modified the Statutory Sick Pay (Medical Evidence) Regulations 1985 (SI 1985/1604) to increase the period that an employee is not required to provide medical information in respect of any spell of incapacity for work from 7 days to 28 days. The Regulations provide that the modified time limit applies to spells of sickness that started during the period from December 17, 2021, to January 26, 2022 (or which started before the Regulations came into force but which had not lasted more than seven days on that date). The measure was intended to free up GP capacity to support the coronavirus vaccine booster programme announced on December 12, 2021, in the light of the surge in Omicron cases.

Means Tested Benefits

7.002 The Social Security (Income and Capital Disregards) (Amendment) Regulations 2021 (SI 2021/1405) came into force on January 1, 2022, and amended (amongst other regulations) the Income Support (General) Regulations 1987 (SI 1987/1967), the Jobseeker's Allowance Regulations 1996 (SI 1996/207), the State Pension Credit Regulations 2002 (SI 2002/1792), the Employment and Support Allowance Regulations 2008 (SI 2008/794) and the Universal Credit Regulations 2013 (SI 2013/376). The amendments cover payments made to a benefit recipient either (a) from a scheme established or approved by the Secretary of State to provide compensation in respect of historic institutional child abuse in the United Kingdom; or (b) under the Windrush Compensation (Expenditure) Act 2020. Such payments are to be disregarded as income and capital and so are not to be taken into account for the purposes of calculating entitlement to the means-tested benefits referred to above. The Regulations also amend respectively the Social Security (Recovery of Benefits) Regulations 1997 (SI 1997/2205) and the Social Security (Recovery of Benefits) (Lump Sum Payments) Regulations 2008 (SI 2008/1596) to ensure that the payments made under the Windrush Act are not to be regarded as compensation payments for the purposes of those two sets of regulations. The Explanatory Memorandum to the amending regulations reveals that four child abuse schemes

195

have so far been approved by the Secretary of State: under the Historical Institutional Abuse (Northern Ireland) Act 2019, the Redress for Survivors (Historical Child Abuse in Care) (Scotland) Act 2021, the London Borough of Lambeth Redress Scheme and the London Borough of Islington's proposed support payment scheme. All provide one-off capital payments. The Memorandum also reveals that payments under the Northern Ireland and Lambeth schemes could have been made prior to January 1, 2022. The application of the disregards provided under SI 2021/1405 to such payments has been authorised by a ministerial direction from the Secretary of State, acting under "common law powers" (see the letters of December 3, 2021 between the Permanent Secretary and the Secretary of State, published on the internet). The Windrush Compensation Scheme has also been making payments for some time. Extra-statutory arrangements agreed with HM Treasury provided for the disregard in practice of such payments in means-tested benefits from the outset.

Those arrangements raise questions as to what a tribunal on appeal should do if it has evidence of receipt prior to January 1, 2022 of a payment that would have been disregarded under the SI 2021/1405 amendments if it had been received on or after that date. The legislation that a tribunal is bound to apply would not allow a disregard of such a payment unless it fell within one of existing "personal Injury" disregards. However, if an express submission from the DWP recorded the practical result of the application of the disregard on either basis mentioned above, it would appear that the issue of the treatment of the payment would not arise on the appeal (see s.12(8)(a) of the Social Security Act 1998) and it is submitted that it would then be irrational for the tribunal to exercise its discretion to consider the issue nonetheless. If evidence of a payment that had not been taken into account as capital emerges in the course of an appeal, but there is no express DWP submission to explain that outcome, it is submitted that a tribunal with knowledge of the arrangements could still legitimately conclude that the issue did not arise on the appeal and decline to exercise its discretion under s.12(8)(a). Memos ADM 21/21 and DMG 15/21 say nothing about these questions.

Competing claims for Best Start Grants or Scottish Child Payment

7.003   From December 23, 2021, the Best Start Grants and Scottish Child Payment (Miscellaneous Amendments) Regulations 2021 (SSI 2021/494) have introduced amendments to the Early Years Assistance (Best Start Grants) (Scotland) Regulations 2018 and the Scottish Child Payment Regulations 2020 to enable Scottish Ministers to have regard to the circumstances of the child in certain circumstances arising from competing claims for benefits in respect of the child.

Suspension of Scottish Child Payment and Child Disability Payment

7.004   The Scottish Child Payment Regulations 2020 and the Disability Assistance for Children and Young People (Scotland) Regulations 2021 (Miscellaneous Amendments) Regulations 2022 (SSI 2022/41) make a number of amendments to the Regulations named in their title, including making provision for the suspension of the benefits in certain circumstances. The Regulations come into force on February 9, 2022.

Adult disability payment

Following the introduction of child disability payment in 2021, the **7.005** Disability Assistance for Working Age People (Scotland) Regulations 2022 (SSI 2022/54) will introduce an adult disability payment from March 21, 2002 to replace personal independence payment ("PIP") for claimants aged at least 16 but, generally, under pensionable age who are resident in Scotland. The Regulations include provision for the transfer of existing PIP claimants to the new benefit, including for cases when people move from England or Wales to Scotland.

The conditions of entitlement to the new benefit will be more-or-less the same as the conditions of entitlement to PIP and it will be rolled out to new claimants over a period of five and a half months. During an initial period of three months, applications will be accepted only from those living in Perthshire and Kinloss, City of Dundee and Western Isles. During the five weeks from June 20, 2022, North Lanarkshire, South Lanarkshire and Fife will be added to that list and, in the five weeks from July 25, 2022, City of Aberdeen, Aberdeenshire, Moray, North Ayrshire, East Ayrshire and South Ayrshire will also be added. From August 30, 2022, all areas of Scotland will be covered. Provision is also made for the payment of short-term assistance where a decision reducing or removing entitlement to adult disability payment is "under review".

The Disability Assistance for Working Age People (Consequential and Miscellaneous Amendment and Transitional Provision) (Scotland) Regulations 2022 (SSI 2022/31) make consequential provision and also provide that, save in limited circumstances, a person who is eligible to claim adult disability payment may not claim PIP.

NEW BENEFIT RATES FROM APRIL 2022

NEW BENEFIT RATES FROM APRIL 2022

(Benefits covered in Volume I)

	April 2021	April 2022
	£ pw	£ pw
Disability benefits		
Attendance allowance		
higher rate	89.60	92.40
lower rate	60.00	61.85
Disability living allowance		
care component		
highest rate	89.60	92.40
middle rate	60.00	61.85
lowest rate	23.70	24.45
mobility component		
higher rate	62.55	64.50
lower rate	23.70	24.45
Personal independence payment		
daily living component		
enhanced rate	89.60	92.40
standard rate	60.00	61.85
mobility component		
enhanced rate	62.55	64.50
standard rate	23.70	24.45
Carer's allowance	67.60	69.70
Maternity allowance		
standard rate	151.97	156.66

	April 2021	April 2022
	£ pw	£ pw

Bereavement benefits and retirement pensions

Widowed parent's allowance or widowed mother's allowance	122.55	126.35

Widow's pension
standard rate   122.55   126.35

Retirement pension
Category A or Category B (higher)   137.60   141.85
Category B (lower), Category C or Category D   82.45   85.00

New state pension   179.60   185.15

Dependency increase for child
The only, elder or eldest child for whom child
  benefit is being paid   8.00   8.00
Any other child   11.35   11.35

Industrial injuries benefits

Disablement benefit
100%   182.90   188.60
90%   164.61   169.74
80%   146.32   150.88
70%   128.03   132.02
60%   109.74   113.16
50%   91.45   94.30
40%   73.16   75.44
30%   54.87   56.58
20%   36.58   37.72

unemployability supplement
basic rate   113.10   116.60
increase for adult dependant   67.60   69.70
increase for early incapacity—higher rate   23.40   24.15
increase for early incapacity—middle rate   15.00   15.50
increase for early incapacity—lower rate   7.50   7.75

constant attendance allowance
exceptional rate   146.40   151.00
intermediate rate   109.80   113.25
normal maximum rate   73.20   75.50
part-time rate   36.60   37.75

	April 2021 £ pw	April 2022 £ pw
exceptionally severe disablement allowance	73.20	75.50
reduced earnings allowance—*maximum rate*	73.16	75.44
retirement allowance—*maximum rate*	18.29	18.86

Death benefit
widow's pension (higher rate) or widower's

	April 2021 £ pw	April 2022 £ pw
pension	137.60	141.85
widow's pension (lower rate)	41.28	42.56

"New-style" jobseeker's allowance

personal allowances		
aged under 25	59.20	61.05
aged 25 or over	74.70	77.00

"New style" employment and support allowance

personal allowances		
assessment phase—*aged under 25*	59.20	61.05
aged 25 or over	74.70	77.00
main phase	74.70	77.00
work-related activity component	29.70	30.60
support component	39.40	40.60

NEW BENEFIT RATES FROM APRIL 2022

(Benefits covered in Volume II)

	April 2021	April 2022
	£ pm	£ pm

Universal credit

Standard allowances

	April 2021	April 2022
Single claimant—*aged under 25*	257.33[1]	265.31
aged 25 or over	324.84[1]	334.91
Joint claimants—*both aged under 25*	403.93[1]	416.45
one or both aged 25 or over	509.91[1]	525.72
Child element—*first child (if born before April 6, 2017)*	282.50	290.00
each *other child*	237.08	244.58
Disabled child addition—*lower rate*	128.89	132.89
higher rate	402.41	414.88
Limited Capability for Work element	128.89	132.89
Limited Capability for Work and Work-Related Activity element	343.63	354.28
Carer element	163.73	168.81
Childcare element—*maximum for one child*	646.35	646.35
maximum for two or more children	1,108.04	1,108.04
Non-dependants' housing cost contributions	75.53	77.87

Work allowances

	April 2021	April 2022
Higher work allowance (no housing element)		
one or more children	515.00[2]	573.00
limited capability for work	515.00[2]	573.00
Lower work allowance		
one or more children	293.00[3]	344.00
limited capability for work	293.00[3]	344.00

1. These 2021 figures do not include the "£20 pw uplift" which increased each of them by £86.67 per month until October 6, 2021 (see the Universal Credit (Extension of Coronavirus Measures) Regulations 2021 (SI 2021/313)).
2. These 2021 figures were increased to £557 pm from November 24, 2021 (see the Universal Credit (Work Allowance and Taper) (Amendment) Regulations 2021 (SI 2021/1283)).
3. These 2021 figures were increased to £335 pm from November 24, 2021 (see the Universal Credit (Work Allowance and Taper) (Amendment) Regulations 2021 (SI 2021/1283)).

	April 2021 £ pm	April 2022 £ pm
Pension credit		
Standard minimum guarantee		
single person	177.10	182.60
couple	270.30	278.70
Additional amount for child or qualifying young person		
first child (if born before April 6, 2017)	65.10	66.85
each other child	54.60	56.35
Additional amount for severe disability		
single person	67.30	69.40
couple (one qualifies)	67.30	69.40
couple (both qualify)	134.60	138.80
Additional amount for carers	37.70	38.85
Additional amount for additional spouse in a polygamous marriage	93.20	96.10
Savings credit threshold		
single person	153.70	158.47
couple	244.12	251.70
Maximum savings credit		
single person	14.04	14.48
couple	15.71	16.20

NEW TAX CREDIT AND BENEFIT RATES 2022–2023

(Benefits covered in Volume IV)

HMRC-administered payments	2021–22	2022–23
	£ pw	£ pw
Benefits in respect of children		
Child benefit		
only, elder or eldest child (couple)	21.15	21.80
each subsequent child	14.00	14.45
Guardian's allowance	18.00	18.55
Employer-paid benefits		
Standard rates		
Statutory sick pay	96.35	99.35
Statutory maternity pay, Statutory paternity pay	151.97	156.66
Statutory shared parental pay	151.97	156.66
Statutory adoption pay	151.97	156.66
Income threshold	120.00	123.00

	2021–22	2022–23
	£ pa	£ pa
Working tax credit		
Basic element	2,005	2,070
Couple and lone parent element	2,060	2,125
30 hour element	830	860
Disabled worker element	3,240	3,345
Severe disability element	1,400	1,445
Child care element		
maximum eligible cost for one child	*175 pw*	*175 pw*
maximum eligible cost for two or more		
children	*300 pw*	*300 pw*
per cent of eligible costs covered	*70%*	*70%*
Child tax credit		
Family element	545	545
Child element	2,845	2,935
Disabled child element	3,435	3,545
Severely disabled child element	4,825	4,975
Tax credit income thresholds		
Income threshold	6,565	6,770
Income threshold for those entitled to child tax credit only	16,480	17,005

Scottish social security assistance	April 2021	April 2022
	£ pw	£ pw
Adult disability payment		
daily living component		
enhanced rate	89.60[1]	92.40
standard rate	60.00[1]	61.85
mobility component		
enhanced rate	62.55[1]	64.50
standard rate	23.70[1]	24.45
Child disability payment		
care component		
highest rate	89.60[2]	92.40
middle rate	60.00[2]	61.85
lowest rate	23.70[2]	24.45
mobility componen		
higher rate	62.55[2]	64.50
lower rate	23.70[2]	24.45
Scottish child payment	10.00	20.00

	April 2021	April 2022
Best start grants	£	£
Pregnancy and baby grant		
first child	606.00	606.00
subsequent child and additional payment for		
twins etc.	303.00	303.00
Early learning payment	252.50	252.50
School age payment	252.50	252.50
Funeral expense assistance		
standard rate	1,010.00	1,041.30
rate where the deceased has left in place a		
pre-paid funeral plan	123.25	127.05
maximum rate for removal of an implanted		
medical device by a person other than a		
registered medical practitioner	20.55	21.20
Young carer grant	308.15	317.70

New Tax Credit and Benefit Rates 2022–2023

	April 2021 £	April 2022 £
Child winter heating assistance	202.00	212.10
Carer's allowance supplement (bi-annual)	231.40[3]	237.90

1. Adult disability payment will be introduced from March 21, 2022.
2. Child disability payment was introduced from July 26, 2021.
3. This amount was doubled for the period from October 1, 2021 to March 31, 2022 (see s.81(4B) of the Social Security (Scotland) Act 2018, inserted by s.1 of the Carer's Allowance Supplement (Scotland) Act 2021).

NEW BENEFIT RATES FROM APRIL 2022

(Benefits covered in Volume V)

	April 2021	April 2022
	£ pw	£ pw
Contribution-based jobseeker's allowance		
Personal rates—*aged under 25*	59.20	61.05
aged 25 or over	74.70	77.00
Contributory employment and support allowance		
Personal rates—assessment phase—*aged under 25*	59.20	61.05
aged 25 or over	74.70	77.00
main phase	74.70	77.00
Components		
work-related activity	29.70	30.60
support	39.40	40.60
Income support and income-based jobseeker's allowance		
Personal allowances		
single person—aged under 25	59.20	61.05
aged 25 or over	74.70	77.00
one parent—aged under 18	59.20	61.05
aged 18 or over	74.70	77.00
couple—both aged under 18	59.20	61.05
both aged under 18, with a child	89.45	92.20
one aged under 18, one aged under 25	59.20	61.05
one aged under 18, one aged 25 or over	74.70	77.00
both aged 18 or over	117.40	121.05
dependent child	68.60	70.80
Premiums		
family—ordinary	17.65	17.85
lone parent	17.65	17.85
pensioner—single person (JSA only)	102.40	105.60
couple	152.90	157.65
disability—single person	35.10	36.20
couple	50.05	51.60
enhanced disability—single person	17.20	17.75
couple	24.60	25.35
disabled child	26.67	27.74

	April 2021	April 2022
	£ pw	£ pw
severe disability—single person	67.30	69.40
couple (one qualifies)	67.30	69.40
couple (both qualify)	134.60	138.80
disabled child	65.94	68.04
carer	37.70	38.85

Income-related employment and support allowance

Personal allowances

single person—aged under 25	59.20	61.05
aged 25 or over	74.70	77.00
lone parent—aged under 18	59.20	61.05
aged 18 or over	74.70	77.00
couple—both aged under 18	59.20	61.05
both aged under 18, with a child	89.45	92.20
both aged under 18, (main phase)	59.20	61.05
both aged under 18, with a child (main phase)	117.40	121.05
one aged under 18, one aged 18 or over	117.40	121.05
both aged 18 or over@	117.40	121.05

Components

work-related activity	29.70	30.60
support	39.40	40.60

Premiums

pensioner—single person with no component	102.40	105.60
couple with no component	152.90	157.65
enhanced disability—single person	17.20	17.75
couple	24.60	25.35
disabled child	26.67	27.74
severe disability—single person	67.30	69.40
couple (one qualifies)	67.30	69.40
couple (both qualify)	134.60	138.80
disabled child	65.94	68.04
carer	37.70	38.85